# A CULTURAL HISTORY OF MONEY

## VOLUME 2

**A Cultural History of Money**
*General Editor: Bill Maurer*

**Volume 1**
A Cultural History of Money in Antiquity
*Edited by Stefan Krmnicek*

**Volume 2**
A Cultural History of Money in the Medieval Age
*Edited by Rory Naismith*

**Volume 3**
A Cultural History of Money in the Renaissance
*Edited by Stephen Deng*

**Volume 4**
A Cultural History of Money in the Age of Enlightenment
*Edited by Christine Desan*

**Volume 5**
A Cultural History of Money in the Age of Empire
*Edited by Federico Neiburg and Nigel Dodd*

**Volume 6**
A Cultural History of Money in the Modern Age
*Edited by Taylor C. Nelms and David Pedersen*

# A CULTURAL HISTORY OF MONEY

# IN THE MEDIEVAL AGE

*Edited by Rory Naismith*

BLOOMSBURY ACADEMIC
LONDON · NEW YORK · OXFORD · NEW DELHI · SYDNEY

BLOOMSBURY ACADEMIC
Bloomsbury Publishing Plc
50 Bedford Square, London, WC1B 3DP, UK
1385 Broadway, New York, NY 10018, USA
29 Earlsfort Terrace, Dublin 2, Ireland

BLOOMSBURY, BLOOMSBURY ACADEMIC and the Diana logo are trademarks of
Bloomsbury Publishing Plc

First published in Great Britain 2019
Paperback edition published in 2023

Copyright © Bloomsbury Publishing, 2019

Rory Naismith has asserted his right under the Copyright, Designs and Patents Act, 1988,
to be identified as Author of this work.

Series design: Raven Design
Cover image: *A money changer negotiating with a client while his assistant checks a coin.*
Chartres Cathedral, stained glass window (early 13th century).
(© Stuart Whatling/Chartres Cathedral, France)

All rights reserved. No part of this publication may be reproduced or transmitted in any
form or by any means, electronic or mechanical, including photocopying, recording, or
any information storage or retrieval system, without prior permission in writing from
the publishers.

Bloomsbury Publishing Plc does not have any control over, or responsibility for, any
third-party websites referred to or in this book. All internet addresses given in this
book were correct at the time of going to press. The author and publisher regret
any inconvenience caused if addresses have changed or sites have ceased to
exist, but can accept no responsibility for any such changes.

A catalogue record for this book is available from the British Library.

A catalog record for this book is available from the Library of Congress.

ISBN: PB Set: 978-1-3503-6718-0
HB: 978-1-4742-3710-9
PB: 978-1-3503-6394-6
ePDF: 978-1-3502-5347-6
eBook: 978-1-3502-5348-3

Series: The Cultural Histories Series

Typeset by RefineCatch Limited, Bungay, Suffolk
Printed and bound in Great Britain

To find out more about our authors and books visit www.bloomsbury.com
and sign up for our newsletters.

# CONTENTS

LIST OF ILLUSTRATIONS — vii
NOTES ON CONTRIBUTORS — x
SERIES PREFACE — xii

Introduction: Approaching Medieval Money — 1
*Rory Naismith*

1 Money and Its Technologies: The "Principles of Minting" in the Middle Ages — 15
*Oliver Volckart*

2 Money and Its Ideas: Payment Methods in the Middle Ages — 37
*Laurent Feller*

3 Money, Ritual, and Religion: Economic Value between Theology and Administration — 57
*Giacomo Todeschini*

4 Money and the Everyday: Whose Currency? — 79
*Richard Kelleher*

5 Money, Art, and Representation: The Powerful and Pragmatic Faces of Medieval Coinage — 99
*Rebecca R. Darley*

6  Money and Its Interpretation: Attitudes to Money in the
   *Societas Christiana*                                              125
   Svein H. Gullbekk

7  Money and the Issues of the Age: The Plurality of Money           151
   Rory Naismith

NOTES                                                                 173
BIBLIOGRAPHY                                                          177
INDEX                                                                 207

# LIST OF ILLUSTRATIONS

## INTRODUCTION

| | | |
|---|---|---|
| 0.1 | A hoard of silver objects and hacksilver, from the Viking Age, found in Denmark. | 4 |
| 0.2 | A silver *denarius* of Louis the Pious (814–40). | 7 |

## CHAPTER 1

| | | |
|---|---|---|
| 1.1 | The young White King learns the principles of minting. Woodcut by Leonhard Beck (*c.* 1480–1542). | 16 |
| 1.2 | *Gros tournois* and *denier* of Louis IX. | 20 |
| 1.3 | The pedlar, from Hans Holbein Junior's *Danse Macabre*, 1524–26. | 22 |
| 1.4 | A set of touch needles, from Georgius Agricola's *De re metallica libri XII*, 1556. | 32 |
| 1.5 | Hindu-Arabic numerals from Gregor Reisch's *Margarita Philosophica*, Freiburg, 1503. | 34 |

## CHAPTER 2

| | | |
|---|---|---|
| 2.1 | *Denarius* of Charlemagne minted at Quentovic. | 43 |
| 2.2 | Panel from the Gniezno doors depicting the purchase of St. Adalbert's body. | 47 |
| 2.3 | Venetian *grosso* of Enrico Dandolo (1192–1205). | 49 |

## CHAPTER 3

| | | |
|---|---|---|
| 3.1 | The parable of the talents—one of many biblical metaphors involving money (New York, Pierpont Morgan Library, Manuscript M.521: Canterbury, 1155–60). | 59 |
| 3.2 | The parable of the lost money (New York, Pierpont Morgan Library, Manuscript M.140, f. 38r: Nuremberg, late fourteenth century). | 60 |
| 3.3 | The parable of the lost money (New York, Pierpont Morgan Library, Manuscript M.385, f. 38r: Bruges, mid-fifteenth century). | 60 |
| 3.4 | Adoration of the coin-like host (Chantilly, Musée Condé, MS 65, f. 189v. France, early fifteenth century). | 61 |

## CHAPTER 4

| | | |
|---|---|---|
| 4.1 | The excavation of a hoard of Anglo-Saxon silver pennies from Lenborough in Bedfordshire. | 81 |
| 4.2 | Silver *denier* of Charlemagne struck at Mainz, 793/4–812. | 85 |
| 4.3 | Silver Short Cross penny struck at York by the moneyer Isaac. | 90 |
| 4.4 | Silver *gros tournois*. | 92 |
| 4.5 | Gold florin of Florence. | 96 |

## CHAPTER 5

| | | |
|---|---|---|
| 5.1 | Byzantine armband with coins. | 102 |
| 5.2 | Byzantine marriage belt with coins. | 104 |
| 5.3 | Latin imitation of a gold *hyperperon* of John III Vatatzes. | 106 |
| 5.4 | Byzantine silver *hexagram* of Heraclius. | 108 |
| 5.5 | Byzantine copper-alloy *follis* of Constans II. | 112 |
| 5.6 | Gold *dinar* of Abd al-Malik. | 113 |
| 5.7 | Anonymous Crusader dirham. | 113 |
| 5.8 | Piedfort of Philip IV. | 116 |
| 5.9 | A copper-alloy imitation of a late Roman *nummus* from Sri Lanka. | 117 |

LIST OF ILLUSTRATIONS

| | | |
|---|---|---|
| 5.10 | Anglo-Saxon penny. | 119 |
| 5.11 | Gold *tremissis* of Visigothic rulers of Spain. | 119 |
| 5.12 | Imitation Byzantine gold *solidus* of Theodosius II from south India. | 120 |
| 5.13 | Imitative *solidus* from Old Buckenham. | 121 |
| 5.14a | Artuqid copper alloy coin of Kutb al-din Ilgazi II. | 122 |
| 5.14b | *Solidus* of Heraclius I. | 122 |

## CHAPTER 6

| | | |
|---|---|---|
| 6.1 | Caricature cartoon of Norwich Jewish taxpayers. | 139 |
| 6.2 | A well-preserved robe made from so-called "Greenland vaðmal" dated *c.*1250–1400. | 140 |
| 6.3 | Harald Hardrade (1047–1066) penny, struck in Norway. | 142 |
| 6.4 | Anglo-Saxon penny of Æthelred II. | 144 |
| 6.5 | Illustrated folio from an early manuscript copy Dante, *Inferno*. | 147 |
| 6.6 | Matthew Paris Long cross design. | 148 |

## CHAPTER 7

| | | |
|---|---|---|
| 7.1 | A hoard of Migration Age gold coins and bracteates, deposited in a rolled silver disk. | 155 |
| 7.2 | A Viking Age hoard of coins and hack-metal with the pot in which it was discovered. | 156 |
| 7.3 | Gold *solidus* of Theodebert II. | 160 |
| 7.4 | A 13th-century penny of Edward I of England. | 167 |
| 7.5 | A scene of almsgiving from the Utrecht Psalter. | 169 |
| 7.6 | Dirham inscribed with runes. | 170 |
| 7.7 | A groat of Henry VII of England, found at Fulford, Yorkshire. | 170 |

# NOTES ON CONTRIBUTORS

**Rebecca Darley** is Lecturer in Medieval History at Birkbeck, University of London. She researches and publishes on the role of coins as social and economic tools, especially in peninsular India and the Byzantine Empire in the first millennium CE. She is currently completing a monograph on the western Indian Ocean in Late Antiquity.

**Laurent Feller** is Professor of Medieval History at the University Paris 1 Panthéon-Sorbonne. His interests are in early and high medieval social and economic history, and his field of specialization is medieval Italy. He is particularly interested in agrarian history and has published *Paysans et Seigneurs au Moyen Âge* (Paris, 2007, 2nd edition, 2018).

**Svein H. Gullbekk** is Professor in Numismatics and History of Money at the Department of Ethnography, Numismatics and Classical Archaeology at the Museum of Cultural History, University of Oslo, Norway. His research focuses on studies of coinage in a broader context of Viking and medieval Scandinavia and particularly the relationship between religion and money.

**Richard Kelleher** is Assistant Keeper of Coins and Medals at the Fitzwilliam Museum, Cambridge. His research interests include monetization and coin use in medieval and early modern Britain, the coinage of the Crusader states, and the secondary lives of coins. His publications include *A History of Coinage in Medieval England* (2015).

**Rory Naismith** is Lecturer in Medieval British History at King's College London. He is interested in early medieval economic and social history, particularly as it pertains to money (coined and otherwise). Major publications include *Medieval European Coinage, with a Catalogue of the Coins in the Fitzwilliam Museum, Cambridge. 8: Britain and Ireland c. 400–1066* (2017) and *Money and Power in Anglo-Saxon England: the Southern English Kingdoms 757–865* (2012).

**Giacomo Todeschini** worked for many years as Professor of Medieval History at the University of Trieste (1979–2016). His studies focus on the development of medieval and modern economics, exclusion from citizenship and market games, and the economic and political meaning of Jews in Christian society. He has researched and lectured as a fellow or member at the École normale supérieure, Paris, the Oxford Centre for Hebrew and Jewish Studies, the Institute for Advanced Study, Princeton, Beijing University, and the Wissenschaftskolleg zu Berlin.

**Oliver Volckart** is Professor of Economic History at the London School of Economics and Political Science. His research interests lie in medieval and early modern history, specifically constitutional history, institutional change, market integration, and the monetary and financial history of the Holy Roman Empire.

# SERIES PREFACE

When the British Museum decided in 2012 to redesign Room 68, the hall containing objects from its Department of Coins and Medals, its curators made a bold departure from how numismatic material had conventionally been displayed. Rather than cases filled with rows upon rows of gold, silver, and bronze coins of European antiquity, the new gallery design featured all manner of objects, not limited to coin or paper currency, capturing the history of transactional artifacts and infrastructures from shells to mobile phones. Each case had a theme: cases on one side of the gallery spotlighted money's institutional supports and issuing authorities, while cases on the other underscored all the myriad ways people use money, not just for exchange or payment but for ritual or religious observance, political contestation, adornment, and storytelling.

The intention in preparing these six volumes was to provide readers with a similar experience, inviting them into the wonder-cabinets of money in all its variegation, multiplicity, and complexity. What emerges is money's irreducible plurality, the multiple stories it tells. Money opens windows into plural economic and moral worlds, too, worlds of value and evaluation, wealth and worth. Never merely coin, cash, or credit rendered in strictly economic terms, money is so much more than the old couplet would have it: "Money is a matter of functions four: a medium, a measure, a standard, a store." Instead, money is always also a medium of communication, a set of instruments with which people exchange messages with one another—about price, to be sure, but also about political conviction and authority, fealty, desire, or disdain. And money is a method of memorializing the past so that relations established among people, institutions, the gods, and the ancestors can be carried forward through the present and into near, distant, and imaginary futures.

Money is in this sense both irredeemably "cultural" and "historical," and so it is apt that this six-volume Cultural History of Money should spotlight money's relation to religion, technology, the arts, and literature, everyday life, metaphysical interpretation, and a wide variety of issues of the age. While many contributors to the first several volumes are numismatists and archaeologists, trucking in the material evidence of coin and bullion, the volumes also contain contributions from scholars of digital infrastructures, literary and legal historians and science fiction scholars, sociologists and anthropologists, economists and artists.

Archaeologists have long bemoaned the fact that the great majority of ancient coins in museums and private collections today were unearthed without any data having been collected on their surrounding context, rendering much of the ancient and even more recent past a mystery. Even where the context for a particular find is present, its interpretation is always ambiguous. In the contemporary period, money is surrounded by context—cables and wireless signals, data protocols and computer servers, lobbying groups' and legislators' voluminous writings, television soap operas and online social media. Yet just as with ancient hoards, we have difficulty escaping our own assumptions about what money is, what people do with it, and the style with which they do so.

Take a basic plastic credit card transaction at a physical till. How many users of this everyday payment device would be able to explain how it works? How would a museum curate this technological assemblage? Moving from the simple act of paying to more involved interactions with money, how might an archaeologist of the future deduce, for example, the practice in some central Asian Muslim immigrant communities known as the "Imam Zamin," which consists of wrapping a coin in a piece of cloth tied about the upper arm to protect a traveler? Or the practice from around 2005–2009 of what people called "doing tuning"(튜닝하다) to a transit card in Seoul, Korea—dissolving the plastic payment card with acetone so as to remove the radio-frequency identification (RFID) antenna and chip, and creatively stitching it into one's pocketbook, bracelet, or the elbow patches of one's blazer, so you can breeze through the turnstile, with style?

Trapped in our own "coin consciousness," we assume money has to be, or that its value should be found in, a tangible thing, despite the fact that our own interactions with it are increasingly dematerialized in digital networks. We hold on to bullionist conceptions of money's worth, despite our bearing continual witness to its fluctuations based on prevailing political whims. We think of money as abstract, even as we use it in the most concrete and interpersonal relations. We believe money equilibrates values, rendering goods and services commensurable with one another measured on one scale of value, even as we use money to demarcate difference—national difference, religious difference, intergenerational difference, differences in class, race, and gender.

The periodization of these volumes is somewhat arbitrary but still Eurocentric. The selection of authors and themes is intended to help disturb this Western-oriented history by globalizing it and insisting on bringing into the frame its political, imperial, and often racial dynamics.

The chapters in these volumes capture money's complexities in both substance and form. In substance, insofar as they attempt a cross-cultural, transhistorical survey of money technologies and cultures that will illuminate its variability and complexity. In form, in that each volume takes up the same thematic areas, but in reading across the volumes one will discover that these themes are themselves complicated by having different eras' understandings of said theme juxtaposed with other eras' often incompatible understandings. Like a ledger book, then—one of the most basic manifestations of money's record-keeping devices—the volume can be read "down," reading the chapters within one historical period, and "across," reading the affiliated thematic chapters from volume to volume. What emerges is an affirmation that money itself is a cultural history.

Bill Maurer
University of California, Irvine

# Introduction

## *Approaching Medieval Money*

RORY NAISMITH

The Middle Ages have, as their name implies, for centuries been seen as an "in-between" period when the supposedly more refined and, to Renaissance sensibilities, familiar classical era gave way to a thousand years of cultural and intellectual backwardness. Such is still the view found in popular consciousness: witness the aggrieved gangster Marsellus Wallace in Quentin Tarantino's *Pulp Fiction* declare that he is going to "get medieval on [the] ass" of a rapist with an assortment of torture devices. Watered-down versions of the same conception of the Middle Ages as an era of violence and unthinking, fanatical religiosity can still even be found in more genteel settings (Manchester 1992; Greenblatt 2011). No one in the Middle Ages themselves of course knew they were "medieval;" the term only emerged, with a pejorative sense, in the seventeenth century as Catholic and Protestant historians constructed competing views of Europe's past (Murray 2004: 4). And while medieval men and women did have a great many misfortunes to bewail, so did most of their counterparts in ancient and modern times. As scholarship of the last two centuries has sieved medieval sources, and constructed and reconstructed views of this period, it has simultaneously highlighted how different the people of the age were in how they viewed the world around them, and also how familiar those people now appear in how they dealt with the challenges life posed (Arnold 2008).

Another product of this modern re-evaluation of the Middle Ages is a sharper awareness of just how arbitrary the label really is, and how pernicious the effect of overarching historical narratives can be; in the words of Chris Wickham, "historical development does not go *to*; it goes *from*" (Wickham 2016: 1–7). Nonetheless, one must start somewhere, and for the purposes of this volume the Medieval Age is taken to cover the period from about 500 to 1400. These dates roughly correspond to the end of Roman rule and rise of Christianity in western Europe at the beginning, and a concatenation of fifteenth-century events (voyages of exploration, development of printing, religious division, and stronger exertion of state authority) loosely associated with the onset of the Renaissance and early modern history at the end. Like every periodization in history, this breakdown can easily be challenged on all sorts of fronts. Its early end can be seen as the latter part of "late antiquity": an alternative division which highlights unity (particularly in cultural history) from around the third to seventh centuries CE (Brown 1971; Marcone 2008). Its later end can be pulled forward to accommodate fourteenth-century humanists, or stretched back to various perceived transformations between the sixteenth and late eighteenth centuries (e.g. Le Goff 2005 and 2012).

These traditional termini for the Middle Ages all imply that the core area of interest is western Europe. Only in the area roughly corresponding to the former western Roman Empire (minus the southern shores of the Mediterranean, and with the later inclusion of areas in central and northern Europe beyond the Roman frontier) does this chronology make much sense. Even thinking in terms of this region as a whole runs against the grain of Roman-period history, when the Mediterranean was a more appropriate unit that remained a zone of varying but constant connectivity thereafter (Horden and Purcell 2000; McCormick 2001; Goldberg 2012; Smith 2015). Roman rule in the form of the "Byzantine" Empire (which always called itself Roman) lasted throughout the Middle Ages in the eastern Mediterranean, although it lost much of its territory to the armies of Islam in the seventh and eighth centuries. The Islamic sphere which ensued cut across former political and cultural divisions, embracing at its height territory extending from modern Pakistan to Spain. For this vast area, let alone for polities beyond such as those of modern India or China, a "Middle Age" on the same terms as western Europe has no intellectual purchase, though the act of comparing networks, societies, and governments across long distances helps to understand the dynamic of local and long-distance contacts (Holmes and Standen 2015).

## VARIETIES OF MEDIEVAL MONEY

Money is a good tool to think with in comparative exercises of this sort, whether within medieval Europe, with other contemporary societies, or with other periods. It was present in some form everywhere. The central meaning of money in much of medieval Europe was a prescribed unit of precious metal, although in practice precious metal did not necessarily change hands in every transaction or make up the contents of savings and purses (see further Chapter 7). This aspect of the Middle Ages is arguably similar to the malleability of money in the early twenty-first century: dollars, euros and pounds are encountered as coins or promissory notes less and less frequently, losing out to cards and electronic transfers based on the same denominations (Maurer 2016). The malleability of medieval money took an altogether different form, however. It could be purely abstract. Law codes from immediately post-Roman western Europe reckon all manner of injuries and slights in monetary terms, from rape or murder through to individual finger-and toenails or teeth. The sums stipulated provided a point of departure for negotiation between the transgressor and victim (or the victim's kin), and reflect a widespread willingness to calculate human life and status in monetary units (Miller 2004). Actual payments might or might not include coins corresponding to the units in question. In some contexts (such as northern Spain in the ninth and tenth centuries) actual coins were vanishingly rare (Davies 2010). Shortage of coin—especially low-value coin—was endemic during the Middle Ages (albeit with some interesting exceptions: see Chapter 1). Complaints to the English parliament about the dearth of farthings and halfpennies became painfully common in the fourteenth and fifteenth centuries (Desan 2014: 124).

This is an important reminder that monetary history in the Middle Ages is emphatically not just the history of coinage; if anything it is more often the history of a lack of an effective supply of cash. For this reason, estimated figures of minting or coin circulation need to be read with caution as a gauge for broader economic activity: they depend on many factors besides demand for coin. The degree of want varied between regions, between town and country, between social groups, and chronologically, both across decades and centuries and, on a more human level, by season. Harvest time brought cash into the hands of peasants; payments of rent drew it out again. This was not a new phenomenon of the Middle Ages. Dealing with limited real coins and an extensive range of "imaginary" ones has simply been commonplace for millennia. Supposed alternatives to coin were in fact the norm for many medieval men and women. People sometimes exchanged "goods of equivalent value" (*res valentes*) including fabric, iron, food, and animals (Davies 2010; Hammer 1997). The range of commodities favored for exchange varied depending on location and social status. The wealthy might even make use of gold and silver, albeit not as coin. There was continual interchange between coin and precious metal in other media such as plate, jewelry and ecclesiastical vessels and ornaments. For the aristocracy, this was a favored way of storing wealth, with the added benefit of displaying it in a prestigious manner, though hard times could always drive gold and silver objects into the melting pot, or even into direct use for exchange purposes. In Viking-Age Scandinavia use of precious metal in this way was standard: even though good-quality foreign coins were available, they were treated simply as round pieces of silver and exchanged or cut up alongside objects. "Hacksilver" was widely used for exchange and storage of wealth, rated and valued by weight (see Chapter 7) (Figure 0.1). Gold and silver coins in the Islamic world were also rated by weight, and as copper became rarer in the Abbasid territories in the mid-ninth century, silver dirhams were cut into small pieces for use as small change (sometimes tested for quality by biting) (Ilisch 1990; Kool *et al.* 2011). Credit of varying levels of formality was inevitably common, and even when early bills

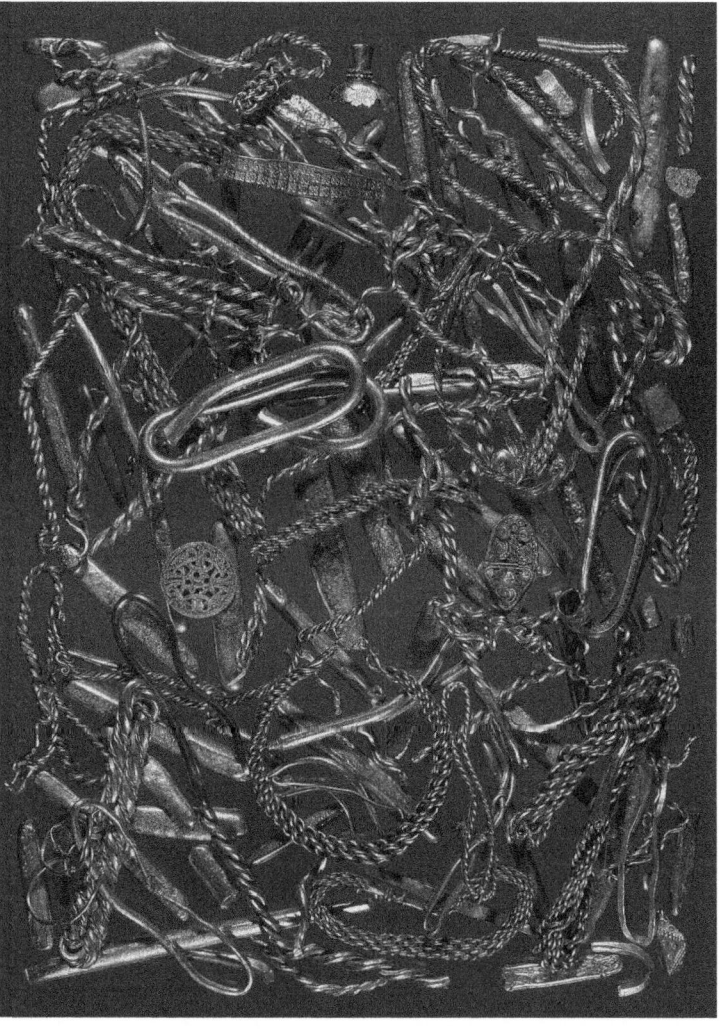

FIGURE 0.1: A hoard of silver objects and hacksilver from the Viking Age (ninth–eleventh centuries). Found in Rebild Skørping parish, Denmark. National Museum, Copenhagen, Creative Commons License.

of exchange appeared in the twelfth and thirteenth centuries (only becoming transferable at a later date) the presumption still was that gold or silver would eventually change hands (Spufford 2008). It was more of a supplement to than a replacement for coin. Availability of credit, at least as recorded in written records, was therefore richest in places with a relatively healthy supply of gold and silver (see Chapter 3).

But even though hard cash was by no means universal, it was still at the heart of the medieval monetary system. Some areas used other commodities as units of account such as slaves and cattle in early medieval Ireland or homespun fabric (*vaðmál*) in Iceland, but even in these cases gold and silver were still known and desirable (see Chapters 6 and 7). Elsewhere, the building blocks of the monetary system were units of gold and silver—pounds, marks, shillings/*solidi*, pennies/*deniers*/*denarii*—which in some cases had never been coined at all, and existed only as a value.

To facilitate understanding of the chapters in this book, it is necessary to have a broad overview of the major features of medieval money (for a similar breakdown from the perspective of use, see Chapter 4). This will be broken down into three chronological phases, each of which will consider the major geographical and other divisions.

## THE POST-ROMAN CENTURIES (*c*. 500–750)

The beginning of the period covered here was heavily overshadowed by the preceding Roman monetary system. With several tiers of currency from the high-value gold *solidus* (and its divisions, the *semissis* and especially *tremissis*) down to diverse copper-alloy denominations, the later Roman Empire catered for multiple levels of monetization. In practice, gold was the prestige money, preferred for state and aristocratic functions, whereas copper-alloy (rated in terms of gold) was uneven in supply and prone to inflation. Production of low-value coins was nonetheless a long-established responsibility of the state.

As Roman rule collapsed in the western Mediterranean during the fifth and sixth centuries, the monetary system endured in a straitened form. Importantly, gold coinage continued to be made and used on much the same level as before. Only in Britain and northern Gaul did it effectively vanish for any length of time. In contrast, Vandal Africa and Ostrogothic Italy preserved more complex monetary and fiscal systems for longer, down to the time of conquest by East Roman armies in the mid-sixth century. Everywhere, gold also continued to be the benchmark in terms of systems of account: the *solidus* held a central place throughout the Middle Ages, even though actual gold *solidi* were already a rarity in the West by the seventh century and eventually became just a unit of account. The preferred coin of the West from the fifth to seventh centuries was the gold *tremissis*: the smallest gold denomination within the traditional framework.

These coins reflected the shifting power politics of the period in a complex way. At first it was rare to recognize local "barbarian" rulers on gold coins explicitly and most instead referred to Roman emperors past or present. Eventually those of Gaul and Spain began to carry current details of production: the name of mint and maker in Gaul, and king and mint in Spain. But of necessity, the gradual constriction of the coinage to very high-value gold pieces meant that exchange based on actual coins fell to a low level; probably the lowest in centuries. Much of the populace must have dealt with coins only rarely.

In this period, minting and monetization were still circumscribed within the borders of the former empire. Gold coins were gradually reintroduced to southern Britain in the seventh century, on the Frankish model, and it was on the northern fringes of the former empire in Frisia and England that an important change took place about 670: abandonment of gold coin (the bullion for which had become scarce) in favor of a similar one in silver. These were the first pennies, adopted soon after in Francia. This zone of gold, and later silver, focused on the North Sea but extending down to the Mediterranean, reflects the emergence of a distinct trading sphere in the north at this stage. Further south, the Lombard and Visigothic territories of Italy and Spain retained increasingly debased gold coinages. The falling quality of gold in coins across the West from the seventh century remains a historical puzzle. Henri Pirenne associated it with a drain of wealth out of the West towards the richer, gold-hungry eastern Mediterranean, but changes in taste and demand closer to home may also have been a factor (Naismith 2014b: 8–20).

The debasement of gold and eventual move to silver in the north contrasts sharply with the experience of the East Roman/Byzantine and later Islamic polities. These maintained the late antique traditions of relatively numerous and high-quality gold coins, closely tied to fiscal incomes and expenditures, and of coinage in other metals. This included copper alloy for low-value denominations (still made on a large scale), while silver was also used sporadically in Roman territory but very widely in the Sasanian Empire and subsequently in portions of the Islamic caliphate.

In the eastern Mediterranean, there is relatively little to distinguish this period from what came before, except of course for the advent of a major new political and cultural force in Islam. The separation of the West, and its eventual evolution of separate monetary regions, is therefore a key development of these centuries.

## THE AGE OF THE PENNY (*c.* 750–1200)

Charlemagne (768–814) and his son Louis the Pious (814–40) played a major part in establishing the broader, thinner form of penny inaugurated around the middle of the eighth century in England and Francia as the dominant western

European currency. It differed from its Merovingian, Frisian and Anglo-Saxon predecessors in openly naming the ruler responsible for overseeing its issue, lending new vigor to the long and close relationship between royal authority and minting (Naismith 2012). Under Carolingian leadership, the silver penny of this form was standardized across the empire, Louis the Pious at one stage going so far as to remove all reference to specific places of production (Figure 0.2).

It was introduced to areas which fell under Carolingian authority or influence, including Italy and northern Spain as well as parts of Germany which had never before seen local production of coinage. A parallel and distinct series of broad pennies was made in southern England, while the northern kingdom of Northumbria stuck with the smaller, thicker model of the early eighth century until its conquest by Vikings in 867.

The silver penny, typically naming the ruler on one face and giving details of place or agent of production on the other, and commonly carrying a cross or other Christian symbols, thus became a hallmark of the Carolingian and Anglo-Saxon world, and of neighbors who imitated them. Expansion of the penny into Bohemia, Ireland, Poland, and Scandinavia occurred between the mid-tenth century and the millennium, as part of a general turn towards the western European mainstream (Bartlett 1993: 280–3, 286–8). Reckoning in pounds, marks, shillings, and pence (or at least translation of native units into these terms) also followed, albeit more slowly: in England the traditional system of twelve pennies to the shilling only became widespread after the Norman conquest of 1066. Although ultimately stemming from the same origin, the silver pennies of this long period varied widely in shape and quality. They developed in almost as many different ways as there were kingdoms, counties, bishoprics, and other polities which took up production. England maintained a comparatively unified currency, as did northern and central Italy, until the twelfth century. Across the former Carolingian Empire, issue of coin—once a royal or imperial prerogative—

FIGURE 0.2: A silver *denarius* of Louis the Pious (814–40), Christiana Religio type. Image © CNG.

gradually moved into the hands of local lords, as one of many rights which could be exercised and negotiated. They could hold the integrity of the coinage hostage, demanding payment from the populace for keeping the currency at familiar levels of quality (Bisson 1979). The Ottonian and Salian emperors in Germany oversaw rapid expansion of monetization in their lands by endorsing this devolved form of currency, and issued numerous diplomas allowing bishops, abbots, and secular aristocrats to produce coin. Some parts of Germany came to favor pennies of very broad, thin fabric in the course of the later twelfth and thirteenth centuries. Struck on only one side rather than two, these so-called bracteates (after the Latin *bractea*, "leaf") developed into one of the most artistically accomplished series of medieval coins. In the mints run by magnates in France, and in those of the towns of northern and central Italy from the twelfth century, the lures of debasement and the pressures of spiraling demand all too often led to the silver content diminishing to vanishing point. The resultant "billon" coins had just a thin veneer of silver on the outside.

In contrast to the overwhelming dominance of the penny in circulation, there was great diversity in units of account: pounds or marks for large values, *solidi/* shillings for multiples of twelve pennies, and a plethora of local variants. An added complication was that the differing values of individual types of penny were widely known: a penny in one location could be rated as two or a half somewhere else, while fixed payments ran the risk of falling (or, less often, rising) in value if the local coinage changed. In practice, therefore, although this was the age of the penny, a penny could mean many different things. There were also some alternatives to it in circulation. Obols or halfpennies existed, and in England and some other kingdoms pennies were cut into halves or quarters on a regular basis to make small change. At the opposite end of the spectrum, silver ingots and gold coins might be used for high-value transactions. Imported gold pieces from the Byzantine and Muslim world circulated alongside locally made specimens. Silver ingots served as a form of metallic traveler's check, to be melted down into local currency as needed (Spufford 1988b: 209–10).

The expansion of the penny was not limitless. As in the earlier period, quite distinct monetary systems prevailed in the Byzantine and Muslim worlds. In many respects these were little changed from earlier times. In Byzantium, there was still a healthy gold coinage tied to prestigious, valuable payments and fiscal expenses, although from the mid-eleventh century the fineness of the gold in these coins started to diminish substantively for the first time in seven centuries (Morrisson 1992: 300). Copper alloy too continued to be extensively used, recovering much of its vigor in the later ninth and tenth centuries after a straitened period between the later seventh and early ninth centuries (Morrisson 2002: 946–62). The Muslim world on the whole still favored a strong gold coinage, with an even stronger emphasis on silver and to a lesser extent on copper alloy, though there was increasing differentiation between polities as rule over the Abbasid caliphate fragmented. Some of the most interesting regions in monetary terms were those which had close contact with several of these cultural spheres. Southern Italy, Sicily, and the Crusader states drew on western European tradition, but also at various times on Byzantine and Arabic practices at the city of Acre coins were produced which bore Christian inscriptions in Arabic, arranged as on Islamic coins; these apparently originated as a response to a ban on unaltered imitations of Islamic coins (with Muslim religious formulas), which had incurred direct sanction from the pope (Georganteli 2012, 152). Further north, the Jewish Volga Bulgars of the tenth century modeled their coin issues on silver dirhams from the Samanid emirate in what is now the area around eastern Iran and Afghanistan, which circulated heavily in the area from the Caucasus to the Baltic. Meanwhile, the first Ukrainian coins (minted around the millennium) were based on Byzantine gold and silver. Gold Byzantine coins also had significant influence on the iconography of coinage in eleventh-century Denmark. Channels of cultural and economic contact, sometimes traveling long distances or crossing in unexpected ways, could be vividly reflected in money during this period.

## SILVER, GOLD, AND FINANCE (*c.* 1200–1400)

The silver or billon penny which was so well established by 1200 did not vanish in the subsequent two centuries that form the close of this volume. It was joined, however, by a more diverse range of other metals and financial instruments which, as a whole, amounted to the dawn of a revolution in the handling of money.

This was a transformation of two parts. The first relates to the appearance of new and more valuable denominations, which together alleviated the problem of merchants and other wealthy individuals having to transport impractical quantities of small silver coin. Larger silver pieces were the first stage in this process. A *grosso* or groat was minted at Venice in the opening years of the thirteenth century, in connection with payments for the Fourth Crusade. Accounting for twenty-four of the existing "pennies," it filled an important niche alongside the smaller coins as a new, larger level of currency. Other cities in northern Italy and southern France soon followed suit; northern France, England, and other major northern European powers did so from the 1260s, German mints from the start of the fourteenth century. A second important addition to the later medieval European monetary system was gold. Although they had never entirely disappeared from western Europe between the eighth and thirteenth centuries, gold coins were a rarity until being revived on a significantly larger scale at Florence and Genoa in the 1250s, building on precedents from southern Italy and Spain and benefiting from more favorable realignment of trade routes from gold-producing regions across the Sahara.

Before long these early gold coins circulated widely, at first in the Mediterranean but in the early fourteenth century further north as well. Imitations of the florin were minted from southern France to Bohemia, and other local gold coinages sprang up in short order, spurred by the opening up of gold mines in Hungary.

The fourteenth century hence saw the addition of another important new tier to the money of medieval Europe. Three of these had emerged: gold, together with "white" and "black" coin, referring respectively to the larger, finer silver pieces and the now badly debased descendants of the penny, by this stage containing little if any silver. Interactions between these levels of money, especially across borders, provide a dizzyingly complex reflection of how extensive and complex the circulation of goods and precious metals within Europe had become.

The second outstanding development of this period was also a response to the problem of how to efficiently and reliably transfer goods, people and money. Written documents (bills of exchange) developed by which a banker would record the receipt of money in one location, and instruct his agent in another location to adjust an account accordingly or make a payment to a named recipient. Bills of exchange had roots going back to the end of the twelfth century, when they first emerged to facilitate transfer of funds between Genoa and the Champagne fairs of northern France. They were widely used in major banking centers by about 1300. Double-entry bookkeeping appeared around the same time; written checks came in the second half of the 1300s, together with negotiable bills of exchange—that is, documents which could be transferred (by attachment of a separate note of paper or endorsement) to a payee different from the one named in the original text. In this increasingly literate and sophisticated world of high commerce, a typical merchant by about 1400, operating along the major commercial routes in western and southern Europe, would probably deal much more often in paper and promises than in hard cash (Spufford 2008: 44–5). But he would have encountered important limits. These innovations were founded on a concentration of literacy and numeracy that could not be matched outside Italy. Within the peninsula, the driving force for change was a close-knit series of mercantile and banking families. Early banking depended on solid foundations of personal trust, in spite of its use of written instruments. Within Italy banking was concentrated in and around major cities, and initially just among the elite; outside Italy it was run mostly by Italians, and was dominated by rich patrons. Bills of exchange tended to flow along certain well-worn paths between a limited number of financial centers: these were quite numerous between Tuscany and the Alps, and extended as far north as London and Bruges, but not east of the Rhine in this period. Large parts of Europe remained unconnected to the world of international banking at the end of the fourteenth century. There were other reasons why written transfers of money could not be used. Very small sums were (at least before about the middle of the fourteenth century, and then only in northern Italy) not practical, but very large sums were also beyond the scope of the system. When Pope John XXII in 1328 had to send 60,000 florins from Avignon to Lombardy to pay a papal army, he had to invest in 150 mounted guards, and still suffered the loss of half the money (Spufford 2002: 37). Nonetheless, a whole new dimension to money had developed, founded on accounts, contacts, and credit. The effect was to facilitate, and thereby multiply many times over, business between merchants at Europe's main commercial centers.

## OVERVIEW OF THIS VOLUME

The present book is not a narrative history of medieval money. This is a job that has been done well by many excellent surveys of the subject (Engel and Serrure 1891–1905; Grierson 1976 and 1991; Spufford 1988b; Kluge 2007), as well as by far too many specific chronological and regional studies to list here. The reader is earnestly encouraged to pursue these general works (and the detailed literature recommended in them) to learn more about what was going on with money at particular times and places. The aim of this volume is instead to place the broad development of medieval money into context by asking the same questions of it as are asked in other volumes of this series. It therefore gives an impression of what was distinctly medieval about money during these centuries. The result is in part a lesson in two perennial aspects of history: origins, in this case of monetary and financial systems which still recognizably underpin those of modern times; and difference, in that those systems are often profoundly unfamiliar and embedded in unrecognizable—even threatening—societies and mentalities. But there is more to the story than that. Money is a way into medieval thought and society. It was how economics impinged on daily life. It was one of the closest forms of contact the majority of people would have with their ruler. It was a way for kings to uphold good governance, or drum up extra income. Its making, giving and taking were laden with symbolism. It was, in short, an unavoidable fact of life for everyone, even for monks and hermits who sought to escape its influence. The seven chapters of this book emphasize the richness of medieval money as a subject in and of itself, rather than as a prelude to another story. They show how use of money was shaped by deeply entrenched religious values and social customs. They also show the opposite: how money affected society, sometimes in very subtle ways which confound the greedy or sanctimonious caricatures that had already gained currency in contemporary rhetoric (and which persist even now).

Chapter 1 by Oliver Volckart (Money and its technologies: The "principles of minting" in the Middle Ages) sets the scene with a masterly survey of the types of money and techniques of manufacture current in the Middle Ages. Considering prices and population as well as the needs and actions of rulers and manufacturers,

Volckart brings a critical eye to the different levels on which medieval money functioned. He highlights the ties between money and other economic processes: the balance of imports and exports, mining, and metallurgical processes essential to the correct fabrication of gold and silver coins. Chapter 2 by Laurent Feller (Money and its ideas: Payment methods in the Middle Ages) offers a deeply penetrating analysis of how money actually functioned in transactions. He looks further at the issues broached above of what money really is, especially at a time when the circulation of coins was marginal. From the eleventh century onward, he sees a stronger commercial side to the use of coin, and enters into further detail on the transformative effects larger silver and gold denominations had for merchants in the thirteenth and fourteenth centuries. Feller also eloquently explains the impact of money and changes in prices on different segments of society, and especially the poorest and most vulnerable. This theme is picked up by Giacomo Todeschini in Chapter 3 (Money, ritual, and religion: Economic value between theology and administration). Expertly interweaving patristic and later literature, he traces the nexus of value and money across a complex millennium, focusing on the rich Christian tradition of thought on wealth. Like Feller, he splits the analysis into earlier and later sections. The first outlines the emergence of a broad orthodoxy on money and its role in the Church and Christian society; the second looks at how that orthodoxy was put under pressure and modified in the period after the eleventh century, as commerce and trade quickened. The perennial challenge of credit (and the threat of usury it brought) receives special treatment given its prominence in the later Middle Ages.

Richard Kelleher in Chapter 4 (Money and the everyday: Whose currency?) turns to the practical experience of money for the population of medieval Europe. Placing the emphasis initially on the variety of finds available for analysis, Kelleher then moves through the Middle Ages, highlighting along the way points when coined money became more or less accessible, or began to serve different roles. He shows very cogently how diverse the forms of medieval money could be, and also how various segments of society would use them differently. Kelleher's chapter highlights the dual perspectives available to the student of medieval money: the tangible one of finds of coin occurring in modern times, with the interpretive challenges they pose; and the inevitably distant and problematic one of how medieval people understood the money they used. These two views are highlighted in a different context in Chapter 5 by Rebecca Darley (Money, art, and representation: The powerful and pragmatic faces of medieval coinage), in which she analyses and critiques the role of money as a vehicle for images and the communication of meaning. Importantly, she does so from multiple viewpoints: that of the immediately intended audience, or rather audiences, including everyone from the immediate intended recipients to contemporaries or near contemporaries who might use coins in a culturally or physically distant setting; that of the patron, who tried to use coins to communicate some sort of very basic or breathtakingly intricate meaning; that of the maker, who had to find a way of bridging these two in practical terms, and who might well have responsibility for including a recognition of local production; and last but not least that of "unintended audiences," including everyone from contemporaries or near contemporaries who might use coins in a culturally or physically distant setting to modern scholars. Calling on examples from a broad range of sources, she offers an unusually deep and multifaceted account of the visual dimension of money which reminds us forcefully that there is no one way to read the representations on a coin.

Svein Gullbekk revisits in Chapter 6 (Money and its interpretation: Attitudes to money in the *societas Christiana*) the question of how money was understood in a culture which was much more steeped in religion than the contemporary West. He looks at what money was, both in contemporary thought and how that measures up to modern readings, taking examples from some of the major thinkers of the Middle Ages such as Gregory the Great and Anselm of Canterbury. The tension between the Church's ideal and the actuality of day-to-day life is brought out very clearly. He offers a particularly interesting case study of the use of coin on church sites in medieval Scandinavia: a window of immense value into the earthy actuality of coin use in the focal point of local Christian society.

Finally, Rory Naismith in Chapter 7 (Money and the issues of the age: The plurality of money) returns to the tension inherent in medieval money. As his title suggests, it meant many sometimes contradictory things at once: a risk to the soul, but a means of expressing pious devotion; coins but also gold and silver in uncoined form, commodities or abstract words and figures, all of which could marry up in unexpected combinations; power in terms of spending, but with important limitations on the simple creation of money by fiat. This chapter also looks at problems concerning finds of coins, a major source in interpreting medieval money: to what extent can these be understood as representatives of deliberate or accidental deposition, or of gift-giving as opposed to commerce and savings, especially in the context of a Christian society with strong strictures on the proper use of wealth?

CHAPTER ONE

# Money and Its Technologies

*The "Principles of Minting" in the Middle Ages*

OLIVER VOLCKART

The young White King very often visited his father's mint and carefully inquired after all the principles of minting, because a mighty king and ruler needs to be acquainted with this art in particular . . . Thus the young White King became most ingenious in minting, considering the use he himself might derive from it, and when he came to rule he ordered the very best coin to be minted, both in silver and gold, better than any other king, and due to his art and experience no other king was his equal in coinage. The same young king also abolished and eliminated all bad and foreign coins in his kingdoms and let new good money be minted in many places, which was to the particular benefit of his people and caused their wealth greatly to grow, as well as increasing his own income from his demesnes . . . And having understood the experience and art of minting, he thought by himself that a king who failed to keep his realm's mines in order did not draw much advantage from them; hence he diligently inquired about each mine's nature and which regulations might maintain it best.

—Schultz 1888: 84, author's translation

This is how Maximilian I (1459–1519), ruler of the Holy Roman Empire from 1486, described an essential part of his education and the resulting policies in his fictionalized autobiography, where he appeared as the "White King." The

FIGURE 1.1: The young White King learns the principles of minting. Woodcut by Leonhard Beck (*c.* 1480–1542); from Maximilian I's Weißkunig (White King). http://digi.ub.uni-heidelberg.de/diglit/jbksak1888/0115

work was lavishly illustrated by leading Renaissance artists. Figure 1.1 reproduces the woodcut that shows the episode quoted at the start of this chapter. Below, we will follow Maximilian in his inquiries. We will examine the "principles of minting" about which he questioned his father's officials as a young man. On that occasion, he not only learned about the tools and implements used to produce coins, but also about fundamental questions of monetary policies. What currency units should a ruler issue? Which metals should his mint use? Should it produce coins that helped increase the ruler's wealth, or that of his subjects? And, last but not least, in what way should the mint be supplied with the raw material needed for coinage? Maximilian, "the last knight," was learning how to answer these questions at the very end of the Middle Ages, when more than a millennium had passed since the fall of the ancient Roman Empire in the West. By his time, emperors, kings and other rulers as well as the many coin-issuing towns and city-states that chequered Europe's political landscape had come a long way, during which their own answers had changed and developed. To a large degree this had happened in response to the changing economic circumstances that affected the demand for money. Before turning to the "principles of minting," we therefore need to examine these circumstances.

As money is not only a store of wealth and a measure of value, but also a medium of exchange, money demand was to a large degree a function of the importance of exchange. That barter was inconvenient was widely recognized in medieval Europe, as was the utility of money as a means of reducing this inconvenience or, in modern terms, the transaction costs involved in exchange (cf. e.g. Biel 1930: 19ff; Johnson 1956: 4.). How often people engaged in markets and how important the purchase of commodities was relative to self-produced goods, influenced both the absolute size and the structure of their demand for means of payment. The questions were, how much money did society need? And how much of this was small change, useful in day-to-day transactions, and how much high-purchasing power money, needed for example in the wholesale trade? It is important to note at this point that causality was not one-directional: While a growth in trade triggered demand for a larger quantity of money and a more differentiated monetary system, satisfying this demand might encourage a further increase in commerce.

The importance of exchange in the early Middle Ages has been debated. Points of view ranged from the hypothesis that markets were practically non-existent to the idea that exchange was flowering as early as the eighth and ninth centuries (cf. e.g. North and Thomas 1971: 782; Verhulst 2002: 113). The large monastic and noble estates of the Carolingian Empire certainly did sell their surplus, and on small weekly markets consumers could buy simple goods. There was also trade across the borders of the Carolingian Empire: with England, North Africa, Spain, and Byzantium (Verhulst 2002: 97ff.). In fact, according to modern research (McCormick 2002: 778), commerce at this time was already expanding from its nadir in the seventh century. However, there is no doubt that its total volume was still very small and that compared to goods people produced for their own consumption, those bought in markets played a minor role.

The "Commercial Revolution" in the sense of the spectacular growth in local, regional and long-distance trade that Robert S. Lopez had in mind when he coined the term, began to take off only in the tenth century (Lopez 1976: 56ff.). First in Italy and then further north, merchants developed new ways to finance their endeavors (Hunt and Murray 1999: 61). In consequence, the

Baltic, Russia, and the Middle East became for the first time firmly linked with western and southern Europe. At the same time increasing numbers of people moved from the countryside into the growing number of towns where they depended on buying the necessities of life. By 1400, the share of people living in places with more than 5,000 inhabitants had increased from practically nothing in the Carolingian age to almost 40 percent in Belgium, 30 percent in the Netherlands, and more than 20 percent in Italy. Even in England it reached 8 percent (Allen 2000: 8ff.).

By that time, Europe was in the throes of the Plague that between its first appearance in 1347 and the end of the fourteenth century killed about half of the continent's population. How this affected the economy and specifically trade and exchange is another current debate. Robert S. Lopez and Harry Miskimin suggested that the late fourteenth and fifteenth centuries were a period of economic depression (Lopez and Miskimin 1962); more recent research points to the growth of per capita output, the proliferation of regional fairs and the advances in market integration that took place at this time (Epstein 1994: passim; Chilosi and Volckart 2011: 769; Broadberry et al. 2015: 205).

There are no hard data, but neither is there any doubt that the absolute volume of trade in Europe was far larger at the end of the Middle Ages than at their beginning. What is more, while there certainly were pronounced regional variations, growth seems to have been almost uninterrupted between the eighth and the fourteenth centuries and seems to have continued, at least in per capita terms, even after the Plague. The wheels of exchange kept spinning faster between the seventh and the fifteenth centuries. To oil them, the European currencies did not only need to grow in volume; they also had to be increasingly complex and versatile.

## CURRENCIES AND DENOMINATIONS

The currency of the Frankish kingdom of the early Middle Ages was initially that of the late Roman Empire, with the focus being on the issue of gold, in particular on so-called *trientes* or *tremisses* that equaled one-third of a Roman *solidus* (shilling). One of the first measures that caused the Frankish currency to depart from the Roman model was the decision to abandon this *triens* in the late seventh century. Instead, the mints in the Merovingian kingdom (as in some neighboring regions such as Frisia) focused on the production of silver *denarii* (pennies) (Grierson and Blackburn 1986: 91ff.). From then on, *denarii* were the only monetary unit issued, with four equaling one old *triens* or twelve equaling one shilling (Spufford 1991: 33ff.). We do not know what triggered the reform. There is no evidence for the principles of minting in the pre-Carolingian period. An outflow of gold to the Arab world and the discovery of silver ore deposits in western France probably played a role, but there may have been at least one other motive: The lower value of the *denarius* implied that it was better suited to small transactions on local markets than the old *triens*; conceivably, this was taken into account when the gold units were discontinued (cf. Verhulst 2002: 88). Until the eleventh century, *denarii* remained the only type of coin issued in western and northern Europe. However, the onset of the "Commercial Revolution" presented rulers with a new challenge: how to meet the demand for complex currencies suited to the requirements of both local and long-distance trade. They had three options, which it is useful to consider systematically (cf. Redish 2000: 18ff.).

The most straightforward solution was to produce several denominations made of the same metal and with the same fineness, but different weights. This was the option chosen by the kings of England. They retained the penny, but from the mid-fourteenth century onward supplemented it with a range of other units. The quarter-penny (farthing) had a quarter of the size, weight, and content of pure silver as the penny, while the penny itself was equally carefully matched to its multiples, of which the four-pence piece, called the groat, became most important (Challis 1992: 701ff.). This may to some extent have addressed the problem of providing larger denominations usable in the wholesale trade, but small purchases still presented a problem. Thus, in the 1350s the average price of a tun (252 gallons) of cider was in the region of 12½ shillings (Rogers 1866: 448), which implies that even the smallest piece of money, the quarter-penny, would buy almost half a gallon. Still smaller coins, however, were impracticable. The quarter-penny had a weight of 0.31 grams (Challis 1992: 701)—less than a tenth of that of the physically smallest modern British coin, the five-pence piece. Anything still smaller would have been impossible to handle. How consumers were able to buy small quantities of relatively cheap commodities is not entirely clear. There is some evidence that late Roman low-denomination coins were still circulating in the fourteenth and fifteenth centuries, as were privately produced jettons (Dyer 1997: 40). However, the use of small-scale credit was probably more important (cf. Nightingale 2004: 51). We need to remember that even at its peak just before the Plague, the total population of England was only about half of that of London today (Broadberry *et al.* 2015: 20). Most people lived in communities where everyone knew everybody else. Under such conditions it was easy to buy small quantities on credit and to settle the balance once a sum had been reached that could be paid using a coin—which was the case for example after three or four pints of cider.

Another problem posed by the English way of structuring the currency was that producing a quarter-penny cost virtually the same amount of labor as minting a groat, whose value was 16 times larger. To save costs, it was therefore tempting to focus on issuing large coins. In consequence, currencies based on the principle that all denominations should have a proportional bullion content therefore constantly tended to be plagued by a shortage of small change

(Sargent and Velde 2002: 49ff.)—if this term is appropriate for coins that had such a comparatively high purchasing power as the quarter-pennies.

The problem of the small size of the lower denominations could be solved by choosing the second and most common option, i.e. by minting them from an alloy of silver and a base metal such as copper, which was comparatively cheap. Nearly all European rulers and cities that issued currencies did this from the twelfth or thirteenth century onward. When, for example, Louis IX (1214–1270)—St. Louis—of France introduced the *gros tournois* in 1266, whose nominal value was 12 *deniers*, the new coin was made of almost pure silver. The *denier* contained about one-twelfth of the amount of silver of the *gros*, but as it consisted of more than two-thirds of copper, its total weight of 1.11 grams made it large enough to handle comfortably (Blanchet and Dieudonné 1916: 225).

However, this option was problematic, too. For one thing, the costs of testing the bullion content of coins increased when the proportion of base metal of which they were made grew. Hence, issuing money with a high content of copper invited counterfeiting (Redish 2000: 21ff.). More importantly, using base alloys to mint small denominations did not address the issue of the proportionally higher costs their production involved. This problem could only be solved if the fine silver content of the smaller coins was reduced disproportionally. Doing this was dangerous, as St. Louis's successors soon discovered. Once consumers noticed that the silver content of the *denier* had been lowered to less than one-twelfth of that of a *gros*, they began trading the larger unit at a premium. Already by the beginning of the fourteenth century, Philip the Fair (1268–1314) had to acknowledge this, issuing a *gros* whose official value was no longer 12 but rather 26¼ *deniers*. The wild fluctuations in the value of the larger silver coins must have made exchange extraordinarily cumbersome, defeating the purpose of issuing a complex currency. Moreover, governments who over-proportionally reduced the silver content of their small

FIGURE 1.2: *Gros tournois* (4.22 grams total weight; 4.11 grams fine silver) and *denier* (1.11 grams total; 0.33 grams pure silver) of Louis IX. https://archive.org/details/manueldenumismat02blanuoft

change, thereby driving up the value of their larger coins, could be drawn down a slippery slope. To depress the labor costs of producing the small units to a sustainable level, they had to keep reducing the proportion of silver in their smaller coins—with no end in sight. Most avoided this trap, but in extreme cases the policy could end in episodes of rampant inflation (e.g. in Austria in the 1450s: Gaettens 1957/82: 40–51).

Moreover, minting authorities that chose this option had to find exactly the right share of base metal in their coinage: It had to be high enough that low-value denominations could be handled with ease, but not so high that the difference between the coin's nominal value and its production costs became too large. Rulers issuing a currency made a profit—the seignorage—from this difference, and if they were pressed for money they tended to focus on minting those coins where it was largest.[1] Hence, if their small coins contained too large a proportion of base metal, they tended to flood the market with small change. Contrary to what two respected economists (Sargent and Velde 2002) have claimed in a book highly esteemed by their colleagues for its analytical rigor, small change was by no means always scarce. Rather, late medieval Europe experienced periodic episodes of an oversupply of small change. From the 1420s to the 1440s, the Prussian estates repeatedly complained about this (Volckart 1996: 92, 99ff.). Further west, in Swabia, the analysis of coin finds suggests that in the fifteenth century up to 40 percent of the total value of money in circulation was made up of half-, one- and two-penny pieces (Schüttenhelm 1987: 429, 559). In late fifteenth-century Lübeck and Hamburg, conditions were similar (North 1990: 84). A Hamburger who in 1487 wanted to buy a barrel (*c.* 47 liters) of wheat using pennies had to count almost 90 of these minute coins that weighed less than one-third of a gram (for the price see Koppmann 1878: 521; for the currency Jesse 1928: 209)—an example which shows that using small change in large purchases involved high transaction costs. Hence, an undersupply of large-denomination coins could seriously impede trade.

This does not imply that the consequences of flooding the market with small change were all negative. The late Middle Ages were the time when small-scale commerce expanded rapidly. Hucksters, hawkers, and pedlars plied their trade buying and selling cheap commodities that satisfied widespread demand: "Poultry, eggs, cheese, fruit, and other food of penny value," are listed in a slightly later Bavarian territorial police ordinance that sought to regulate this trade; an Austrian ordinance adds "ironmongery, salt, woollens, and linen" (1553: LXIX; Schwiedland 1899: X). As these small merchants were itinerant (Figure 1.3 shows one of them carrying all his commodities on his back), local credit arrangements that depended on buyers and sellers interacting regularly could hardly develop. Small-scale trade would therefore have stagnated if consumers had not been supplied with low-value money that allowed them

FIGURE 1.3: The pedlar (from Hans Holbein Junior's *Danse Macabre*, 1524–26). https://archive.org/details/dancabre00holb

paying "penny values." The economic effects of this development can hardly be overrated. Hucksters reached places and people whom large merchants never visited, supplied consumers with goods that otherwise would have been impossible to buy, and thereby contributed to the shift from self-sufficiency to a market-based economy (cf. Braudel 1979: 58ff.).

While in countries such as England even small silver coins had a fairly high purchasing power, satisfying the need of wholesale trade with silver alone was difficult, in particular as prices seem to have universally risen once the "Commercial Revolution" began (Abel 1986: 19). However, there was a third option that rulers and urban governments could choose and that offered a solution to this problem: They could supplement silver with coins made of gold. Both Genoa and Florence began doing this in 1252, and within decades cities and princes from all over western and central Europe followed suit (Lopez 1956: 223ff.). Many authorities tried to integrate the new gold units into their traditional silver currencies. The city of Florence, for example, gave its golden *florin* the value of one silver *lira*, St. Louis his *écu d'or* that of half a *livre tournois*, and the city of Lübeck its *gulden* that of half a mark (Blanchet and Dieudonné 1916: 225; Jesse 1928: 214; Lopez 1956: 223). They all introduced bimetallic currencies where the ratio between the value of gold and silver coins was legally fixed.

However, the price of gold and silver depended on supply and demand, and as both never moved entirely in step, the relative prices of the two metals were bound to fluctuate. It did not take long for this to cause problems. Monetary theory traditionally supposed that fluctuations in the price of gold expressed in silver or in that of silver in gold would result in coins made of the metal whose value was rising being withdrawn from circulation to be sold as bullion. Bimetallic currencies were therefore assumed to have a constant tendency to revert to monometallism. However, this outcome is likely to come about only if two conditions are met: First, as culling coins, melting them and selling the metal is not costless, people will engage in monetary arbitrage only if the difference between the legal and the market ratio of the value of gold and silver is large enough to cover the costs they have to bear (Flandreau 2002: 492). Second, the local political authority needs to monitor market exchange closely enough to be able to enforce the legal ratio between gold and silver money. If this is not enforced, there is no incentive to withdraw those coins from circulation whose metal is appreciating on the market. Rather, they circulate at a premium (cf. Redish 2000: 30). This is what happened in most late medieval polities. Florence, for example, proved unable to stabilize its *florin* as equivalent of the *lira*: On the market, the gold coin had a flexible exchange rate in Florentine silver money (Spufford 1986: 1-25), with both metals effectively constituting different and parallel currencies issued by the same authority. Likewise, Lübeck's repeated attempts to fix the value of its gold *gulden* in its silver mark failed (Jesse 1928: 214). Using gold for large purchases still made sense, but the transaction cost savings were lost which a bimetallic currency with stable relationships between its denominations made of gold and silver had promised.

Many authors believe that the supply of high-purchasing power gold coins played a crucial role in the "Commercial Revolution" (Vilar 1984: 36), and to some extent this was certainly the case. A number of gold coins issued from the thirteenth century became popular all over western Europe, notably the *florin*, which was imitated by a large number of authorities (Berghaus 1965: passim; Giard 1967: passim). Venetian *ducats* and their Hungarian imitations played a similar if more limited role in east-central Europe (Volckart 1996: 47, 60, 212). Still, the commercial effect of gold should not be overrated. Peter Spufford (Spufford 1991: 240) already suspected that the increasing quantity of money in the high Middle Ages helped trade more than the new forms in which it circulated. More recently, statistical analyses have found that trade links between the Hanseatic towns of the late fourteenth and fifteenth century benefited more from the use of the same silver currencies than from the availability of popular gold coins (Volckart 2016: 26)—a finding that points to the overwhelming importance of local and regional small-scale exchange, which in total far outweighed large and generally better documented long-distance transactions.

In sum, medieval rulers who reacted to the growth in exchange by issuing currencies composed of several coin types faced a number of dilemmas. Using silver alone made it difficult to cover the whole range of denominations that consumers required; alloying it with copper invited counterfeiters, exposed the currency to the danger that the ratio between its denominations would become instable, and might provide incentives to focus on issuing small change, and minting both gold and silver amounted in most cases to issuing two parallel currencies that would circulate at flexible rates. In each case, consumers continued to face high transaction costs: less high, certainly, than if the early medieval one-denomination currencies had been retained, but higher than expected when complex currencies were first created.

On top of this, consumers had to cope with additional problems. Authorities did not always follow the lofty principles that Maximilian claimed to have learnt in his father's mint; rather, they often issued money to make a profit (the seignorage mentioned above). Secretly reducing the bullion content of the coinage—debasing it—allowed rulers to increase their profit. When this happened, coins of the same nominal but diverging intrinsic values tended at least for some time to circulate side by side, creating uncertainty among consumers and increasing transaction costs. In practice, therefore, which types of coins consumers encountered depended only in part on the desire of political authorities to satisfy the increasingly heterogeneous demand for money: Its supply could always be affected by their wish to increase their revenues by debasing the coinage.

## BULLION: FEAST AND FAMINE

How much seignorage rulers and governments received depended on how expensive producing coins was, and this, in turn, depended to a large extent on how much they had to pay for the coins principal component, i.e. for the gold or silver. Whereas they did have some choice when they had to decide whether and how to satisfy the demand for complex currencies, most of them faced far more restrictions when supplying their mints with bullion. In principle and with very few exceptions, which will be discussed below, there were only two possibilities: Either an authority controlled its own gold- or silver-mines whose output it turned into coins, or it had to use imported bullion. In the short term, an authority might experiment with various policies designed to increase the inflow of precious metal. In the long term, however, imports were only possible if the rulers' or governments' subjects produced sufficient goods for export in return for gold or silver, or if they provided services—e.g. in the transit trade— for which the subjects of other authorities were willing to pay.

The link between access to bullion mines and minting was close from early on: The importance of the silver ore discovered in western France for the development of the silver penny has already been mentioned. Since the 960s, silver deposits newly discovered in the Harz Mountains gained particular importance (Hillebrand 1967: 109), and 200 years later the Saxon Ore Mountains and Kutná Hora/Kuttenberg in Bohemia became the centers of European silver production (Castelin 1973: 1ff; Schwabenicky 1994: passim; Steuer 2004: 133–6). Production figures do not exist, but the general impression is that until the fifteenth century, all other mines remained comparatively unimportant. The fourteenth century saw a decline in output of at least some mining districts (Bartels 2000: 166), the fifteenth the discovery of new deposits and the opening of new mines, which resulted in the silver mining boom of the decades between 1460 and 1550 (Munro 2003: 8). Gold, by contrast, was nowhere in Europe produced in large quantities: From the twelfth century onward, there were mines in the Alps, Silesia and Hungary, but most of the metal was imported from Africa and Asia (Vilar 1984: 33ff, 47).

We do not know which ways the bullion took from mine to mint before the late Middle Ages. However, from the twelfth century onward mineral resources were counted everywhere among the rulers' "regalian rights" that were supposed to generate revenues (Thieme 1942; Hägermann 1999/2003). Mining itself was entrusted to organizations called *gewerken* whose members initially may have worked below ground themselves but later engaged primarily in finance, selling for example shares that by the fifteenth century were freely traded (Ermisch 1887: XCIff.). The *gewerken* sold a fixed percentage of the bullion they produced at a fixed price to the ruler, whose mint then had to buy it at a similarly fixed but higher price (Schirmer 2006: 92; Wolfstrigl-Wolfskron 1903: 65).

Given the uneven distribution of deposits of gold or silver ore, few governments could rely on mining to supply their mints: In the late Middle Ages, the kings of Hungary, the Habsburg rulers of the Tyrol and some other German princes, e.g. the dukes and electors of Saxony and the counts of Mansfeld, were important in this field. All other rulers depended on the import of bullion, and this normally required a positive balance of trade. The supply of bullion to the English mints, for example, always depended on England producing enough goods for export: This is why the wool and textiles trade with the Netherlands played such a crucial role in English politics. The kings of England sought to improve the situation by pursuing what have been called "bullionist" policies: Not only did they prohibit the export of gold and silver but they also tried to attract as much precious metal as possible. For example, a statute first published in 1340 required merchants to bring 1⅓ pound of silver plate to the London mint for every sack of wool they shipped (Munro 1972: 36). A more subtle way to reach the same aim was manipulating the exchange rate: If gold was to be issued, the mint would offer higher rates (in silver) for foreign gold coins and raw metal; if it planned to intensify the production of silver coins, it offered more gold in return for that metal (Munro 1972: 29).

Other rulers pursued similar policies, though generally with less success. Thus, the Teutonic Order in Prussia was well aware of how western European rulers supplied their mints. In the 1420s, the Order imitated such measures, trying to safeguard the gold supply by setting the rate its official exchange offered to above the market rate. However, while by the late Middle Ages the kings of England were able to enforce their policies, the Teutonic knights failed: their rudimentary bureaucracy was incapable of making sure that enough gold reached the mint (Volckart 1996: 144ff.). In any case, most medieval lordships were far too disorganized to even consider pursuing policies as sophisticated as the kings of England, whose mint published the price at which it would buy precious metals and then waited for members of the public to supply it with bullion. Most mints were left to their own devices, with their head officials, the mint masters, trying to persuade merchants to sell gold and silver at the best possible rate. Occasionally, for example in early fifteenth-century Prussia, the mint master would even engage in commerce himself, using the profits to subsidize minting (Volckart 1996: 147). As he could of course not buy silver whose market value was higher than the nominal value of the coins he intended to produce, such practices had at best a limited effect: They could help cover the labor costs of minting, but not much else.

There were some further approaches. In the first place, any ruler would be able to increase the supply of bullion by debasing his currency. As long as the public did not become aware of the reduced bullion content of his coins, his mint would be able to offer a higher nominal price for the gold and silver it bought. Even when experienced merchants and money changers did notice that the coins they received from the mint had been debased, they might still accept them: If they expected to be able to pass them on to other consumers, whose ignorance or weak bargaining position they could exploit (cf. Rössner 2012: 574ff.), they would be willing to take them on much the same terms as pre-debasement money.

A related policy relied on the fact that most European polities (with the at least temporary exception of England) lacked clearly defined currency borders, which implied that many coins circulated outside their territory of origin. If a ruler copied a popular foreign coin, reducing its bullion content and changing the original design just enough to avoid exposing himself to the accusation of counterfeiting, he would have a good chance of finding consumers willing to accept it at its full face value. The most famous instance where such a measure was employed was the "war of the gold 'nobles,'" that is, the imitation of English nobles by the Duke of Burgundy toward the end of the fourteenth century, which was designed to increase the inflow of gold into the Burgundian Netherlands (Munro 1972: 47ff.). However, similar policies were common in particular in parts of Europe such as the Holy Roman Empire, where a large number of currencies circulated side by side (Volckart 2009: 105). If the ruler whose coins were threatened by underweight imitations reacted by debasing his own money, the result could be rounds of competitive debasements, "*guerres monétaires,*" as Girard (1940) called them, that in some cases could lead to extreme monetary instability.

Finally, some rulers were able to exploit their favorable geographical location. The archbishops of Cologne, Trier, and Mainz, and the Count-Palatine, for example, jointly produced the so-called Rhinegulden, which became the most widespread commercial gold coin in the Holy Roman Empire and beyond. Obviously, the four rulers did not control any gold mines; and while Rhine wine was increasingly popular in the late Middle Ages, its export did not generate sufficient revenues to supply their mints with gold. However, the archbishops and the Count-Palatine did control much of the Rhine, which in the late Middle Ages developed into a transcontinental trade route of European importance (Chilosi and Volckart 2011: 773). The customs posts that they maintained along the river demanded—occasionally by extortionate means—payments in gold, and this allowed supplying their mints with raw material and minting Rhineguldens (Weisenstein 1995: 171). Thus, if a ruler's territory straddled an important trade route and was costly to circumvent, he did not depend on a favorable balance of trade. Neither did he need to resort to manipulating exchange rates, debasing his coinage or imitating the products of foreign mints: Rather, he could exploit commerce to supply his mint, which would thus be in a position that allowed it to produce a currency that was stable enough to become popular over a wide geographical area. Still, instances such as this were rare. Normally, the need to acquire the bullion necessary to keep up minting—and the stream of revenues derived from the mint—tended to water down the principles that Maximilian claimed to have learnt from his father's officials: Most medieval currencies were far less stable than the one he claimed to produce.

## ORGANIZATION OF MINTING

The previous section has shown that mint officials could enjoy different degrees of autonomy when it came to supplying the mint with bullion. In fact, how autonomous they were—that is, to what extent they were bound to follow directives of the political authority that officially enjoyed the right to issue a currency—differed in other fields, too. During the Middle Ages, rulers and governments experimented with a wide range of organizational options. One end of the spectrum was taken up by closely controlled officials who received fixed salaries. Semi-independent entrepreneurs occupied an intermediate position: They might have to produce coins according to a prescribed standard and to pay a prescribed seignorage into the ruler's coffers but could in all other respects autonomously organize minting. The extreme end of the spectrum was taken up by entirely independent entrepreneurs who were free to determine monetary policies themselves. This implies that, on occasion, rulers were not even able to pursue their own policies in a core field of economic activity; it indicates that mint organization was closely linked to issues of constitutional development and state formation.

One striking feature of the early Frankish coinage—the *trientes* or *tremisses* mentioned above—is that from about 570 the coins usually do not bear the name of the Merovingian kings ruling at the time they were minted. Rather, they are marked with the name of the mint and of the person who produced them, i.e. the moneyer. This not only reflects the fact that the Merovingian kings never claimed a monopoly of minting; it was also a consequence of the breakdown of the state-run mints of late antiquity that ceased to be regularly supplied with bullion. In this situation, individuals—some of them wealthy and of relatively high standing—took over, producing coins as well as they could (Grierson and Blackburn 1986: 98–101). Many aspects of their currency are still poorly understood. Thus, the fact that moneyers marked their products with their names suggests some sort of accountability—but if they were accountable, then to whom? Hardly to the Merovingian kings, who do not even seem to have been willing or able to determine basic features of the Frankish currency such as the content of bullion of the *trientes* (Grierson and Blackburn 1986: 109). Still, the seventh-century Frankish way of producing coins must have worked well enough to appear attractive to other rulers: seventh-century Anglo-Saxon England adopted the strongly moneyer-based organization of mints (Naismith 2011: 40).

A large degree of organizational autonomy was not a feature of early medieval mints only. One aspect of the breakup of the Carolingian Empire was the spread of the right to issue coins, which was acquired—or successfully claimed without the consent of a king or emperor—by a large number of secular and spiritual authorities. In order to ensure that their agents followed directives, many of these regional rulers entrusted their mints to servile members of their households, so-called *ministeriales*. However, as in other contexts—*ministeriales* were widely employed in all branches of administrations—lords tended to lose control of their agents (Bosl and Weis 1976: 76ff.). Where mints were concerned, this happened all the sooner because many were located in towns whose political clout grew in the high Middle Ages. With the rise of commerce, the economically independent inhabitants began to form communes which became increasingly interested in restricting the power of their lord (Ennen 1972/87: 122ff.). This affected the mint officials' status: Their former servility lost all practical importance, though they continued to acknowledge a formal link with the towns' overlord. A twelfth-century poem reflected this: "I am a moneyer, the mint here is my rightful fief" it has one such quasi-official claim, "God knows I need to flatter no one, being wealthiest in this town" (von der Hagen 1850: 112).

Early on, rulers who had installed *ministeriales* to manage their mints lost their right to appoint the mint master, which was taken over by cooperatives formed by the persons involved in the work of the mint. These cooperatives, called *serments* in France, *ministeria* in Italy and *Hausgenossenschaften* in Germany (Jesse 1930: passim; Spufford 1988a: 15ff.), became increasingly well organized, admitting new members by co-optation only and gaining a large number of privileges. By the twelfth century, they exercised an almost unlimited jurisdiction in matters relating to coinage: counterfeiting, offences against regulations concerning the exchange of currencies etc. (Jesse 1930: 60; Travaini 1988: 45). In France and Italy their members continued to be directly involved in the process of minting. In Germany, they focused on the monopolies they enjoyed in the bullion trade and currency exchange. Monetary standards might still be determined by the lords of the cities or increasingly by autonomous urban governments, but the corporations supplied the mints with raw material and financed the production of coins (Jesse 1930: 61ff.).

When the costs of minting grew—for example because mint output had to be increased at short notice—the corporations occasionally turned out to be unable to raise the capital that was required to finance production. In such cases, rulers might reassert their control, only to give it away by farming out their mint. This happened all over Europe and seems to have been increasingly common from the fourteenth century onward. Farms might last for varying numbers of years—from one in France to up to five or more in Germany and Italy—and both their degree of formalization and the terms under which they operated differed hugely between localities (Spufford 1988a: 17; Travaini 1988: 49ff.). The underlying principle, however, was the same everywhere, with William Turnemire's contract with the English government from 1279 being a typical example. William pledged to "cause money to be worked for the present in four places," i.e. at London, Canterbury, Bristol, and York,

> And in each of the aforesaid three places, Canterbury, Bristol, and York, he shall have under him a master to keep the said mint and its appurtenances; and he shall at his own expense bear the expenses and payments of his men in those places . . . So that the said Master William shall bear all the charges

and expenses in the said four places, and shall deliver the money to the king . . . ready in every respect at his own expense. And the king shall give him for every pound of sterlings seven pence.

—Johnson 1956: 59ff.

The farm holder would thus be responsible for financing and organizing every aspect of production; his profit would consist of a share in the regular seignorage.

William Turnemire was French, which was rather unusual, as Italian firms were particularly active in the management of mints. In Hungary, for example, entrepreneurs from Florence and Padua dominated mint farming in the fourteenth century, being also engaged in transferring Papal revenues and political subsidies to Rome (Stromer 1973–75: 87ff.). The Frescobaldi firm, likewise from Florence, was running the mint of Merano for the Bishop of Trent and the Count of Tyrol, the mint of London for the King of England and the mint of Castel Capuana for the King of Naples. Other Italians were active in Dublin, Toulouse, Lübeck, and Wrocław/Breslau (Spufford 1988a: 17). In the 1430s, the Teutonic Order in Prussia negotiated with the Alberti of Florence—at that time one of the largest trading companies of Europe—eventually deciding against this option, however (Volckart 1996: 110).

So far, no one has systematically examined under which conditions rulers and urban governments farmed out their mints. Lack of capital was one obvious factor, but an analysis of a related phenomenon, i.e. tax farming, suggests that other issues may have played a role. According to Edgar Kiser (1994: 290), pre-modern rulers used their own administrative apparatus when they were able to adequately monitor and sanction the behavior of their tax-collecting officials. When direct control was impossible or too costly, they resorted to farming because this provided them with a reliable income and gave their agents a strong incentive to collect taxes. In other words, market relations—farms—prevailed when high monitoring costs made hierarchies inefficient. Often, the situation in minting was similar. In particular in late medieval western and southern Europe, some mints had a huge output: Already in the 1220s, the Canterbury mint produced well over 3 million pennies per year, which amounts to about 11,000 per day or more than 1,000 per hour, if we assume a working year of about 275 days and a working day of 10 hours (Spufford 1988a: 20; cf. Penn and Dyer 1990: 366; Clark 2005: 1308). The Flemish mint output about a hundred years later was even larger (Blockmans and Blockmans 1979: 83). Under such conditions, monitoring production was a major task. As we will see below, producing coins was a complicated process that offered numerous opportunities for fraud and embezzlement. A ruler might employ a technical official—an assayer—to check the correct weight and fineness of the coins. In addition, he might try to increase transparency, for example by inviting representatives of urban elites to witness the assaying process—an option chosen, for example, by the grandmaster of the Teutonic Order in 1380 (Volckart 1996: 49ff., 396). However, making sure mint officials did not defraud him by manipulating the costs of raw materials and wages or by underreporting the quantity of money they produced with the aim of paying less than the agreed seignorage was a different matter. Farming out the mint reduced such difficulties. If a ruler could make potential farmers bid against each other, he could even auction off the farm for a lump sum, which he would receive in addition to the seignorage. This probably accounts for the popularity of mint farming in the late Middle Ages.

However, there were parts of Europe where small mints proliferated. In the Holy Roman Empire of the fifteenth century, for example, even important estates such as Saxony or Brandenburg preferred maintaining several relatively small "workshop mints," not least because sending money over large distances was dangerous in times when the enforcement of public peace left much to be desired (Ilisch 1988: 159). Moreover, most mints belonging to smaller estates such as counts, barons, abbeys, or towns operated only intermittently. Farming out such mints was impractical: it would have been unattractive for the potential farmer and unnecessary for the minting authority that was still capable of monitoring the mint personnel's performance given the small scale of production. Hence, most mint masters worked under conditions that began resembling those of modern public officials. They received a fixed and contractually determined salary, part of which was normally intended to cover the wages of their staff, too (Ilisch 1988: 163ff.). They were also regularly sworn in to their office. The oath the mint master of the town of Braunschweig took in about 1400 was typical: he promised "for the present year to faithfully preside over the mint, to the good and the benefit of the council and the whole town, and not to seek my own advantage above the salary that the council grants me" (Bode 1847: 187).

## MONEY AND METALLURGY

Coin production itself required not only organizational skills but also expertise in metallurgy. Determining the amount of pure gold or silver in an alloy was one of the most important tasks. The simplest way of doing this made use of a pair of instruments that allowed checking the fineness of precious metals: touch needles and a touchstone. The touchstone was a dark, smooth, stone-like basalt; the edge of the coin that was to be tested was scraped over it, leaving a colored streak. This color was then compared to that of the streaks left by the touch needles made of gold and silver of varying and known degrees of fineness. The method allowed the fine silver or fine gold content of coins to be determined with an accuracy of about 2 to 3 percent (Redish 2000: 22). Anything more

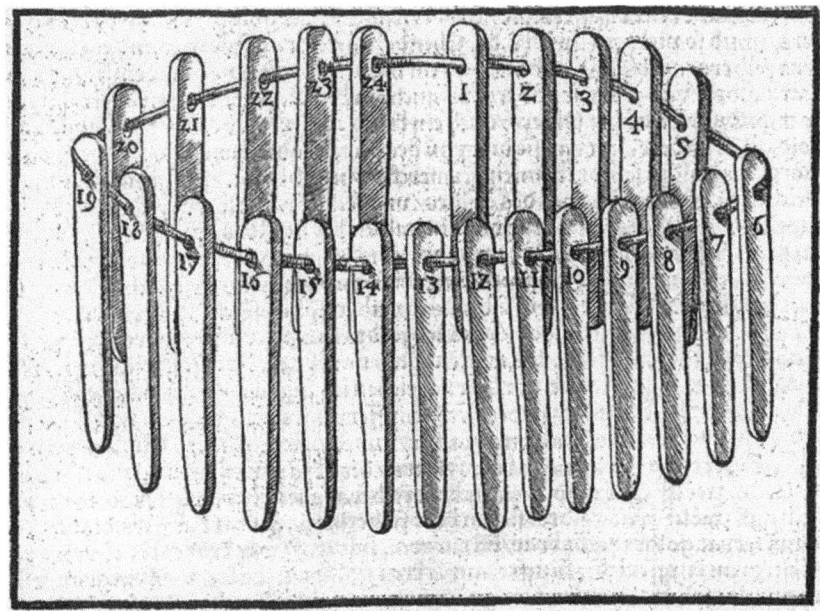

FIGURE 1.4: A set of touch needles, Georgius Agricola's *De re metallica libri XII* (1556). http://www.deutschefotothek.de/documents/obj/88960409/df_tg_0000409

precise required melting the coins with lead, which would amalgamate with the base metals they contained and which would also be absorbed by the porous earthenware of the crucible. The pure gold or silver remained at the bottom of the pot, with the metal's high surface tension forming it into small beads that were weighed and set compared to the original weight of the alloy (Emmerig 2006: 8).

Professional money changers, merchants and on occasion even peasants paid careful attention to the fine silver or gold content of the coins they were handling: Touchstones and touch needles were widely known. Consumers sometimes tried to exploit minute differences between individual specimens of the same type of coins by culling, melting and selling those whose bullion content was highest. This could end in speculative crazes which could ruin whole currencies. Hermen Bote, a late fifteenth-century chronicler from Braunschweig, described such an episode: according to him, merchants were the first who "traded and bought money for money or goods that were bullion and silver, and in this way became exceedingly rich, until at last the common burghers learned this trade too: Whoever had a good silver penny or a *gulden* of full weight solely looked to his advantage, until finally the peasants, too, learned this, so that no good penny, *groschen* or *gulden* would stay in circulation: whenever one appeared it was withdrawn" (Bote 1880: 410).

To prevent such developments, it was essential that coins were produced as uniformly as possible, with deviations from the legally defined bullion content being kept to a technically unavoidable minimum. This, in turn, required precisely mixing the alloy of which the coins were minted—a complicated task that was not made simpler by the use of widely diverging regional metrological systems, none of which was based on decimal relations between their respective different units. Thus, the most common unit of weight used to measure precious metals was the mark (locally different, anywhere between 190 and 280 metric grams) that was divided into 24 carats when measuring gold, and into 8 ounces, 12 *deniers* or 16 lots when measuring silver. Smaller units were e.g. the quentin ($\frac{1}{64}$ of a mark), the engels ($\frac{1}{160}$ of a mark), the grain ($\frac{1}{288}$ of a mark) etc. These units did not only denote weights, but also percentages: Thus, the carat was one twenty-fourth or 4.2 percent, the quentin one sixty-fourth or 1.55 percent and so on.

A problem set by a mid-fifteenth-century mathematical textbook shows how complicated manufacturing an alloy was using such units of measurement:

> Item, a mint master plans to alloy 36 marks of silver whose fineness is 8½ lots with 53 marks 9 lots whose fineness is 8½ lots and 68 marks 12 lots with a fineness of 9¾ lots in such a way that the resulting bullion is 6¼ lots fine. He has old coins whose fineness is 3½ lots and which he wants to add to the alloy. The question is: How much of this aforementioned coined silver does he need to use in order to produce silver that is 6¼ lots fine?
>
> —Vogel 1954: 118

Solving equations such as this (using Roman numerals and at best with the help of an abacus) was part and parcel of every mint master's work.

Once mixed, the alloy was cast into ingots that were hammered until they reached the thickness required for the future coins. These so-called flans were produced by workmen such as the one shown sitting and hammering a sheet of metal in the middle of the woodcut illustration to Maximilian I's autobiography (Figure 1.1). The next step was cutting coin-sized pieces of metal (blanks) from the flan; the woodcut shows that this was done with shears, one of whose arms was fixed to a base such as a workbench (on the left of Figure 1.1). The weight of the blanks of gold and large silver coins was individually checked and adjusted (*al pezzo*, to use the technical term), again using shears to cut off superfluous metal (underweight pieces went back into the crucible). The blanks of small coins were tested *al marco*, that is, the moneyer checked whether a prescribed number of them had a prescribed total weight, ignoring variations among the individual pieces (Emmerig 2006: 13). If the alloy contained a high proportion of base metal, the blanks might be left for some time in a vat with wine scale acid. This would dissolve the base metal at their surface, leaving a

FIGURE 1.5: Using Hindu-Arabic numerals became common only at the end of the Middle Ages; before then, people used calculating boards with counters or, at best, an abacus (from Gregor Reisch's *Margarita Philosophica* (Freiburg, 1503), fol. 79 verso). https://archive.org/stream/gri_c00033125008256329#page/n161/mode/2up

thin coating of pure gold or silver. Finally, the blank was placed between two steel dies, each of which was engraved with a negative of one side of the design of the coin. The lower die was fixed to a wooden block; the upper was placed by the moneyer on top of the blank and hit with a hammer—a process that transferred the dies' design onto the coin (this is what the workman on the right shown in Figure 1.1 is doing, cf. Emmerig 2006: 16ff.). In the course of the production process, the metal was regularly reheated to keep it from splitting. Like treating the blanks in acid, this caused a loss of weight which by the late Middle Ages was carefully recorded at each stage (as shown in the background of Figure 1.1). Even in small mints, the whole process was characterized by a highly developed division of labor that despite the absence of mechanization allowed a fairly large output.

## CONCLUSION: THE WHITE KING AND HIS MINT

Figure 1.1 shows the young White King visiting such a small workshop-like mint. However, through his marriage to the daughter of the last autonomous Duke of Burgundy in 1477, Maximilian became ruler of the Netherlands, the most developed part of Europe outside Italy. Flanders, Holland, and Brabant had an advanced minting culture: in the late 1470s, the quantity of money their mints issued equaled on average more than nine tons of fine silver per year; ten years later it was still almost seven tons per year (Munro 2009: 78). We are therefore probably right to regard the woodcut from Maximilian's autobiography at least in part as an artistic simplification: even before he became ruler of Burgundy, the Habsburgs controlled the rich silver mines of the Tyrol whose output they turned into coins (Moeser and Dworschak 1936), and this must have happened in mints that had more staff than the few persons shown in Figure 1.1. Once lord of the Netherlands, Maximilian became familiar with "factory mints" (Spufford 1988a: 19ff.) operating on a vastly larger scale. Still, the general economic, political and administrative principles that he had learned as a young man in his father's mint remained the same, and the woodcut that illustrated his autobiography shows an important part of them.

CHAPTER TWO

# Money and Its Ideas

*Payment Methods in The Middle Ages*\*

LAURENT FELLER

Examining payment methods in the Middle Ages implies examining the role of money in transactions, as well as the role of commercial exchange in the medieval economy. In more general terms, this question is tied to the importance of money in social life and its capacity to connect or oppose groups and individuals in the course of transactions. First, the issue of money stems naturally from economy, but the medium it establishes can perform functions other than those linked to value, as it puts individuals in contact with one another (Feller 2014). Medieval economies did not all make use of coins all of the time, and they also relied on all kinds of other objects to arrange a payment. Using non-monetary objects was common enough that one must wonder how sustained and continual growth could be compatible with an uneven use of monetary instruments, sophisticated forms of barter, and the use in exchanges of various objects valued at a fixed rate (Spufford 1988b). On the other hand, in peasant societies of that time, not many things resulted in an exchange of currency. The mutual aid necessary for survival in poor societies entailed the exchange of services, oftentimes in the form of unpaid labor which was nonetheless assessed and recorded as a debt: paradoxically, labor and skill served as a means of exchange or barter in that this labor or service was paid back through another labor or service, without the mediation of objects, and without seeking direct acquisition of money or objects.

Examining methods of payment equally leads to questioning the relevance of an intuitive view of economic life in the period spanning the sixth through the sixteenth century. As far as economic and monetary history is concerned, such a view allows for an account that can be integrated into the widely accepted general narrative in which money passes from being rare or rarely in demand to being the ultimate desired object, whether through the mechanisms of seigniorial levy or taxation, the organization of trade, or wage distribution. To claim that it is money rather than a service or an object that is coveted or desired is to liken the economy of the late Middle Ages and its history to contemporary economy, where money is seen as an end in itself rather than a means of obtaining other things (Testart 2001: 51–53). Such a claim certainly supposes, at the risk of being anachronistic, that economic life was shaped by a desire for wealth accumulation, which was far from evident in the Middle Ages. Pushed to its logical limit, this position would validate evolutionist hypotheses according to which an economy based on gifts, pillaging, and redistribution by those in power would be succeeded by an essentially trade-based economy.

One of the functions of money is to be a medium of exchange, and therefore a means of payment. Yet, in the Middle Ages, all sorts of non-monetary objects were offered and accepted as a means of payment during transactions (Feller 1998a and b). Objects were thus exchanged directly for other objects, or services for objects or other services, which was not incompatible—quite the opposite—with the existence of oftentimes sophisticated measurement and appraisal procedures, and with the fact that the two parties were fully aware of the monetary value of objects involved in the transaction. This implies accepting the existence of non-monetary payments, and that in a wide range of situations money was not expected, or if it was, it could be accompanied by other objects. In the context of the late Middle Ages, what comes to mind is a wage, which was not always paid in cash but rather in foodstuffs, clothing, or any other object that could help sustain the employee's livelihood (Beck, Bernardi and Feller 2013; Feller 2018b).

When discussing payment methods, it is important to mention a large number of cases in which, during a market transaction, money was not physically used even if it was present in the background for the purposes of appraisal. In fact, it was a common practice during the early Middle Ages to measure the value of goods with the help of a monetary standard. The transaction itself took place *in appretiatum* or by monetary substitutes (*in res valentes*); it was settled, in other words, with the help of non-monetary objects whose value was assigned through an agreement between the parties, or through a more general convention resulting in the transformation of these objects into money. In this context, the question of bartering, namely of an exchange that has not been settled through a medium or a formal appraisal, remains open: many undocumented exchanges could have taken place in this way, through a particular agreement rather than according to a general convention. We will see, however, that in many cases, resorting to non-monetary objects does not necessarily imply that the practice of appraisal was absent, but rather that medieval merchants possessed a sophisticated knowledge of the value of the objects in question.

This means that wages, which from the thirteenth century onward became an important part of payment, were paid partly in kind rather than in money, and that this monetary component was subject to continual reappraisal.[1] However, it is widely accepted that the choice of payment method determined the nature of the relationship established between buyer and seller: it was not presumed to be neutral, nor did it result in the suspension of any existing relationship between the parties. The payment agreement was part of a verbal exchange, which concluded the transaction but did not necessarily put an end to the relationship. The former might have continued, and might have actually helped shape the latter: clearly, accepting an animal as a form of payment for land allowed the buyer paying with an ox to play the role of a patron to his clients. In this case, he provided ways of continuing the exploitation of the land, and the economic value of the ox was added to the established relation of dominance. Similar observations can be made in the case of arms. Moreover, the land took on a monetary function insofar as it incorporated farmers' savings. It was a store of value that could be mobilized in order to acquire things that could not be produced through the land's exploitation, or something that could not be purchased directly on the market with the land's produce (Feller, Gramain and Weber 2005: 78–85).

Two very different phases should be clearly distinguished within the long period of the Middle Ages. The first period goes from the sixth through the eleventh centuries. Its distinctive characteristics are quite well known, but it should also be characterized by its relation to a currency that was undoubtedly less rare than traditionally believed, as well as to commercial and non-commercial exchanges (Pestell and Ulmchneider 2003; Loveluck 2013). The second period spanning the eleventh through the fifteenth centuries is precisely the period of the development of commercial exchange and of transformations in a number of economic structures. It was marked by, among other things, the diversification and multiplication of payment methods, and by a more widespread use of the monetary instrument, without that actually being the only method used. In fact, monetization of the economy was central to this period, even though money did not define every transaction in general.

## TO SETTLE OR TO PAY? FORMS OF PAYMENT IN THE EARLY MIDDLE AGES

In the latter half of the twentieth century, the development of studies of the early Middle Ages led to divergent and sometimes contradictory viewpoints. On the one hand, the earliest historiographers claimed that local trade was marginal, and as a consequence currency was not frequently used for everyday purchases. On the other, they insisted on the idea that only long-distance trade had any economic significance and should be considered in the context of the development of the Western world, excluding the possibility that wealth accumulation could be achieved through the production and marketing of goods. From the 1960s onward, a re-evaluation of local trade and a widespread application of perspectives from economic anthropology to the history of the early Middle Ages have considerably altered, though not unified, views on the role of money in economies and societies of the period (Despy 1968; Toubert 1983).

In fact, local trade was long considered to be marginal between the sixth and the eleventh centuries. Self-consumption was sufficient to cover peasants' needs, and there would be no need to rely on periodic markets to sell foodstuffs or buy finished goods. Basic needs were met by the domestic production of food and clothing. The issue of agricultural techniques and tools, and consequently that of metallurgy, was dealt with negatively and pessimistically by confirming the scarcity of iron and farming tools (Duby 1962; Fossier 1981). The question of whether there was a market for iron farming tools was circumvented by blaming the poor state of agriculture of the early Middle Ages and the people's inability to change their situation. Doubts as to the capacity for local trade of low-value goods were reinforced by the weakness and apparent unsuitability of monetary circulation. Thus, at least up to the Carolingian era, the only possible trade would take the shape of barter, and as a consequence would be simultaneously less developed and diversified than it would have been otherwise had an appropriate currency circulated (Duby 1973a). Finally, as far as the dominant class was concerned, their needs were largely met through dues paid on tenures, and, above all, through exploitation of their own demesne property through direct farming by the landowner: the image of a poor aristocracy was thus being established (Bonnassie 1990: 141–2). Needs for luxury goods were in turn met by high-value international trade with transactions settled in gold. The latter came, to a large extent, from profits made by war and redistributions of largesse carried out by rulers. There was a complete disconnection, therefore, between production and work on one hand, and aristocratic consumption on the other, as only the latter required a more or less systematic use of currency.

Since the late 1950s, however, the view that luxury goods did not necessarily circulate through commercial exchange, has finally gained acceptance (Grierson 1959). At least in the case of the elites, the economy offered a significant place for the acquisition and redistribution of luxury goods as gifts (Keller 2013). Objects of value circulated vertically in the form of rewards and incentives offered to the nobility by sovereigns or, more generally, by superiors to inferiors. In these circumstances, money served mainly non-commercial purposes: it was used for gifts and compulsory payments such as fines, or was accompanied by other objects, since gifting money created specific, oftentimes complex problems.

The political circulation of wealth was reciprocal. Every year, the nobles sent *munera* to their king, as did defeated people as a sign of their submission, thus ensuring the proper functioning of this circulation marked by reciprocity within the political society of the early Middle Ages (Nelson 2010). However, this circulation could stall in the case of a lost war when the conquerors become prey, as happened in the ninth century. Reciprocity also worked between peasants and lords by way of eulogies—compulsory gifts given as a thanks for the granting of tenure, qualified by Duby as "necessary generosities" (Duby 1973a: 63).

In this context, there was hardly any room for horizontal exchange such as the market trade of goods mediated through money. As a result, economic life functioned in parallel closed circuits. The first, that of the peasant economy, was characterized by production aimed at meeting the most immediate food demands for producers and their lords. Only rarely or marginally did this circuit resort to commercial exchange, and in most cases it did so without recourse to the monetary instrument. The aristocratic economy constituted the second circuit, which only participated in commercial exchange in a very secondary way, since the majority of needs were met through renders collected from agricultural production, and through a constant exchange of gifts between the sovereign and the nobility, thus ensuring a steady supply of luxury goods. Testaments and chronicles in many cases help us understand how these goods were allocated. Ecchard, the Count of Mâcon, for example, in his testamentary disposition of 876, distributed movable and immovable property—jewelry, arms, and books—among his relations and friends according to their rank and esteem (Bruand 2010). Similarly, at the beginning of the eleventh century, Meinwerk, the Bishop of Paderborn, distributed luxury objects among aristocrats with whom he had business relations, in return for their gifts (Feller 2013).

One can clearly see the shortcomings of this way of presenting the economy of the early Middle Ages, which risks transforming it into a variant of the economies studied by anthropologists in the most impoverished societies on the planet, while disregarding what we currently know about the reality of monetary circulation thanks to material, archaeological evidence. Between research on an exclusively monetary economy imposed, to some extent, by a free-market tradition, and the image of a moneyless economy, which anthropology could tempt us to construct, the reality established by archaeological finds is something else entirely.

## ARCHAEOLOGICAL REALITIES

Documentary reality and archaeological documentation in particular present us with a different landscape. In the 1990s, British archaeologists established the category of "productive sites" (Pestell and Ulmschneider 2003). Numerous sites, identified thanks to the use of metal detectors, contained a quantity of coins sufficient to at least partially reconstruct a map of places where trade—namely markets and fairs—took place on a regular basis, whether or not they were linked to the local population, to sites of power, or to centers of production and consumption. From that point onward, the goal of research has been to re-contextualize these finds within a larger economic and geographical context. In any case, the emergence of "productive sites" on the historiographic scene settled the debate that is crucial to our understanding of economic activity in the early Middle Ages, namely the capital importance of local markets in economic development. These exchanges involving agricultural surplus, tools, and clothing did take place at marketplaces where, at least in England, activity continued to increase after the 700s (Pestell and Ulmschneider 2003: 1–10).[2] Thus, beginning in the eighth century, the use of money as a medium of trade became widespread. This chronology corresponds to the abandonment of gold coinage, the opening of mines in Harz and Melle, as well as to the development of commercial exchange in the North Sea economic area.

Yet numerous difficulties and gray areas can be identified. It is particularly challenging to see a link between "productive sites" and large-scale trade, which on the periphery of the North Sea and the English Channel is structured around *emporia*. The development of these exchanges happened concurrently in the British Isles with the more rapid and intense circulation of Frisian *sceattas*, which were quickly melted down and imitated by the Anglo-Saxon kingdoms (Blackburn 2003: 34) at the same time that the *denarius* (*denier*) made its appearance on the continent. It becomes quite clear how *emporia* could be connected to larger economic systems shaped by the immense monastic and aristocratic land properties of the Frankish world (Devroey 2003: 161–9 Wickham 2005: 680–8). These *emporia* or *wic* were oftentimes sites of exchange coupled with minting workshops, as in the case of Quentovic. In fact, such on-site availability of payment instruments was one of the operating conditions of these institutions. It is no accident that one of the most beautiful examples of Charlemagne's *denarii* was minted in Quentovic (Figure 2.1). It was much easier to collect tolls in those places precisely because currency was available there. However, these institutions were fragile and did not withstand geo-political changes. Beginning in the eighth century, they suffered from the Franks' policy of expansion into Frisia: marginal to the system of augmenting aristocratic possessions, and with little military protection, they were also sensitive to those changes in the political and military environment that could influence the direction of commerce. In fact, a large number of them, including Quentovic and Dorestad, were abandoned by the ninth century or were moved—sometimes only by a few hundred meters—as happened in London, from the Strand to the City. Yet new trading venues began to emerge starting in the tenth century. Such was the case of Exeter, whose founding was an example of the durability of commerce despite the displacement of supply routes (Maddicott 1989).

FIGURE 2.1: *Denarius* of Charlemagne, minted at Quentovic (Grierson and Blackburn 1986, no. 749; Fitzwilliam Museum, Cambridge).

Details are missing, however, such as the material traces of trade routes that exist in written testimonies but which are insufficiently or incompletely documented by archaeology. If money circulated, we have to work backwards in order to find the objects obtained with that money. Yet the analysis of archaeological evidence found at coastal and riverside sites in England shows that such goods as earthenware and glassware traveled considerable distances, from the Rhineland to English and Danish *emporia* on the North Sea, without ever penetrating inland (Loveluck 2013, 2016). In other words, these "productive sites" are not yet well connected to the archaeological sites associated with consumption. Such elite sites as Flixborough were linked in their own right to trading networks bringing them in contact with distant lands, but these were not the same networks, and the luxury objects found there did not necessarily pass through *emporia* (Loveluck 2016). We find ourselves in a double impasse here, the first having to do with the circuit of goods exported through *emporia* and their links to commercial exchange, and the other with the circuits of elite consumption themselves. How far did the goods exported by *wic* penetrate inland? Did they reach beyond the coasts and river ports? Where did social elites acquire their goods, and how was the circulation of objects implemented?

## THE AVAILABILITY OF CURRENCY AND THE CHOICE OF PAYMENT METHODS

In this economy, while money was materially present, it was not necessarily an indispensable *medium* of commercial exchange. Participants entered and left the monetary system depending on context and their own needs. As

J.-P. Devroey reminds us, they had a whole range of possible ways to put goods into circulation (buying and selling, gifting and counter-gifting, barter), and they did not hesitate to use them all (Devroey 1993b: 353).

In this regard, Georges Duby cites two apparently contradictory examples (Duby 1973a: 69). In the 850s, the abbot of Ferrières, Lupus Servatus, was looking to acquire lead to resurface the roof of the abbey church. For this purpose, he solicited a gift from Æthelwulf, the King of Wessex, and in exchange committed to increasing the number of prayers said for the sovereign at his establishment (Levillain 1927–35: 71, no. 84). Shortly before, in the 830s, looking for ways to get the same kind of improvements to the roof of the Basilica of Saints Peter and Marcellinus, Einhard certainly negotiated a purchase of lead for the sum of fifty pounds from Abbot Fulk of Fontenelle (Hamp (ed.) 1889: 127–8, no. 36). It turns out, the same object could be achieved in a number of ways, and Carolingian administrators were able to mobilize all known forms of putting goods into circulation, including barter, gifts, and money-based commercial transactions. In the case of Lupus, it was an exchange of objects of different natures: lead, a quantifiable material object, for prayers, an immaterial, non-quantifiable good; in other words, a promise of salvation in the beyond. This was obviously a transaction that had nothing to do with commerce. Einhard, on the other hand, was engaged in quantification, measuring of commercial value, negotiation, and trade, which put his act in the category of commercial exchange mediated through money.

While reviewing different forms of payment used in Galicia in the tenth century, W. Davies was struck by their diversity and by certain forms of regularity in given geographical locations (Davies 2002 and 2007). She noticed in particular that close to the monastery of Sahagún in Castile, in order to settle purchases of parcels of land, the parties involved in the transaction would use grain rather than money or small livestock, and that they also occasionally resorted to clothing and beverages. Such choices seem to defy explanation and should probably be linked to the value assigned to the objects by the parties: it is possible that clothes had more value than foodstuffs and were therefore more sought after. Similarly, the use of certain goods as a form of payment—such as small livestock or beverages (cider or wine) that were easily obtained in this region but were less common than grain—addressed immediate consumption needs. Perhaps this was the result of a dialog between the parties involved, referring to the intention of the sale whose main motive could have been obtaining food.

Aside from the objects themselves, the existence of "ghost money" was probable. In León, Davies found payments made in *argentei*. This currency corresponds to what Luigi Einaudi called imaginary currency, rather than to anything that was or could have possibly been minted in early medieval Spain (Einaudi 1936). Regarding the *argenteus*, Davies proposes a hypothesis according to which we are witnessing a phenomenon that can be characterized as resilience; a term referring to an object that no longer exists physically but is preserved through memory and economic use. As it happens, the *argenteus* was a currency minted in the fourth century that was equivalent to twenty-five *denarii*. It no longer circulated in the tenth century but its name continued to be used to designate other monetary units. Davies believes that what is being referred to here were fragments of dirhams used to supplement sums paid during land purchases. A similar problem existed in the case of the Italian *mancus* in the ninth and tenth centuries. But this coin, which was used exclusively as an accounting currency, did not refer to a unit in present or past circulation (Rovelli 1992).

Money could also be used as a gift, even though cash gifts were sometimes regarded with suspicion, as in the anecdote told by Einhard in the *Translatio sancti Petri et Marcellini*. A man came to Seligenstadt to offer (*quasi pro dono tribuit*, "he gave as if in place of a gift," according to the text) an exact sum of money, forty *denarii*. First, Einhard asked him with some vehemence who he was and what he wanted, before having him explain how, why, and under what circumstances he managed to get the money that he now wanted to offer to the saints (Waitz (ed.) 1887: 249). The donor explained that this was the result of a wish made during his illness, which was cured by their miraculous intervention. The offering was the result of a commercial transaction—the sale of a pig— carried out precisely with the goal of offering the revenue to the saints. The purpose of the sale was to be able to offer, for lack of land, some money instead of an animal. In a way, the commercial transaction made for this purpose was sanctified. The giver did not look for any immediate reciprocity, since the benefit of having being cured was already obtained by him before the offering: it was about repaying a truly immeasurable debt, and not about merely buying something (Naismith 2014b). The use of money was unexpected in this context due to the ambiguity of the gesture, which resembled a purchase.

While money was available for various uses, the available quantity of coins was not always sufficient to meet demand. It is now widely accepted that the coinage of money, starting with the *sceattas* of the eighth century (Naismith 2014b), boosted the development of rural markets (Despy 1968; Toubert 1990; Devroey 1993a and b), and that the nature of seigniorial rents was such that it was necessary for peasants to have access to these markets: small sums were frequently required to pay land taxes called *cens* (Latin *census*), alongside dues proportionate to the harvest that were paid in kind or in the form of work. But there was oftentimes not sufficient cash, and in numerous cases other arrangements had to be made, due as much to inadequate circulation as deficient earnings or savings.

In the 840s, while managing his bishopric's property, Frothaire, the Bishop of Toul, was faced with a delicate situation. Not the least of its causes was a famine provoked by a series of bad harvests (Parisse 1998: 113, n°11). Having realized that his tenant farmers were not able to pay off their *cens*, whether in cash or produce, he required them to work on his own lands, all the while complaining that it was a costly arrangement for him: he had to feed the serfs who, according to the bishop, were not particularly good workers (Ibid.: *Unde nec censum ab eis debitum exigere possum nisi in opere manuum, pro quo rursus a me pascuntur et nec sic recuperari utiliter queunt*). Here, labor serves as a substitute for other forms of payment, which proved to be inadequate. It equally serves as a pretext for an act of charity, saving the serfs' lives by providing them with meals in exchange for work. In short, the failed harvest provoked a complicated situation in which the function of payment for the *cens* was switched from money or agricultural goods to work, and then from work to food—as part of an exchange inside of a domain whose proper functioning implied the creation of multiple profit opportunities (the exploitation of his land as well as that of his tenants), transforming anything that might have value, essentially labor and food, into a means of payment.

## FURTHER MONETIZATION OF THE ECONOMY

The monetary reform imposed by Charlemagne provided the Western world with a robust and flexible system that proved to be astoundingly sustainable. While it could be used to evaluate any sum, it was not adequate to settle every transaction. Even if it sometimes had submultiples (obols and pictes), the *denarius* would not have multiples until the thirteenth century. As a consequence, large payments were quite impractical, or had to be carried out with the help of ingots.

At the end of the tenth century, for example, the King of Poland, Boleslaw, wanted to buy back the body of St. Adalbert, the Bishop of Prague martyred by the Slavs (Hardt 2016). In order to obtain his remains, Boleslaw had to pay a substantial sum which he settled mostly in silver ingots, and incidentally in silver coins. The bronze doors of the cathedral of Gniezno depict this transaction: on one of the panels, ingots and coins are weighed on a scale as was the norm (Figure 2.2).[3] It was not a purchase of just any merchandise, but a ransom paid for a relic held prisoner. The use of objects without specific monetary value could be justified insofar as the relic, embodying the sacred, could not be the object of a commercial transaction: it needed to be completely insulated from mercantile exchange. It was therefore a payment made for an object whose value could not actually be measured. Here, the use of the silver's weight has an obvious justification, apart from practical reasons for the Prussians whose economy did not necessarily rely on money: one could not assign value to a sacred object.

Yet weight value seems to have been one of the features of exchange in the early Middle Ages, with the ingot being one of the well-attested payment

# MONEY AND ITS IDEAS

FIGURE 2.2: Panel from the Gniezno doors depicting the purchase of St. Adalbert's body, Creative Commons License.

methods. If it was hallmarked and inspected by a political authority, it was considered genuine currency. Otherwise, the weight and the hallmark of such objects were verified on an individual basis, which greatly diminished their usefulness, since the ability to quickly recognize a coin's value was an important part of its effectiveness as an instrument of exchange. Peter Spufford places fifty *solidi* as the limit short of which the use of the ingot was not possible and coins could not be replaced (Spufford 1984: 388).

The function of the ingot was manifold. It served as the store of a universally accepted value, and was easily converted into liquid assets. Travelers of high social rank carried them in much the same way that one would later carry traveler's checks in dollars. Spufford cites the example of a Germanic prelate from the early thirteenth century whose itinerary was marked by multiple transactions—eleven in total—conducted in different cities, allowing him each time to obtain the local currency necessary to cover his expenses (Spufford 1988b: 209–10). These ingots were standardized even if they were not necessarily certified: they always weighed the same, and, if they did not have a distinguishing mark, they were nevertheless guaranteed by the rank of their bearer, in this case, a bishop. Their provenance gave the trader indications of their pure silver content, which would obviously not be easy to verify otherwise given the absence of markings. In the sophisticated procedure of barter in which iron bars rather than silver ingots were used, as we see in the Pyrenees in the fifteenth century (Verna 2010), the identification of the mine where the iron was extracted and of the shop where it was molded allowed necessary information to be gathered on the quality of the metal to be exchanged, and on its commercial value and potential use. While the silver ingot was used as a store of value rather than a form of payment, that could not be said of the iron bars, which were used in both commercial transactions as well as in salary payments. In the example of the traveling bishop, the rank of the bearer was the essential guarantee of the object's quality, while in the example of the iron bar, it was the information on the object used as a means of exchange—easily verified in the local context—which guaranteed its value to the parties involved.

The prelate used standard weight ingots in order to avoid being encumbered by the excessive quantities of cash needed to cover his travel-related expenses. Occasionally, however, coins, even in large quantities, were preferred to all other forms of payment. This was probably true in the case of taxes. In 1286 in Valencia, for instance, a royal tax of £3,300 was levied, and it was paid off entirely in silver *denarii*. One of the explanations of this choice could be the fact that the authorities did not want to increase the cost of the tax by transforming money into ingots or, in other words, by buying ingots with this money. But above all, if they guaranteed the perfect correspondence between the amount requested and the amount paid through the exclusive use of coins, they did not in any way certify its real value, as these *denarii* could come from different minting workshops, which made it difficult to verify their origin (Furió and Garsia Marsilla 2014). Indeed, it presented a considerable mass and volume: thirty-one bags, each containing between 24,000 and 26,000 *denarii*, for a total of around 800,000 coins (typically 792,000), corresponding to an estimated weight of 775 kilograms. The issue was not so much the weight as the difficulty of handling all of these bags filled with currency of such low purchasing power.

However, at the beginning of the thirteenth century, multiples of the *denarius* came into use. The best known and the most robust was the *grosso* (Fr. *gros*, Eng. groat) first minted in Venice, corresponding to two grams of pure silver, and worth twenty-four *denarii* (or two *solidi*) (Figure 2.3). If we are to believe Martin da Canal, a chronicler of the period, the coin was struck in order to pay the salaries of masters of the shipyard who were at the time building a fleet to take Crusader armies to the Holy Land for the Fourth Crusade (Martin da Canal, *Les Estoires de Venise*, ch. XXXVII: ed. Limentani 1972: 46–7). The link between increasing monetary mass and the development of salaried activities, despite being of major importance, should be questioned here. Indeed, the increased demand for labor implied an increased money supply coming from the state, which was supposed to provide the public with the means of clearing

FIGURE 2.3: Venetian *grosso* of Enrico Dandolo (1192–1205) (CNG).

payments and to serve as a guarantor, that is to say, to respond to economic demands and requirements for equitable trade relations. The case of the Venetian Arsenal offers a good illustration of this. The newly minted currency was adapted to suit the procurement of supplies, the payment of large salaries, and the balance of fixed-price contracts negotiated with artisans. In fact, Martin da Canal speaks of the payment of the master artisans, making no mention of their salaries but referring often to their expenses, which simultaneously included payment for the supplies used, as well as the salaries paid to the workers performing manual labor.[4] In order to do that, the masters had to use coins with a lower purchasing power than the *grosso*, which had been newly released by the Venetian mint. Since the workers did not have permanent room and board, their most immediate need was to be able to pay for their everyday expenses, namely small coins necessary for buying food, clothing, and lodging.

Public authorities acted equally as guarantors of fairness during transactions. In urban economies, the non-payment of salaries, their delay, or instances of salaries being paid in merchandise, were easily equated with usury. At least this was the way the *Arte della lana* corporation looked at things in 1377 when it prohibited even partial salary payments in kind, as happened with payments in cloth (Rodolico 1889: 88–91).

Concerning large payments, the Western world was in better shape at the beginning of the thirteenth century. Beginning in 1250, gold coinage was slowly returning, even though silver was still dominant and widely used in commercial trade, whether as ingots or coins. Gold was used for payments within Europe as well as during trade with the Middle East. Between the ninth and the twelfth centuries, silver mine discoveries were rare, if not completely absent. To some extent, the mines of Melle and Harz satisfied the needs of a limited increase in circulation. In the tenth and the eleventh centuries, however, the Western world seemed to rely on its own reserve of precious metals—the result of a favorable trade balance, which may have been a surplus from the export of raw materials and the slave trade (McCormick 2002; Manzano 2013). Evidently, replacement currencies and elaborate forms of barter needed to be developed. Thus, between the tenth and the twelfth centuries, grain volumes and livestock could be used in Spain to settle commercial transactions (Gautier-Dalché 1969; Davies 2002 and 2007). In an arbitrary but consensual manner, monetary values were thus assigned to animals such as the ox or to quantities of wheat.

Things began to change in the middle of the twelfth century when new mines opened up in Saxony in Meissen, in Austria near Salzburg, in Freiberg, in Friesach, and in Italy near Volterra. From the 1160s until the mid-fourteenth century, new sources of supply were appearing regularly, resulting in a permanent, constant, and regular influx of precious metals (Spufford 1988b: 109–31). Yet this new abundance was accompanied by profound qualitative changes linked to the abundance and availability of money. On the other hand, the opening of Saharan trade routes allowed limited access to the gold of Sudan. This precious metal was quickly put into circulation in the form of ingots, as explained above, but also in the form of new coins such as the *grosso*, minted in the most economically active zones, and having a stronger purchasing power. In one way or another, this influx of currency is linked to the price inflation that took place in the late twelfth century, and was fraught with consequences. Nick Mayhew reminds us that this period was associated with a sharp increase in prices, and massive developments in the activity of monetary workshops all over Europe (Mayhew 2013a and b). All of this happened without manipulation of the currency: prices, monetary production, and commercial activity advanced together, and this had consequences for the entire European economic system.

## PRICES, TAXES, AND MERCHANDISE

The price hikes and the parallel emergence of urban markets also led to modifications of the seigniorial tax system inherited from Carolingian times, which was shaken by the need to adapt new modes of revenue extraction (Hilton 1992: 32–3; Feller 2009). It was no longer enough to levy labor, land taxes, and a little cash to maintain the revenues of a large institution or an aristocratic family. In addition, it was necessary to adjust to changes brought about by the emergence of urban markets. The noticeable movement of prices provoked mixed, if not contradictory, reactions depending on whether or not the lords were willing to engage in trade. Oftentimes, taxes to be paid in cash were converted since lords preferred fixed rents, either in cash or in kind. Labor service was largely commuted, which simply meant it was convertible into money, while the *champart* (a share of the harvest) was often replaced by a usage fee in cash. These two trends forced peasants to commercialize their products and to direct their flow according to the information gathered at the markets. Their perception of urban food consumption (types of cereal and meat in demand), as well as information on artisans' raw material needs could modify the nature of their production, without any mediation imposed by a lord. Initially, this conversion of taxes resulted in a drop in the producer's standards of living, since it more or less systematically corresponded to heavier taxation on their tenures. However, once it forced them to project their activity onto the market, it ended up being profitable, since from now on they had access to current information. Eventually, the fixed tax levied in currency allowed peasant producers to take advantage of monetary depreciation, the impact of which was not immediately visible, especially the spike in prices that came with it.

Things were different in the case of a fixed tax to be paid in kind. Here, the producer was further removed from the market, and it was the lord alone who benefited from the development of urban consumption and price fluctuations, both up and down. Production risks were transferred solely onto the peasant, while the lord, having quantities of merchandise at his disposal that were known in advance, could make the best of urban consumption by speculating on grain prices whenever he liked. His only concern was marketing. In short, in the late twelfth and early thirteenth century, the acceleration of currency circulation and the growth of the precious metal stock went hand in hand with a profound reconfiguration of the seigniorial taxation structures. The methods imposed on peasants for paying their taxes thus evolved depending on the lord's perception of the changing economic situation (Bourin 2009).

The movement and valuation of goods took place in complex circuits, which depended on surrounding social and political contexts. However, it should be taken into account that objects could have successively or concomitantly multiple positions in trade, and could have been desired for their trading or practical value. Whatever these objects were, they could serve as forms of payment or as goods in a market transaction. All of this took place in the context of the diversification of activities, and in a climate of relative monetary abundance that made changes to the revenue structure possible and opened the way to changes in consumption—that of dominant groups of course, but not exclusively so—while the use of objects as a means of payment or as a store of value continued to be the norm. They assumed or could assume a monetary function, as in the case described above where they served as a salary substitute.

## GOODS, WAGES, AND THE POOR

Luxury goods multiplied in the late Middle Ages and, along with them, the ostentation of wealth: the sumptuary laws decreed between the fourteenth and the fifteenth centuries are the clearest example of that (Muzzarelli 2003). In fact, in the latter half of the fourteenth century, there was a certain improvement in living conditions, which could seem paradoxical and oftentimes dramatic in a society profoundly marked by all kinds of difficulties. Yet, it did take place. Access to goods, especially clothing, which up until then was reserved for the social elites, became possible. On the other hand, the richest invested more and more in objects that were clearly meant to display and signify their fortune. Political and religious authorities reacted violently by prohibiting the flaunting of excessive luxury for moral and economic reasons, especially when it came to women's clothing and jewelry. The display of luxury was considered indecent in a society profoundly affected by misery. In addition, it diverted money from productive investment by immobilizing it in unproductive, sterile, and therefore useless objects: luxury was seen as a way of hoarding and immobilizing wealth, which, in a Christian society, in order to be profitable, was meant to circulate. All the Italian cities, as well as the major states such as the Kingdom of France, came up with laws of various severity, which in reality were poorly complied with because they were impossible to enforce.

But in reality, the proliferation of goods affected all levels of society, and many goods were present in even the most modest of households. They marked the general rise in standards of living, while permanently maintaining a monetary function. Savings in the form of money were indeed rare; it was rather objects that served to store value. When needed, they were converted into cash or exchanged for other goods or services. For instance, Boccaccio's novellas abound in the sometimes comical situations in which objects were used one after another in exchanges as a guarantee or a form of payment.[5] The development of the second-hand market, in respect to clothing in particular, followed suit. There were markets of this kind in every large city—the best known found in Valencia—with all types of clothing, from luxury items to the most worn-out rags (Garcia Marsilla 2013). Indeed, just as in modern times, servants' wages could take the form of gifts of used or old-fashioned clothing in place of cash, gifts that were destined to find their way back to the marketplace. For their own part, the poor sold what they had, whether the items of clothing in question became unnecessary due to bad fortune or there was a need to make the most of everything they owned in order to overcome a downturn. Incidentally, these people acquired the bulk of their clothing at the market.

Naturally, objects also served as collateral for loans. This was the case in Petrarch's quarrel with his old schoolteacher over a book (it was exceptionally valuable since, according to his own account, it contained the manuscript of Cicero's *De Gloria*), which he lent to him so that it could be pawned. Lending money directly was not appropriate among friends, while pawning a borrowed or entrusted object to a third party did not pose particular problems.[6] Seizing objects from a house in case of bankruptcy, or more frequently for non-payment on a loan, shows that movable possessions were always susceptible to being turned into cash assets (Smail 2013). In other words, this climate marked by monetary abundance could equally transform the living conditions of the lower classes, whether urban or rural, by giving them access to goods that, in addition to having use value, could also have a reserve and savings capacity, or the capacity to conserve value. In times of monetary difficulties, particularly during major shortages of billon currency at the end of the Middle Ages, this monetary function of property objects was seen as vital to survival.

We have already mentioned the issue of wages. Both in urban and rural economies, the remuneration of labor was fast becoming widespread. This issue was being discussed at the beginning of the early Middle Ages, as evidenced by the statutes of Adalard of Corbie (d. 827) (Semmler (ed.) 1963). Labor was already being considered a quantity that corresponded to a measurable value, even though one might have run into difficulties measuring and especially verbalizing this value. As we have seen earlier in the example of the ninth century, the interplay between money and goods or food was constant in payments related to labor, while labor itself was still considered a means of payment until the late Middle Ages. Mutual assistance among villagers included mutual evaluation of work, reciprocal commitments to loan tools, and the provision of labor services (Wilmart 2016). The available examples are still very few but are very convincing.

On the other hand, the question of remuneration is never clear or simple. Journeymen were normally paid in cash, but not exclusively. Often—if not always—a portion of the wage was not monetized. Instead, one could be compensated in meals or in kind in proportion to the harvested product or other completed work, and, quite frequently, in clothes. Thus, in a survey conducted in 1338 by the Hospitallers on their Provençal domains, the workers' pay comprised consumed meals and foodstuffs, a portion called *salarium*—generally consisting of a quantity of wheat allocated depending on the rank, scope of responsibilities, and expertise of the worker—and lastly, a sum of money allocated for clothing (Duby 1962; Beaucage 1982). Here, we see a whole range of payment methods used for remuneration of labor. Finally, wages, always tailored in the Middle Ages, were paid based on the reputation, skill, age, gender, and strength of the worker in question. Sometimes, this resulted in notable differences on construction sites of the late Middle Ages, which were justified precisely by the master's unequal appraisal of individual workers (Pinto 2013).

On the other hand, rank was marked as much by wage level as by the form of payment, and the choice of currency allocated for payment. On major construction sites, the main contractor was paid in gold once a year: the salary of the main architect thus became a veritable annuity. For the duration of the construction, he might also receive, in addition to his compensation, a canon's emolument or prebend, which was obviously as honorific as it was remunerative

(Victor 2013). As has been mentioned earlier, workers were paid in billon—a completely different form of payment, which in their case did not have a symbolic value.

The use of two metals—gold and silver—increased the possibility of having it both ways while also making various payment manipulations possible. A remarkable example is offered by the *studium* of the city of Perugia where the commune paid teachers' salaries in silver, but based the calculation on gold: the exchange rate applied in this case to the teachers' salaries was much more favorable than the one applied to the city suppliers, which was equally indicative of the esteem held for teachers when assigning their pay. While it seemed to be low from an accounting point of view, in reality it was elevated thanks to the exchange rate applied to a teacher's salary (Zucchini 2008).

Finally, in the complex double and even triple systems that emerged in the twelfth century, new moneys of account appeared and started to play a key role in the often sophisticated currency exchange operations necessary to reach an agreement on the amount to be paid. This simultaneously provoked speculation on exchange rates and established hierarchies within the communal personnel. Thus, in Perugia, all wages were calculated in a *florenus da camera*, the distinctive characteristic of which, aside from being a pure accounting fiction, was to have different values depending on whether the commune made or received a payment. By taking advantage of the difference in exchange rates, the commune was able to save on expenses while using payments for purposes that were not directly financial.

## CONCLUSION

Permanent features present in the variety of forms of payment used during the Middle Ages were the capacity to denote the value of things, and a remarkable ingenuity in finding ways to make trade possible in an economy marked by constant calculation, estimation, and valuation. Settling exchanges in a balanced manner, giving value to labor through remuneration, estimating rank, and establishing hierarchies were some of the many functions performed by the different forms of payment mobilized by the players in economic life. However, the choices were limited: the abundance or rarity of currency limited the possibilities that the complex trade structure could in theory allow. On the other hand, the development of commercial economy, the progress made in artisanal production, and improvements in the organization of seigniorial taxation paved the way to a truly sophisticated system of processing payments. The payments remained open-ended, however, in that they were never (or rarely) made with the goal of a full settlement. The participants did not look for ways to break free from one another but—on the contrary—to establish and reinforce close long-term ties. In all of its complexity, the attitude towards labor and its compensation is characteristic in this regard. Far from being considered a merchandise that could be acquired without a debt, it offers all the signs of an intentionally permanent relationship with all of the benefits in kind (meals, tips, gratuities, and clothing) highlighting its long-term character. Payment also reflected the existence of a hierarchy between people through the choice of the currency used (gold, silver, or billon), or the objects involved in a payment. Convenience played a role: bringing ingots along during travel was obviously more practical than equipping oneself with a multitude of currencies of different origin and low purchasing power. Finally, this question brings us back to the polysemic, multiform character of medieval exchange: at times commercial, at times non-commercial, at times a bit of both depending on the context and the intended purposes of each of the parties involved, which were rarely exclusive and which, depending on the economic setting, could take on different meanings.

CHAPTER THREE

# Money, Ritual, and Religion

*Economic Value between Theology and Administration*

GIACOMO TODESCHINI

The link between "money," in terms of both abstract *pecunia* and specific coins (*nummi*), and "religion," that is to say rituals relating to and institutionalized relations with the supernatural, was crucial in the medieval West. From the first beginning of European Christianization to the end of the Middle Ages, Western intellectuals and rulers began to represent religious mysteries in economic terms and simultaneously to attribute a sacred meaning to the cycles of economic life controlled by the social groups that could be identified as protagonists and guarantors of general wellbeing.

## MONEY, DEBT, AND VALUE FROM LATE ANTIQUITY TO THE TWELFTH CENTURY

The notion of "debt" existing both between living and dead, and between human and divine, is perfectly visible in many different kinds of religious cultures and habits (Malamoud 1983, 1988). Nevertheless, in the Jewish and Christian West the concept of debt as legal and ethical obligation assumed a specially monetarized, namely quantifiable aspect ambiguously linking the everyday economics and the economy of salvation (Anderson 2009). The close analogy established, during the twelfth century, between the charismatic power of the consecrated host to embody divine Value and the coin's capacity to express the value of things, is the culmination of a more ancient tradition describing mystic and metaphysical events in economic and monetary terms. Comparison of the sacred pieces of bread in the small, round shape of the host of Christian tradition with a coin of gold, silver, or copper (Morrison 1961) in fact had nothing to do with the material (corn or metal) forming the host and the coin, but instead with the abstract and physical power of both the host and the coin to denote religious Value and economic value simultaneously. The eleventh-century Eucharistic definition of transubstantiation as a result of the consecration of bread by priests recognized by the Roman Pope as authentically ordained gave rise to the idea that the host through consecration actually became the real body of Christ (and not simply an apt sign to symbolize it). This idea implied that the invisibility of Christ's Body was not contradictory to his real presence in the consecrated bread and in its symbolic reshaping: the host. The possibility of comparing the arithmetic power of coins to represent earthly value (and values) with the metaphysical power of the host to represent divine Value was thus directly linked to eleventh-century conceptions of the Eucharist (Shell 1982; Rubin 1991; Bedos-Rezak 2000; Todeschini 2000; Kumler 2011; Travaini 2013), which asserted that consecration of bread converted it into Christ's Body independently from the visibility of this extraordinary transmutation of substance.

In other words, from the eleventh century, liturgists and canonists, experts respectively in religion and law, began to create and circulate a specific religious language shaping the understanding of "Value" as an abstract and invisible quality embodied in a visible sign/object: the coin or the host. At the same time, the countable and measurable quality of this sign/object, that is to say its own concrete appearance, weight, size, and material, implied that "value"—even if intangible and immaterial—could be verified through the seal impressed on hosts and coins, and as a consequence might be calculated and infinitely reproduced (Shell 1982; Bedos Rezak 2000). Reproducibility of coins and hosts as symbols of value/Value implied that value and Value could be reproduced and simultaneously reappear in innumerable different places. It seems therefore incongruous to assume—as today sociologists of religions do (McKinnon 2013)—that "market rationality" (free market rationality, to be more specific) would be embedded in economic metaphors as the inner substance of religious discourse, or, on the contrary, that "religious rationality" as a discourse used economic metaphors to express its own meanings more clearly. From a historical and linguistic point of view this antithesis makes no sense. In fact, as will be discussed below, Western religious and economic lexica can be understood by those studying their specific manifestation in historical sources as a complex linguistic system shaping a unique and indivisible discourse both religious and economic. The economic metaphors and metonymies which structure Western Christian religious-economic discourse can therefore be understood as a formal and even essential characteristic of that discourse, laying the foundation for what the modern and most of all post-capitalist West will recognize on the basis of its own epistemology as a double and, perhaps, interconnected language (Todeschini 1994, 2002) (Figures 3.1–3.3).

The more visible linguistic recapitulation of this discourse on value, and things embodying value's substance, is shaped by some liturgical pronouncements produced between the eleventh and twelfth centuries by authors belonging to the ecclesiastic world of French and German reformers of the Church and supporters of the primacy of the Roman bishop: Ernulf of Beauvais Bishop of Rochester, Bernhold of Constance and Honorius of Autun (or of Regensburg) (Ellard 1943; Kumler 2011) (cf. Figure 3.4). The most renowned of these was the one contained in the *Gemma animae* or *De divinis officiis* ("The gem of the soul" or "On the divine rituals") by Honorius of Autun, written around 1120. When discussing the shape that bread consecrated by

FIGURE 3.1: The parable of the talents—one of many biblical metaphors involving money (New York, Pierpont Morgan Library, Manuscript M.521: Canterbury, 1155–60). http://corsair.themorgan.org

FIGURE 3.2: The parable of the lost money (New York, Pierpont Morgan Library, Manuscript M.140, f. 38r: Nuremberg, late fourteenth century). http://corsair.themorgan.org

FIGURE 3.3: The parable of the lost money (New York, Pierpont Morgan Library, Manuscript M.385, f. 38r: Bruges, mid-fifteenth century). http://corsair.themorgan.org

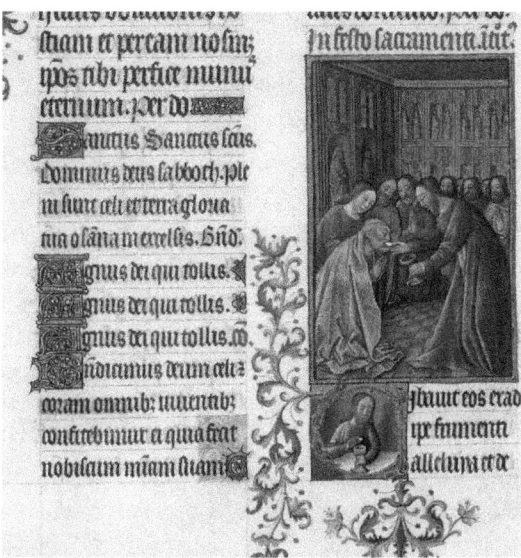

FIGURE 3.4: Adoration of the coin-like host (Chantilly, Musée Condé, MS 65, f. 189v. France, early fifteenth century). Wikipedia, Creative Commons License.

the priest during the Mass should assume (*De forma panis*), Honorius wrote that:

> The Bread then is shaped in the form of a coin, because Christ, the Bread of Life, was delivered for a sum of money, and it is He who, as a real Coin, will be given as reward to the workers in the vineyard. So, the image of God is represented in this Bread because the name and the image of the emperor too are engraved on the coin, and through this Bread the image of God is returned to us, and our name is inscribed in the book of life.
> —Migne 1844–64 ed., vol. 172, col. 555B; Ellard 1943; Bedos-Rezak 2000; Todeschini 2000; Kumler 2011; Brett 2012[1]

Even if, in this form, the formulation used by Honorius is conceptually and linguistically innovative, it is possible to reconstruct its origin and formation by looking back to more ancient theological concepts rooted in monetary metaphors of the relation between humans and God (Herz 1958; Bogaert 1973; Toneatto 2012), such as those formulated by Augustine of Hippo. In turn these metaphors were related to the proto-Christian linguistic tradition of describing the Incarnation of Christ through economic images. Some precepts directly attributed to Christ by the first Christian Fathers were also characterized by the use of monetary terms to express moral obligations. One particular *agraphon* (saying attributed by the Greek and Latin Fathers of the Church to

Christ) had proven crucial. It asserted that good Christians should be "similar to skilled money changers" (probati nummularii, "dokimoi trapezitai"), that is to say as expert in distinguishing good from evil as money changers are in distinguishing good from bad coins (Resch 1889, 1906; Rahner 1956; Todeschini 1994). Augustine as well as other Church Fathers like Ambrose of Milan, Basil of Caesarea and Clemens of Alexandria built extensively on this tradition of describing religious choices and spiritual life as a whole in economic terms. Augustine, more than other authors, in his sermons and treatises made use of economic metaphors to describe Christian duties and salvation, as well as sins and perdition. Among Augustinian economic images shaping spiritual or metaphysical realities, the representation of human beings as coins minted by God is of primary importance and has left a rich legacy extending down to modern times.

This representation of the creation of humans utilizes the image of true and false coins to underline strongly an analogy between authenticity and faithfulness or, alternatively, between probable inauthenticity and infidelity. This association of human beings with coins is then developed through a detailed description of the way authentic and trustworthy coins and humans can lose their authenticity even if they are perfectly "true." Loss in both cases can be the effect of "rubbing" (*defricatio*), which removes the image of the emperor from the coin and that of God from the soul (and body?) of humans. The obliteration of these images authenticating coins and human beings, caused by the rubbing of coins against soil and of humans against sin, will eventually annihilate the sign indicating the real belonging of coins and human beings to the economic and religious society conceived both as a market and a Church. The impossibility of deciphering the sign on the coin and on the human body and soul made these "objects" absolutely valueless: worthless things. In short, since Patristic times, Christian linguistic custom had associated coins and human souls and bodies by suggesting that their own worthiness derived from the impression made on them by the Lord, and that this mark had a specific economic meaning. In fact, the Augustinian emphasis on the monetary character, both of coins and humans, introduced into Christian theological and economic discourse the possibility of representing religious and moral values in terms of monetary value (Anderson 2009).

The widespread Patristic image of the Price of Redemption represented by the Passion of Christ was powerfully reinforced through the emphasis placed on the monetary meaning of human beings. The possibility of both specific, historical coins and all mankind losing their authenticity and value made economic language eminently suitable for depicting analogically the real and legal belonging of men and women to the Christian people, and for imagining the person of Christ as the central figure of a "sacred commerce" (*sacrum commercium*) connecting religion and accounting (Herz 1958):

Look, Christ suffered, the merchant offered his price. The money he handed over was his blood, the blood he shed. He carried our ransom money in a purse; he was pierced with a spear, the purse spilled out, and the price of the whole world gushed out.

—Augustine of Hippo 2000: 238; Poque 1960, 1984; Bynum 2007[2]

The importance of coins and money for Christian thinking before the sixth century is also apparent in the well-known religious invectives written by Church Fathers against Jews and Judaism. Indeed, among the arguments supporting this conflict about the *verus Israel*, the Jewish interpretation of Holy Scriptures (*hebraica veritas*) was described (by Ambrose of Milan, in the late fourth century, for example) as a devalued and worthless money, a "money" that had lost its own worth in consequence of the Jewish misunderstanding of its own real meaning and value.[3] Through this connection between correct understanding of religious truth and the value of faith, the idea of minted coins as the shape of money most appropriate to represent worthiness was confirmed, while at the same time money's value and meaning was seen as strictly connected to one's ability to recognize it (Schreckenberg 1982; Ambrose of Milan 1985a).

## MANAGEMENT OF MONEY AND WEALTH BEFORE THE "COMMERCIAL REVOLUTION"?

The notion of debt and indebtedness as a key concept for understanding the relation between earthly life and metaphysical entities is crucial for many different religions. The idea itself of "creation" implies a supernatural power giving shape to reality and therefore providing an origin for the indebtedness of living creatures to their creator (Malamoud 1983; Anderson 2009). Nevertheless it is hard to deny that the mainstream Christian religious perspective since its origins has conceptualized relations between humans and God in monetary terms, and represented the foundational event of the entire Christian narrative—the Passion of Christ and resulting Redemption of humankind—using money as a measure of values and Christ's sacrifice (namely the blood of Christ: Bynum 2007); as quantifiable value compensating that of the original sin which in turn was represented as a bond (*arrha*) possessed by the Devil since the beginning of times. Even if elements of this connection between money and salvation can be found in Jewish Scriptures, and particularly in the Mishna *Pirqe Avot*,[4] it seems clear that the Western development of representations linking money (and coins) and religious life directly depends on Christian transformation of the notion of indebtedness; a notion which results from the physical death and resurrection of God in order to extinguish the debt shaped by the original sin committed by the first human creatures (Anderson 2009).

On the linguistic basis established by Christian Fathers, the relationship between money and religion, that is to say between monetary logic and the dialectic of Salvation, notably developed during the early Middle Ages. In this period (sixth–eleventh centuries), the growing patrimonies of monasteries and dioceses were described, by ecclesiastic writers and especially by the ecclesiastic laws gradually composing what will be called Canon Law, as sacred wealth economically representing the Body of Christ itself. During the same period, on a different textual but similar narrative basis, the ongoing construction of the figure of Judas as a complex character summing up different kinds of infidelity and untrustworthiness, came to define more closely the monetary meaning of religious faithfulness. From Latin Church Fathers to Christian authors of the sixth to the eleventh centuries such as Cromatius of Aquileia, the Venerable Bede, Isidore of Seville, Hraban Maur, and many others, and also in the continuing stratification of conciliar canons, the "avarice" of Judas was increasingly portrayed as an effect of his incapacity to understand the real value of Christ, so that the thirty silver coins paid to Judas for Christ's betrayal/selling were depicted as an absurdly low sum of money which came to signify not only Judas's untrustworthiness but mainly his inability to appreciate and understand Value. Subsequently this characteristic would become a stereotype identifying "false" Christians, namely those whose lack of faith corresponded to ignorance of criteria for the correct estimation of social values (Todeschini 2010, 2011).[5] In this way, the capacity to correctly appreciate the value of everyday things and the Value of sacred things and persons finally could emerge. This monetary/moral discernment had been affirmed in the *agraphon* attributed to Christ as a central characteristic of good, faithful Christians: it was this quality that definitely made a man or woman into a true citizen of the *civitas Dei*, and, consequently, a reliable participant in the economic exchanges embedded in the earthly side of that holy City.

Indeed, the close connection between Christian administrative languages related to the managing of ecclesiastical property and Christian theological languages expressing the logic of the metaphysical economics of Salvation formed the core of a deeply ambiguous Western economic vocabulary, perpetually fluctuating between transcendent and everyday governmental meanings. It was as a result of this ambiguity that, for example, monastic rules from the fifth to the twelfth centuries, could affirm the religious importance of "rationally" managing the sacred goods of Benedictine houses. The growth of Cluniac monasticism after the tenth century and the Cistercian monastic reform during the twelfth century introduced differences and controversies to the pre-existing Benedictine tradition but did not eliminate this religious/economic semantic nexus; rather they transformed it by placing a different emphasis on the mystic significance of economic choice and investments. In fact, beyond the polemic between Cluniacs and Cistercians (exemplified by the works of Peter the Venerable of Cluny and Bernard of Clairvaux) about the correct use of monastic wealth and incomes by abbots, what clearly connects these two different discourses is the vocabulary and conceptual syntax they have in common. In both cases monastic wealth was described as a sacred store of wealth consisting of land, coins, buildings, and precious objects whose administration is at the same time earthly and divine; the crucial difference between these two monastic points of view rather has to do with the use of this holy wealth, namely with the economic criteria which regulated the investment of monastic revenues (Bredero 1971; Rosenwein and Little 1974; Rosenwein 1989; Brittain Bouchard 1991; Devroey 1993; Noell 2008). Nevertheless, although from a Cluniac perspective these incomes should be spent on liturgical apparel, marbles for decorating the churches and on the seigneurial life of the monks in general, while from a Cistercian perspective the wealth of a monastery should be systematically reinvested in land and improvement of its administration, in both cases the problem was how to rule holy monastic goods so that their own religious and economic value could be truly preserved and enlarged (Little 1978; Brown 2015; Naismith 2015). In both cases sacred goods and their economic value needed to be venerated as a manifestation of divine power and magnificence.

The intimate link between religion and money, that is to say between monetary value and spiritual value of things and persons, had its roots in the theological language of Salvation and, at the same time, was embodied by ordinary administrative ecclesiastic and monastic rules organizing the economic life of territories managed by bishops and abbots. This linguistic equation, nonetheless, became socially pervasive from the ninth century. It became the starting point of ordinary Western Christian economic languages for two main reasons: the solid and durable relation between political and ecclesiastical powers formally inaugurated by Carolingian emperors; and the legal codification of the sacred wealth of churches and monasteries as patrimony of the poor (*res ecclesiarum sunt patrimonia pauperum*). Justinian's Code, in the sixth century, had enshrined the close connection between imperial substance and ecclesiastical properties. It was, however, after the alliance forged between the Carolingian emperors and the bishops of Rome around the middle of the eighth century, that an exact equivalence of ecclesiastical possessions and revenues with the imperial treasury was affirmed by imperial and episcopal *capitularia* (Magnou Nortier ed. 1993–7). All at once, on the basis of more ancient canonical definitions, the administration of church goods was legally defined in collections of canons composed between the seventh and eleventh centuries. The new practice in the management of wealth was for income from different sources to be expended in different ways: for the building or restoring of churches, for the sustaining of clerks, for the managing of dioceses, and for the subvention of the poor (Brown 2012; Toneatto 2012). The formal destination of one part (normally a quarter) of ecclesiastical revenues originating from gifts, acquisitions, inheritance, tithes (Lauwers ed. 2012), and economic transactions to the needs of the poor, that is to the supporting of *minus potentes* (all those, the majority, who were lacking in power), transformed the seigneurial protection of the poor traditionally performed by ecclesiastical lords and churches into a kind of sacred accounting. This in turn directly emphasized the close relationship between administration of holy goods and social welfare, and at the same time demonstrated the sanctity of Christian economic organization that derived from the correct managing of ecclesiastical wealth. The consequence of this linguistic and political alchemy was the sacralization of Christian economic language and rationality beyond and outside the exclusive circle of the sacred economy concerning churches, monasteries, and imperial domains.

## MONEY AND FAITH IN A QUICKENING ECONOMY (ELEVENTH–FOURTEENTH CENTURIES)

The intricate connection between religion and money in the Western Christian world became even more highly developed during the so-called "economic revolution" of the central Middle Ages (tenth–thirteenth centuries) (Naismith 2015). Problems connected with the correct management of Church goods or its opposite, simony (i.e. commerce of sacred properties and charges), and formal definition of the inalienability of ecclesiastical land, combined to emphasize the fusion of economic and religious logic. The growing trans-territorial charismatic power of the papacy characterizing the Gregorian Reform movement played a direct role in the categorization of religious institutions (churches, monasteries, confraternities, hospitals, religious Orders, etc.) as nodes in a model moral and legal economy. Secular powers from the twelfth up to the fourteenth century on the whole accepted the clerical affirmation of sacred patrimonies as a higher form of public administration. This sacred and institutional economy therefore became synonymous with right economy, and economic justice could appear as an obvious attribute of the sacralization of economic transactions, the core of which could be represented as spiritually crucial. This process of sanctification of the economic interplay of the growth and safety of ecclesiastical and monastic goods was deeply embedded in the more general reorganization of local markets, which itself was related to the growth of seigneurial economic policies encouraging exchange and favoring commerce both for fiscal and entrepreneurial reasons. However, it is very difficult to neatly differentiate the Western growth of a "lay" economy performed by landlords, money changers, and merchants, from the parallel growth of a sacred economy shaped by the organization of the huge possessions of churches and monasteries. This was the responsibility of ecclesiastical administrators and emerged alongside the remodeling of Western ecclesiastical institutions into a new collective and a relatively centralized political/economic whole, the Church, whose leading power, the pope, through canonical definition of usury, acceptable forms of credit and the difference between simony and right transactions, aimed to define the very notions of economic righteousness and legitimacy. Even if experts in Roman Law from the twelfth and thirteenth centuries onward began to produce definitions of credit, money and economic contracts in general that in some cases were different (Piergiovanni ed. 1993; Quaglioni, Todeschini *et al.* 2005) from those codified by Canon Law assembled between the ninth and twelfth centuries, many crucial economic categories and ecclesiastical representations established during previous centuries and summed up by Canon Law became an integral part of standard legal and institutional economic rationality in both medieval and modern times. Indeed, these categories and representations, especially those connected to the central idea that the holiness of money was confirmed by its capacity to express sacred values like those managed by ecclesiastical powers, became established as the starting point of late-medieval Christian economic ways of thinking.

Indeed, a huge part of market life—that which was controlled by sacred institutions—did not adhere to the common rules concerning exchange. The fact that sacred goods of churches and monasteries (including land and relics, vessels, and buildings) were seen as inalienable objects, that is to say as representatives and fragments (Geary 1990; Bynum 1991) of a Value both commercial (i.e. calculable) and spiritual (i.e. unpredictable), was then enormously influential on the entire logic of evaluation, particularly on the definition of the crucial notion of right economic evaluation and "just price." On the one hand, the economic exceptionality of sacred commodities and the impossibility of expressing their price in terms of a simple relationship between "supply" and "demand," suggested to lay participants in ordinary markets that sometimes prices could be shaped by unquantifiable elements and qualities (as for example those which belonged to a charismatic subject). On the other hand, the partition of markets into distinct but intercommunicating spheres, the sacred and the secular, as well as (from the eleventh century) the prohibition against laypeople administrating, buying, and selling the holy goods of churches (and thereby committing the sin of simony), paradoxically came to legitimize (as Humbert of Silva Candida wrote around 1060) markets and economic exchange among the laypeople who continued to respect the difference between sacred and ordinary economic spheres (Todeschini 1994).

The ancient Christian monetary metaphor which described—according to Basil of Caesarea and Ambrose of Milan (Ambrose of Milan 1985b; Toneatto 2012)[6]—circulation and good use of riches through the image of water that by its flowing becomes pure and potable and thus useful and productive (whereas hoarded money is compared to stinking and useless stagnant water) during the Church Reform in the eleventh century was used to support arguments against simony. The crime was depicted as a sacrilegious form of thesaurization, which desecrated holy wealth by obliterating its correct use. In this way, desecration, uselessness, and hoarding of sacred wealth came to be seen as complementary aspects of the same economic and moral abuse, and revealed the misunderstanding of Christian economic complexity which characterized infidels and false (that is to say untrustworthy) Christians. The idea that rational use of wealth and money was synonymous with its appropriate spending, and that the principle of rational correctness in spending was founded on recognition of the difference between sacred and ordinary value, became a foundation of the Christian religious and economic right to participate in markets. From the eleventh century onward, economic interaction between ecclesiastical and lay institutions, as well as clerics and merchants, expanded continually, and representation of the value and price of commodities as something only partially consisting of quantifiable attributes became a widespread economic concept. Money in turn began to be viewed as an object whose ability to quantify values included the marvelous power to calculate the hypothetical, spiritual value of sacred things. Ancient Christian metaphors of Salvation as wondrous exchange and repayment of a debt through the coin shaped by Christ's blood, began during the medieval economic "revolution" to metamorphose into the possibility of describing money as actually able to represent conjectural values like those symbolically characterizing sacred objects and charismatic powers.

The so-called "economic revolution" of the Middle Ages—the acceleration of economic life in the Christian West from the eleventh century (Poly and Bournazel 1991)—coincided with two apparently divergent phenomena: the "conversion to poverty," that is to say the widespread assumption of evangelical poverty as an exemplary Christian lifestyle, and the diffusion of credit and financial contracts as an ordinary way of doing business. Historians, with rare exceptions (Little 1978; Todeschini 1994, 2009a), normally did not pose the question concerning the relation between these two apparently different novelties. It is however important to perceive the subtle but strong and close link that connected the mystery of Christian poverty as a specific economic choice governing the use of resources, and the systematic recourse to credit as economic technique transforming markets in networks of obligations based on reciprocal trust. In both cases money as coin tended to disappear from the scene and vanish from sight. It was replaced by forms of reasoning based on the use and hypothetical value of useful and marketable things that, though systematically keyed in to money as a universal measure of values, made the value of all things into something computable in a probabilistic way. The first step in this direction was apparently represented by the eleventh-century redefinition of the meaning of institutional possession of ecclesiastical goods and, consequently, by the reshaping of the role of ecclesiastics and monks as administrators and holders but not owners of sacred patrimonies.

The discovery of evangelical poverty as a model of Christian life, and the reconstruction of the figure of Christ as suffering poverty and no longer as a triumphant Deity and role model for emperors and mighty sovereigns, was an effect of the progressive estrangement of the ecclesiastical sphere from the seigneurial and imperial one, a development which began around the middle of the ninth century in the French-German Carolingian area. The culmination of this process came in the second half of the eleventh century, during the so-called Gregorian Reform (Gilchrist 1972; Capitani 1990; Tellenbach 1993) and its more dramatic episodes. On the one side the Schism of 1054, which separated western and eastern Church and clearly opposed the Roman pope to the Byzantine emperor, and on the other the Roman synod of 1059 which established new rules for the election of the pope and his essential independence from the power of German Western emperors (Szabò-Bechstein 1985), were the final steps in distinguishing the style of rule represented by lay landlords, kings, and emperors from that personified by priests, bishops, and popes. This new form of ecclesiastical power codified by the most notable Gregorian Reformers as charismatic power governing both territories and souls, depended on three main fundaments: the celibacy of clergy; a deep liturgical renewal which affirmed the supernatural potency of priests when celebrating the Mass and producing the "Eucharistic miracle" (Browe 1938; Rubin 1991; Bynum 2007)—the real presence of Christ's Body on the altar—every day and everywhere; and, finally, the firm distinction between wealth institutionally pertaining to churches and monasteries and substance owned by individual clerics.

This third aspect of the Gregorian "revolution" was often summed up through narratives comparing the individual "poverty" of priests, bishops, monks, and abbots, with the affluence of the institutions such as dioceses, monasteries, and parishes which they skillfully ruled. Peter Damian, Humbert of Silva Candida, and Hildebrand of Soana (who was elected Pope Gregory VII in 1073), as well as many other protagonists of the Reform, repeatedly and insistently underlined in their letters, treatises, and pamphlets the ethical, pragmatic, and governmental superiority and efficiency of power managed by charismatic leaders who had chosen a lifestyle based on abstinence from riches. Refusal of luxury and wealth distinguished the clergy from lay seigneurs and identified them as the evangelical poor. Indeed, during this recodification of the model of clerical life, the deeper meaning of the sin of simony was labeled as directly dependent on avarice (*avaritia*), namely on an individual's perverse desire to become owner of an institution's consecrated wealth and thereby to transform public and holy riches into a piece of a familial or private property. Establishment of "poverty" and pauperization as the main characteristics of the renewed ecclesiastic lifestyle (Little 1978) thus served to promote new forms of economic rationality. This dovetailed with the shaping of administrative practices founded on the link between the relative economic insignificance of bishops and abbots, their economic asceticism and probable sanctity, and the magnificence and profitability of the mobile and immobile substance that they handled. From the Gregorian Reform and its fight against simoniacs, through the Cistercian redefinition of the monastic criteria of management of lands and revenues during the twelfth century, to the Franciscan debates about correct use of wealth, money, the price of commodities, and markets, "poverty" (from *paupertas* to *usus pauper*) became the key concept in religious thought, widely used to pursue and deepen the relationship between money and the different aspects of value embodied in material things (Bériou and Chiffoleau eds. 2009; Todeschini 2002, 2009a; Lenoble 2013).

## CREDIT AND CHRISTIANITY

During this period, marked by the distancing of ecclesiastical economic ideas from those of the seigneurial sphere (eleventh–thirteenth century), credit became the main form of economic transaction, undertaken by lay businessmen as well as religious and secular institutions (*Credito e usura* 2005; Bougard 2010). Merchants, farmers, monasteries, churches, cities, and kingdoms, and indeed the popes themselves, were more and more involved in credit relations; that is to say, in a system of obligations created by lending and borrowing, buying and selling of rents, promises of payment, and payments of interest. It is perhaps not so imperative to establish a causal relation between the shift of ecclesiastical economics from the eleventh up to the thirteenth century and the concurrent growth of a credit economy in Europe, as past scholars often did. Nevertheless, it would be incongruous to deny the simultaneous emergence of these two historical phenomena in post-Carolingian Europe, from north-central Italian cities to French-German domains and the newborn kingdoms of France and England.

On the whole, the development of an economy of credit coincided with the growth of a new economic jurisprudence embodied both in Canon and Roman Law (Santarelli 1984; Prodi 2008, 2009). This was concerned with the contractual subtleties implied in the multiplication of financial relations in markets, and reshaped the social meaning of money payments and money (*pecunia*) as a tangible sum of coins (*nummi*). This reconsideration was consistent with the religious relativization of money and wealth that emphasized the role of institutions as charismatic subjects authorized to cultivate the sacred wealth of churches through a "profit economy" whose accounting logic was simultaneously political and probabilistic. Christian credit economy, as it developed during the twelfth century in the most commercially active areas of Europe, had at its core a system of dealings held together by trust (*fides*). This semantically ambiguous word (Todeschini 2002; Prodi 2008) indicated both the trustworthiness of those who as partners were involved in a business relationship, and the mutual recognition of each other's belonging to a kinship with a boundary marked by the acceptance of political and religious rules as well as by ritual behavior increasingly controlled by the ecclesiastical territorial leaders. The ancient Christian linguistic practice of describing metaphysical concepts through economic lexica came to be, at this stage, the starting point of a form of economic reasoning which hardly distinguished religious belief from economic reliability. To trust somebody became at once the beginning of a credit relationship and a recognition of the other as a member of a community that was both mystic and institutional.

A good overview of this conceptual and linguistic mélange can be gained through a close reading of the juridical and legislative documents (mostly produced by ecclesiastical authorities) regulating, during the twelfth century and at the beginning of the thirteenth century, credit contracts like lending of money at interest, forward sale with an increase in price and contracts associating a lender and a merchant (the so-called maritime loan). Papal letters, conciliar acts, comments on Canon and Roman Law, and from the thirteenth up to the fourteenth century Scholastic treatises and academic disputations (*quodlibeta*), represent this congeries of new or renewed contractual relations whose defining features were credit and hypothetical definition of values (what will be the exact value of a commodity in the future? What is the value of a sum of money someone lends to someone other?). These practices served to differentiate licit from illicit contractual forms, specifically by establishing which kind of contract had an economic meaning that could be viewed as compatible with the religious and political organization of Christian territories (McLaughlin 1939–40; Langholm 1992). The solution of this dilemma was not, as historians have too often stated in the past, a generic and absolute prohibition of credit contracts based on lending at interest and therefore on the productivity of money, but rather an accurate differentiation between credit forms that could be articulated through the vocabulary of trust and exchange of values. This vocabulary was especially suitable for representing and ruling the post-Gregorian charismatic political community, and also credit forms whose public and institutional meaning was unclear or blatantly inimical to the stricter interplay between religion and power: *usura*, usury was the word that, generally after 1120, was used to designate this kind of sacrilegious economic otherness (McLaughlin 1939–40; Noonan 1957; Langholm 1992; Todeschini 2012).

Indeed, the mutable medieval definition of usury (Siems 1992) and the medieval focus on fruitfulness or sterility of money hinged on the religious and political representation of money and coins that had been fabricated right through the Western Christian Middle Ages, beginning in Patristic times. Since money had been perceived and described both as an abstract and physical object, both as a metaphor of metaphysical Values and a measure of ordinary values, the problem of money's capacity to generate more money during the so-called "economic revolution of the Middle Ages" was placed in the linguistic category concerning the institutional "common good" (Kempshall 1999; Lecuppre-Desjardin and Van Bruaene 2010; Gamberini et al. 2011). It became part of a public discourse intended to rule markets and territories including them in religious and political terms. From this perspective, a strong distinction was established both in Roman and Canon Law from the first half of the twelfth century which distinguished credit forms with the goals of safety and growth of institutional (that is to say sacred) patrimonies from financial transactions intended to increase individual or "private" wealth without any visible positive effect on the economic health of society.

The shift from money as virtuous profit of a credit transaction to money as a usurious by-product of the sale of coins was therefore not produced, as classical economic historiography of the twentieth century maintained (Noonan 1957; De Roover 1971), by abstract medieval misunderstanding of the productive nature of money (imagined as a sort of everlasting natural law), but rather by the medieval and governmental varying perception of money. According to this fluctuating point of view, money had neither the same meaning, value, or reproducibility when it was managed and manipulated by those who were recognizable as protectors and protagonists of social and religious holy order, as when it was managed and manipulated by those whom law and common opinion perceived as untrustworthy and greedy usurers. The real problem was thus detecting the deep nature and significance of economic behaviors and choices so that it would be possible to understand what money as a sign of value was signifying. As the first part of Canon Law, the so-called *Decretum Gratiani* (composed around 1120–40), clearly stated (on the basis of Emperor Justinian's seventh *Novella*), money resulting from the pledge of holy commodities and money acquired by bishops and abbots through earmarking Church lands and their periodic revenues—namely money earned both by lenders and borrowers involved in credit transactions which improved the administration of sacred institutions—was indisputably holy money: it quantified values and profits whose transcendent meaning was directly related to the wellbeing of the Church, the *societas Christiana* and mystical subjects institutionally embodying Christ on earth.

In contrast, as the second and third Lateran Councils in 1123 and 1178 declared and as both confessional and juridical literature underlined in the twelfth to thirteenth centuries, money sold by manifest usurers (*usurarii manifesti*) and borrowed by common people as well as interest paid from borrowers to lenders as the price for that money, represented forms of unnatural, sinful, and meaningless money. Values denoted by the latter money were immaterial because of their irrelevance in the mystical, political, and religious context shaped by the holy supranational community of Christians. In this case, but only in this case, the Aristotelian saying (Langholm 1979) "money does not breed" (*pecunia non habet partus*) becomes meaningful from the medieval institutional, canonistic and on the whole legal viewpoint. Indeed, it was only when money was sold and made fruitful by "manifest usurers," commonly designated as doubtful Christians, heretics, infidels, and mostly outsiders, that it lost its wonderful power of representing sacred (that is to say political and institutional) values and decayed into a dead and sterile item of coined metal. In most cases, however, medieval juridical and theological discussions about usury concerned the multitude of contracts whose public nature and institutional utility, regarding who belonged to the sacred Christian space, was unclear and controversial (Todeschini 2002, 2011). It was precisely in these cases that money and its value, particularly its ability to produce wealth independently from human work, definitively became a mark of participation in the ritual and economic community of Christians. To understand fully this link between religious belonging, that is to say probable election, and money, it is useful to consider on the one hand the twelfth-century canonistic texts dedicated to financial and profitable investments performed by ecclesiastic institutions, and on the other the so-called "exceptions" to the forbidding of usury recapitulated and codified in the middle of the thirteenth century by the *Summa* of Henry of Segusio, cardinal and bishop of Ostia (and then ordinarily called "Hostiensis") (Henry of Segusio 1574).

The *Summa decretalium* by Bernard of Pavia (Bernard of Pavia 1860, 1956), a collection of canon laws composed around 1190, is a good example of the sanctification of money and economics implemented by canonists. Bernard, in this authoritative textual assemblage, explicitly stated the right of consecrated clergy to alienate and exchange ecclesiastical mobile and immobile goods as well as the revenues derived from those possessions.[7] With reference to the *Decretum Gratiani*,[8] the notion of the inalienability of sacred wealth was reshaped by Bernard through the recalling of some legislative texts promulgated in the middle of the fifth century by the emperors Leo and Anthemius, inserted by Justinian in his Code (1, 2, 14; 1, 2, 21) in the sixth century, recapitulated by Justinian's *Novella VII* in 535, and finally annexed to the *Decretum* around 1140.[9] This imperial law established the right of churches to pledge and consequently to alienate sacred goods when the ecclesiastical institutions were indebted. A second textual sequence in Bernard's *Summa* transformed a complicated sequence of canons,[10] aimed at prohibiting the alienation of church goods (with the exception of cases concerning the care of the poor and urgent necessities of the churches according to a passage of Ambrose of Milan)[11] into an administrative formulation listing four situations allowing the alienation of church goods (*sunt quatuor causae quibus res ecclesiasticae licite alienantur*): necessity (*causa necessitatis*), care (*causa pietatis*), utility (*causa utilitatis assequendae*), and the avoiding of an economic loss (*causa inutilitatis vitandae*).

It is important to note the combination of terms such as *utilitas* and *inutilitas* with *necessitas* and *pietas*, which bestowed on the two economic words an ethical/religious and even institutional meaning; at the same time the two ethical/religious terms assumed a more defined economic meaning through this association. Bernard's elaboration and interpretation of previous Canon Law regarding economic abuse performed by those heretics who, like simoniacs (*symoniaci*), were commercializing sacred properties, turned upside down the sense of norms against economic heresy and produced a systematic formulation of administrative principles. Immediately after the quoted passage, Bernard presented at length some basic economic strategies,[12] intended to facilitate the profitable alienation of ecclesiastical goods: the contractual logic suggested by Bernard was shaped by the possibility of investing revenues of ecclesiastical lands so that these periodic sacred earnings could produce some profits.

On the whole, this process of cataloging allowed the performance of administrative rules inside of Canon Law's sections intended to define the sacrosanct institutional organization of churches. From "precary" (*precaria*) (the cession from a church to a layman of use of land previously donated to the church, in return for a periodic payment) to "pledging," Bernard, as well as other canonists like Rufinus of Bologna, Stephen of Tournai, and subsequent authors of thirteenth-century Canon Law, show how ecclesiastical goods and rents could be fruitfully reinvested. Lending, pledging, interchanging, and selling appear, from this perspective, as legitimate and, moreover, spiritual techniques suitable for maximizing holy wealth. The canonistic determination to differentiate "simoniacal," namely heretical, from sacred and authorized economic administration, gave rise to an increasingly subtle analysis of specific forms of transaction. The outcome of this procedure is the discovery of many categories of legitimate credit investments embedded in different kinds of contractual relations which were thought to be conducive to the wellbeing and growth of the holy institutions.

A good example of this logic is offered by contracts of exchange between different ecclesiastical domains. The need of a bishop or abbot to exert closer control over immobile properties pertaining to his own estate but situated too far from his principal domain, sometimes was the reason for the exchange of a distant property belonging to one church or monastery for a closer piece of land belonging to another church or monastery. Such an exchange, however, prompted close scrutiny of the value of exchanged goods in light of their relative utility. Since this kind of commutation was based on the principle of a sacred (and political) utility, a church could legitimately give to another church lands and money compensating the hypothetical difference in value, which in turn derived from the relative and probabilistic estimation of land values. The value of landed property, in other words, had to be assessed in relation to the holy needs of the church which proposed and advanced the exchange. Cases of this kind, frequently recalled by Canon Law (*Decretales Gregorii IX* 1959), were thus the occasion for legitimizing investments based on estimates of probable economic values: a holy profit could originate from assessment of the market value of sacred commodities.[13] In this case, and also in the pledging of ecclesiastical land and the sale of rents produced by sacred assets, the difference between given and earned value was rationalized and legitimized through the notion of institutional utility of the transaction. Condemnation of lending at interest and the principle of maintaining an equivalence of value between exchangeable objects were bypassed by playing on the notion of public and sacred economy. Thus Canon Law came to condemn forms of private economy characterized by the greediness of wicked and unfaithful people increasing their wealth by damaging the common good through wounding the holy Body of Christianity; it also portrayed the holiness of the institutional economy whose essence was recognizable in the proper aspiration of the Church to maximize the sacred wealth of Christians. The last quarter of the twelfth and the beginning of the thirteenth century were characterized by abundant papal economic legislation which depended on canonistic and scholastic arguments (McLaughlin 1939–40; Baldwin 1959; Schnapper 1969; Langholm 1992; Schmoeckel 2014). From the time of Alexander III up to the decrees of Innocent III and the resolutions of the fourth Lateran Council in 1215, as well as through many commentaries on the *Decretum Gratiani*, Canon Law finally legitimated and bureaucratically formalized many forms of credit contracts entered into by canonically ordained clergy. In these cases, money and profit turned out to be the sign and consequence of sacred entrepreneurship.

However, in the course of defining the sacred economy practiced by holy institutions, another process of economic categorization of money took place. It concerned the types of lending at interest and credit transactions that were permitted inasmuch as interest could be considered compensation for damages actually suffered or risked by the lender (the so-called *damnum emergens*: Langholm 1992; Ceccarelli 2001, 2007; Todeschini 2009b). The formulation of "exceptions" to the ban on usury grew up from the twelfth to the thirteenth century in Canon and Roman law, and they were recapitulated and transmitted to the economic Western tradition by the *Summa aurea* completed around 1253 by the main canonist of the thirteenth century: Henry of Segusio (Henry of Segusio 1574),[14] born around 1200, bishop of Sisteron in 1243, archbishop of Embrun in 1250, papal chaplain and finally cardinal-bishop of Ostia since 1262 until his death in 1271. Although historians have often represented Henry's sequence of contractual cases authorizing lending at interest and credit transactions as a list of "exceptions" to the absolute and indisputable ban on making money fruitful that was characteristic of the medieval "mentality," a closer reading of Henry's text allows interpretation of some situations in which the payment of interest is permitted not as an "exception," but rather according to specific rules legitimating as publicly useful and sacred certain kinds of credit transaction performed by both laypeople and clerics. For mnemonic reasons the list of cases that might allow the charging of interest, namely admitting a surplus on loaned money, was versified by Henry in a poetic stanza:

*Feuda, fidejussor, pro dote, stipendia cleri,*
   *venditio fructus, cui velle jure noceri,*
*vendens sub dubio, pretium post tempora solvens,*
   *poena nec in fraudem, lex commissoria,*
*gratis dans, socii pompa: plus forte modis datur istis.*

To take these terms in order:

- *Feuda* was the return of a fief to the church as security for a loan with rents going to the lender without being deducted from the capital;
- *Fidejussor* was compensation for those who put up security for clerics in debt to merchants;
- *Pro dote* denoted fruitful property given to a bridegroom by the father in law as security on unpaid dowry;
- *Stipendia cleri* were revenues from pledges placed with clerics in view to recovering abusively subtracted ecclesiastical benefices;
- *Venditio fructus* was land revenue sold in advance: fruits in excess of payment reaped by the buyer, justified in light of uncertainty;
- *Cui velle jure nocere* was the charging of usury to heretics and infidels as performance of just war;
- *Vendens sub dubio* was selling at a higher price now in anticipation of probable higher value acquired later;
- *Pretium post tempora solvens* was a late payment charge to cover possible damages;
- *Poena nec in fraudem* was a penalty charge for not executing a contract;
- *Lex commissoria* was a clause allowing a seller to regain possession of property by refunding the original price, with fruits accruing to the buyer;
- *Gratis dans* was interest paid voluntarily as a gift by the debtor;
- *Socii pompa* was money or property leased for purposes of display;
- *Plus forte modis datur istis* denoted cases in which greater reimbursement was permitted.[15]

What is important to grasp is that credit cases listed by Henry of Segusio are not random and unconnected situations, but a sequence that has a visible and comprehensible meaning. It becomes evident if we pay attention to the probable protagonists of these contracts and to their socio-economic position and role in the hierarchized order that characterized twelfth- to thirteenth-century Christian society. Indeed, this sequence of financial eventualities suggests that money becomes fruitful, that is to say generates a price/value higher than its numeral substance, when certain human and institutional subjects are managing it: churches or ecclesiastical institutions (*feuda, stipendia cleri, fidejussor, venditio fructus*), families bonded by a wedding contract recorded through a notarial document (*pro dote*), and most of all professional businessmen interacting with churches as well as with other professionals in the market (*venditio fructus, pretium post tempora solvens, fidejussor, poena nec in fraudem, lex commissoria, socii pompa, gratis dans*). One case (*cui velle jure noceri*) recalls an ancient Patristic statement declaring the legitimacy of usury as a weapon (Nelson 1969) useful in fighting "natural" enemies including infidels such as Muslims and Jews, and therefore underlines the potential political meaning of financial transactions. The whole series of economic situations stylized and synthetically portrayed by the legal formulas employed by Henry of Segusio makes money's value something hypothetical and enigmatic. In other words, money turns out to be fruitful (Ceccarelli 2003) when manipulated and invested by subjects thought to be acting as protagonists of the "common good" of the Christian *respublica*, and looking after the health and growth of Christian society as a community mystically personifying Christ's Body. In a similar way to both the religious and public meaning ascribed to ecclesiastic entrepreneurship, Henry's contractual summation eventually states the public role and institutional function and, consequently, the religious relevance of prominent lay families, merchant bankers, and mercantile companies in thirteenth-century European cities through recognizing the value of productive capital (and therefore the existence of a potential value) embodied by their own money.

## CONCLUSION: CHRISTIAN ECONOMIC LANGUAGE AND LAY ECONOMY

The broadening of western European religious conceptual and political space from the twelfth to the fourteenth centuries, namely the strengthening link between public administration, sovereignty, and sacralization of ruling powers on the model shaped by the papacy, gradually fostered the incorporation of merchant bankers and the business they managed into the mystic sphere of spiritual economy previously associated with churches and monasteries. Relevant twelfth- and thirteenth-century financial phenomena include the commitment of fiscal income to lay merchant companies by the papacy (Dini 1999), the increasing connection between administration of public revenues and public debt (Armstrong 2003), and also the assumption by these merchants of the role of bankers to the Holy See as well as to the French and English kings. These developments plainly contribute to explaining, from a political and pragmatic viewpoint, the religious meaning assumed by money and economic matters during the later medieval centuries. The ancient Christian vocabulary which used economic and monetary images to construct metaphors of religious and transcendent concepts was both revitalized and actualized by the late-medieval identification between religion, politics, and the consequential representation of institutional economy in terms of "common good" and affluence of States represented as sacred bodies seeking to stay healthy (Kaye 2014). Circulation of money could henceforth be represented through the organic image of blood circulation and the misuse of money performed by unauthorized non-spiritual agents like "manifest usurers" and Jews could be described through the medical metaphor of the tumor blocking that virtuous and vital circulation (Bernardino da Siena 1956: 383–4; Todeschini 2016). If on the one hand those who helped this circulation were perceived as promoters of the wellbeing of a sacred Christian society, on the other the "evil usurers" were thus identified as unbelievers and heretics able to contaminate and infect Christian social Body.

A well-known intellectual and politician of the fifteenth century, the German prince-bishop Nicholas Cusanus in his *The Ball Game* (*De Ludo Globi*) written in 1463 (Nicholas of Cusa 1998: 137–49), reworded for the umpteenth time the Augustinian metaphor that represented human beings as God's coins. He fantasized about real coins, like papal florins, and imagined that if they had been living entities they would have been capable of recognizing the pope as their own creator by virtue of the mint mark. In the same way true Christian believers and citizens had become skilled in understanding that God was their own almighty Coiner by virtue of the mark of resemblance He engraved on them.

CHAPTER FOUR

# Money and the Everyday

*Whose Currency?*[1]

RICHARD KELLEHER

During the Middle Ages coins, stamped with the images and inscriptions conceived by the authorities that issued them, became an important medium in the broader cultures of exchange of which they were a part. It is recognized that cultural meaning is deeply embedded in ideas of money and monetary transactions (Bloch and Parry 1989: 1) and thus, while we might explore the different ways that money was used during a person's life, it is equally valid to look at the lifecycle of the coinage as object. In the midst of everyday—ordinary and commonplace—experience, we find a spectrum of variation along cultural, temporal, and spatial lines dictated by the individual's occupation and gender, social status, and age, thus the "everyday" experience is something multifaceted and diverse. Medieval coinage was, more than any other common artifact type, consumed by a broad cross-section of society, and therefore provides a wide range of contrasting economic and social experiences from the great magnate down to the rural villein (Kelleher 2018).

This chapter surveys the broad European trends seen in the production and use of money across the period, highlighting key developments in the monetization of society and questioning the nature of an "everyday" experience of money. The evidence at our disposal comprises documentary, archaeological and material, mediated through written texts (including legal, religious, and literary sources); hoards, single finds, and coin finds in other contexts; and numismatic sources. All these find categories are, by their nature, interdisciplinary and available in varying degrees of abundance and detail across the Middle

Ages. This chapter emphasizes the numismatic and archaeological evidence, discussing its nature and adaptability for use in everyday life in medieval Europe. The hallmark of money in daily affairs was availability (ability to meet prices for daily transactions in the marketplace, small or large) and universal acceptability within the context of prevailing economic conditions.

Numismatists have avoided offering explicit definitions of "monetization," instead drawing on the work of economic historians. The concept of monetization, insofar as coin finds can be used as evidence, is a broad and often complex one and is bound up with arguments about the emergence of a money economy and the commercialization of society (Bolton 2004; Britnell 1995; 2004). According to Britnell, monetization, evident in the increase in coins in circulation in England between 1158 and 1319, is one of the three indices of commercialization (1995: 7; 2004: 76). Does the use of coins, evidenced by the spread of single finds, constitute what we can term a money economy? Jim Bolton has warned of the dangers of assuming that a "money economy" emerged in tandem with the use of coins, and argued that a convergence of circumstances was required for this to occur. For example, he cites the need for a steadily growing population which stimulated demand for land, goods, and services as essential components in this development alongside other stimuli such as advancements in law and legislation, the emergence of markets and fairs, and the growth of the urban population. Also vital was an increase in the availability and use of money (Bolton 2004: 4–5; 2012: 22–3). Textual evidence for the use of money is found in a number of sources across the Middle Ages; be they charters, polyptychs, or saints' lives in the early period or, in increasing quantity from the thirteenth century, official mint documents (Mayhew 1992; Naismith 2014b: 4; chapters in this volume). These sources can prove problematic for appreciating the everyday use of money in society; the early documents provide an elite or church perspective, while later mint records tell us only about production, rather than consumption.

Coin-find evidence is a legitimate source for providing a different perspective to the documentary record, and one which has the capacity to offer insights into matters of both economy and the agency of humans and objects (Kemmers and Myrberg 2011: 87). In the past thirty years the growth in metal-detecting has led to the creation of large, publicly accessible databases of coin finds in Britain and the Netherlands.[2] A strength of this data is that each coin represents a single "loss event," and the nature of accidental loss is such that, with some important caveats, it can provide a non-biased sample that should represent a given coin "population." A site of particular importance for the interpretation of single finds is Rendlesham in Suffolk. Here, a systematic program of metal-detecting and targeted excavation has recovered an exceptionally large assemblage of sixth- to eighth-century coins identifying an economically complex and socially diverse royal central place (Scull *et al.* 2016).

FIGURE 4.1: The excavation of a hoard of Anglo-Saxon silver pennies from Lenborough in Buckinghamshire. © Portable Antiquities Scheme.

Hoard evidence has been central to the numismatic discipline from its earliest days and has shaped the conceptual development of numismatic seriation and methodology. Like the single finds each hoard is representative of an event; however, unlike the single finds, these events were often structured and intentional, and thus provide a different kind of window into everyday monetary affairs.

Hoards were (with few exceptions; see next section) intended to be recovered by their depositors—and it was only through some unhappy (and probably unknowable) set of circumstances that this did not occur. Numismatists' proclivity for classification has extended beyond coins to encompass hoards. Several scholars have attempted to classify hoards based upon their content and/or context, with various, and often unsatisfactory, results. Philip Grierson saw hoards as belonging to one of four categories (Grierson 1975: 131–5). The first are "accidental losses" in the form of purses or small bags of coin which usually comprised the currency of the day. The second category is "emergency hoards," which are described as often having the same contents as accidental losses but sometimes in large sums. His third category, "savings hoards," were accumulated over time, selecting the best specimens available to the hoarder. The last category, "abandoned hoards," was an unsatisfactory term for those hoards that were buried with no intention of recovery. Mark Blackburn was critical of Grierson's categorization and presented an alternative approach which focused on how the elements of the hoard were originally assembled (Blackburn 2005a: 13). In some cases, hoard patterns show clear connectivity with historically attested periods of unrest and upheaval, although such functionalist interpretations are now unfashionable and beset with problems (Rovelli 2004: 242). The hoard record is defined by the complex interplay between levels of hoarding events in a given period, and the circumstances that might have affected their non-recovery. Like single finds, hoards have the potential to cast light on the monetary realities at different levels of society; the huge Tutbury hoard found in 1831 near the English castle that shares its name was clearly the war chest of the great fourteenth-century magnate Thomas of Lancaster who was in open rebellion against his cousin King Edward II (1307–27). The find, of up to 360,000 silver pennies, was lost or buried as Thomas fled Tutbury following the Battle of Burton Bridge in 1322 (Kelleher and Williams 2011). Other hoards are linked to more humble individuals; excavations at the deserted settlement of West Whelpington in Northumberland yielded a small hoard of five silver coins (Evans and Jarrett 1987). In recent years, scholars have drawn on prehistoric archaeology and evolved more interpretive theoretical approaches to hoarding (van Vilsteren 2000; Myrberg 2007; 2009).

## "EVERYDAY" MONEY IN MEDIEVAL EUROPE, SIXTH–ELEVENTH CENTURIES

The landscape of coinage and currency in medieval Europe in the period under discussion owed its origins to the Roman tradition. The monetary systems which emerged as the faltering imperial administration in the West contracted, and then collapsed, were modeled on, and inspired by, the fifth-century Roman template. At the top was the *solidus*, a gold coin which had been introduced by Constantine in 309. The *solidus* was the economic workhorse of the imperial administration. Generated by the vast agricultural estates of the elite, and used by the state to maintain the army and civic and public services, it was vital to the functioning of the empire (Spufford 1988b: 7–8). If you were rich, *solidi* paid your land tax and allowed you to purchase luxury goods, but it was by no means an everyday coin for the vast majority of the Empire's inhabitants. At the opposite end of the scale were low-value denominations in copper known as *nummi*. The ratio of *nummi* to *solidi* fluctuated across the sixth century, rising from 7,200 in 539 to 12,000 in 565 (Spufford 1988b: 8). The virtual absence of any denomination between these two extremes was problematic and stemmed from a shortage of silver which led to the virtual disappearance of silver coins during the sixth century.

It was into the void left by the collapse of the Roman administrative machinery that the barbarian "successor states" emerged in the late fifth and sixth centuries. In Britain, uniquely, coin supply ceased altogether, but hoard and single find evidence shows that clipped silver *siliquae* circulated in significant numbers in the first half of the fifth century, extending coin use beyond the period of official supplies from Roman mints (Abdy 2006: 94–5; Naismith 2017: 31–4). Away from Britain, mints in the western part of the Empire fell into the hands of barbarian kings who struck their own pseudo-imperial coins, and followed these with national coinages intended to reflect the new states' independence (Blackburn 2005b: 661). This process saw the virtual extinction of the minting of copper coins (apart from issues in North Africa and Italy), while gold output was largely limited to the smallest denomination, the *tremissis* (Grierson 1991: 9). Thus, the barbarian kingdoms of western Europe produced monometallic coinage systems based on the *SOLIDUS* and *tremissis* (Blackburn 1995: 539). The Byzantine Empire of the sixth century enjoyed a relatively flourishing monetary economy underpinned by a coinage of gold (in three denominations), and a system of five bronze denominations introduced by Anastasius (491–518) in 498 (Grierson 1999). A peak in the volume of sixth-century coin finds from excavated cities in the lower Danube and eastern Mediterranean, particularly at Athens, Sardis, Caesarea, Carthage, Sadovec, and Histria, seems to support this analysis, although the contrasting average value of losses across the sites, and the source mints represented in the assemblages, suggest fluctuating levels of supply and use (Guest 2012: 112–19). Only in CE 615 was a silver coin (the *hexagram*) added to bridge the gap between the high and low value coins.

Anglo-Saxon gold coinage of the seventh century was limited in scope, but large numbers of Merovingian gold coins survive today. These were struck at hundreds of mints and suggest a "very substantial and active currency" (Blackburn 2005b: 672). As the seventh century progressed, bullion shortages led to a significant reduction in the fineness of Anglo-Saxon and Frankish gold coins, down to 25 percent or less (Blackburn 1995: 539). The earliest dateable silver coins from Francia are those of Childeric II of Neustria (662–75) which were struck 673–5. Naismith suggests that the transition from gold to silver in England began at, or perhaps even before, this date (Naismith 2017: 85–7). The small, thick silver pennies (often erroneously called "*sceats*" or "*sceattas*") were produced at a multitude of commercial hubs across southern and eastern England, and on the continent. Together these formed a "tightly integrated monetary continuum" spanning the North Sea (Naismith 2017: 88). Understanding the extent to which this coinage circulated within, and penetrated through, different levels of the social strata of the North Sea region has occupied and often exasperated scholars. That they were an important part of everyday life is hinted at by the many metal-detector finds from English "productive sites" (see papers in Pestell and Ulmschneider 2003, particularly Blackburn). Excavation has provided a valuable perspective on the provision, chronology, and use of the early pennies. During excavations of the thriving eighth- and ninth-century trading center at Ribe, archaeologists recovered an unusually well-stratified sequence of finds, including more than 200 early pennies (Feveile 2008). Of these, 85 percent were of the Wodan/monster type (Series X), which has led to Ribe being identified as their minting place. Furthermore, the phasing of the finds suggests that they grew to dominate the currency pool in the town as the eighth century progressed and they were still being lost in the early ninth century, well beyond the traditional timeframe for the use of such coins in England and Frisia.

If the coinages of the sixth and seventh centuries had their origins in late antiquity, the currencies of Latin Christendom that would emerge in the tenth and eleventh centuries were conceived in the fundamental remodeling of the currency brought about under the Carolingians. In 754/5, shortly after he deposed the last Merovingian king, Pepin reformed the coinage. The small, thick Merovingian-style *deniers* were replaced by coins on a broader, thinner flan restored in weight. Following the precedent set by Visigothic and Lombard coinages, the reformed issues identified the royal authority and usually the mint of issue (Blackburn 1995: 548). Charlemagne's important reform of the 790s increased the weight of the *denier* to 1.7g, while also standardizing the design with the Karolus monogram (Figure 4.2). The number of mints was reduced from more than 100 to 40. The most productive site for Carolingian coin finds anywhere in Europe is Dorestad, close to the northernmost branch of the Rhine in the province of Utrecht. The abundant site finds of Charlemagne's monogram type and the *Christiana Religio* type of Louis the Pious suggest a prolonged and steady rise in economic activity there from the 790s to the 830s, and Dorestad as a significant location in empire-wide trade networks (Coupland 2010: 98–100). Charlemagne's influence can be seen beyond the boundaries of the empire in Anglo-Saxon England, in the coinage reform of Offa of Mercia. This reform introduced a full silver broad flan penny (*c.* 96 percent; 1.3 grams), which included the king's name and title, and the name of the moneyer for the first time. In Italy, Byzantine influence gave way to Carolingian, with the replacement of the Lombard, Papal, and Beneventan coinages of debased gold by silver. Despite increases in coin production in the eighth century, its use was limited to a largely urban and elite minority.

Charlemagne was crowned emperor by Pope Leo III on Christmas Day 800, and this auspicious occasion cemented Carolingian political supremacy in much of northern and western Europe. An empire-wide reform of weights and measures ensured uniformity of currency throughout the empire (Blackburn 1995: 543). The silver penny dominated the monetary system but whether it was an object of everyday experience is contested, as is the extent of monetization

FIGURE 4.2: Silver *denier* of Charlemagne (768–814), struck at Mainz (793/4–812) with the cross on steps reverse type © Fitzwilliam Museum, Cambridge.

in the Empire. Coupland's recent survey shows a monetary landscape dictated by geographical and temporal factors, with clear regional differences. Single-find, hoard, and documentary evidence show that coinage was more common in the West Frankish kingdom, a pattern reinforced by the establishment of new mints between the Seine and the Rhine. By contrast, Brittany and areas east of the Rhine show fewer finds and mints (Coupland 2014). A similar picture emerges south of the Alps, where Carolingian hegemony failed to bring the region into the mainstream economic dynamic of the imperial center (Rovelli 2009: 75–6). However, the introduction of *obols* (halfpence), which account for 16 percent of the Carolingian single finds, is an indicator of the diversifying uses of coinage among the general population. In the West, gold coin was virtually non-existent beyond the minting of pieces meant for presentation or ceremonial use. However, to the south and southeast of Charlemagne's polity, monometallism was not the norm. In the Byzantine lands and the Abbasid Caliphate, gold and base metal coins were struck in some quantity. In central and southern Italy, the currency zones were more nuanced, reflecting the region's position at the confluence of western European, Byzantine, and Muslim cultures. In the south the principal coinages were those of Benevento, which declined in fineness over the century, and the Byzantine outposts at Naples and Sicily (to 878). Money use in England in the ninth century was divided on a north/south axis. In the north, the coinage of small, thick silver pennies (known falsely as "stycas") became increasingly debased to the point at which they contained no silver at all. The Danish capture of York in 867 ended this Northumbrian coinage for good. The English coins that replaced the "stycas" in the ninth century were less suitable for use in daily transactions due to its greater value; each penny was priced well beyond most of the commodities and services offered in ninth-century England. The coinage in the southern English kingdoms of Wessex and Mercia was of quite different character, and had been based on large silver pennies—after the Carolingian fashion—since c. 760. Two reforms under Alfred in the third quarter of the century improved the debased silver pennies from barely a quarter fine to a standard weight of 1.6g. In the Danelaw, the currency was of a more diverse character, exemplified by the mixed content of hoards such as the Ashdon, Essex find of Anglo-Saxon, Viking, and Carolingian coins (Blackburn 1989). In the ninth century, relative levels of coin use remained constrained by factors of supply in northern Europe.

In the tenth century, coinage in the West continued to be dominated by silver. However, the quantity of coinage available and levels of use greatly declined. Spufford attributes this to three factors: a deteriorating balance of payments with the east caused by a reduction in the slave trade; the diversion of silver into church treasuries; and the Scandinavian invasions (Spufford 1988b: 60). Only in those regions under Islamic rule, such as Spain and Sicily, or within the Byzantine Empire, did gold coin circulate in any meaningful sense. Western European gold coins were produced only in exceptional circumstances. The Carolingian model of coin production continued into the tenth century, but developed in different ways in France and Germany. The breakdown of imperial political authority was accompanied by decentralization of minting rights, either by usurpation or grant. In France, the legacy of the Carolingian system can be seen in a continuation in coin types and over the century comital usurpation of minting rights led to the emergence of immobilized coins which, frequently and frustratingly, defy dating and seriation. In Germany, the axis of power shifted from the Rhineland and Bavaria to the east and north, following Henry the Fowler's assumption of the throne in 918. The rich silver mines of the Rammelsberg at Goslar in the Harz Mountains encouraged the establishment of a prolific mint there, which boomed from the 990s with the striking of considerable quantities of Otto-Adelaide Pfennige (Spufford 1988b: 74). In addition to the establishment of new imperial mints, minting rights were granted to others, most often bishops and abbeys. In Bohemia, minting increased substantially, with issues drawing inspiration from the Bavarian, Papal, and English prototypes which must have been encountered through trade in the principal towns of the kingdom.

The decentralization of coin production seen in France and Germany was in direct contrast to the English experience of ever closer centralization. At the start of the century, coinage was produced under the authority of the kings of Wessex and Mercia, and in the southern Danelaw and Scandinavian Northumbria. In about 973, King Eadgar was able to reform the coinage, bringing uniformity in design to the issues of *all* the English mints. Viking expansion had begun to impact coastal western Europe in the ninth century in different ways: in the North Sea zone the Dorestad mint had closed after several Viking attacks, while settlement in parts of Britain and Ireland resulted in the introduction of Viking coinages at York and Dublin. The "bullion economy" that emerged in ninth-century Scandinavia, in which coins and precious metal objects were used for exchange and to store wealth, was also found in those areas of Britain and Ireland under Scandinavian influence in the early part of the century, and famously exemplified by the hoards from Cuerdale in Lancashire and the Vale of York (Williams 2011a). Likewise, the expansionist northmen brought a new monetary reality to the northern lands with the mass importation of Islamic silver. Their eastern trade networks attracted large numbers of central Asian dirhams from Transoxiana via the Bulgars and Khazars. These constitute the majority of coin finds from Scandinavian trading sites such as Kaupang in Norway, Birka and Uppåkra in Sweden, and Paviken in Gotland, where they succeeded European coins from the third quarter of the ninth century (Blackburn 2007a: 53); in the tenth century, the composition changed radically as Samanid and Volga Bulgar imitations took precedence (Blackburn 2007a: 39–40). At the newly discovered urban Viking site in the vicinity of the famous Gokstad ship burial in Vestfold in Norway, the ninth- and tenth-century silver dirhams were all fragments, mostly weighing 0.5g or less (Gullbekk 2014). The nature of fragmentation suggests that the silver employed as a means of payment would be adapted to everyday demands in the marketplace. Within the Viking world small fragments of silver dirhams were used intensively everywhere, including Viking campsites such as Torksey and Repton in England. In the Slavic lands, silver was the preserve of elites and merchants involved in long-distance trade. Two trade routes have been identified; hacksilver and coins went from the Baltic to Pomerania and from Kiev to Eastern Poland, Mazovia, and Great Poland. In the late tenth century, the use of ever smaller fragments of coins intensified (Bogucki 2011: 146). Despite the extension of minting to eastern Europe, the widespread adoption of coin was limited. Perhaps the most dynamic aspect of the century was the hacksilver economy of the Vikings, which drew huge numbers of silver dirhams into northern Europe, and exported them across Scandinavia, the Baltic, northern Britain, and Ireland.

Coinage in the eleventh century was affected to varying degrees by the great events of the time. The silver penny was adopted by states newly won for Christendom in northern Spain, Scandinavia, and Hungary. There was an unsatisfied increase in demand for coined money over much of Europe, during the second half of the century in particular (Grierson 1991: 65). While the penny remained pre-eminent, other denominations did begin to appear, suggesting a demand for flexibility in the values of coins issued by the mints. In the northwest, gold coins were limited to ceremonial issues, such as Anglo-Saxon pieces struck using penny dies under Æthelred II (978–1016) and Edward the Confessor

(1042–66). However, the influence of Islamic gold on those states bordering the Caliphate led to the minting of imitative dinars in Barcelona, Salerno, and Amalfi. Coins valued at less than a penny, which had been struck intermittently in Francia from 700 and in England and Italy from the ninth century, were increasingly experimented with. These were mostly in the form of round obols or halfpennies, but pennies cut into halves and quarters were known in England, with even smaller fragmentary pieces in eastern Europe. In Germany in the eleventh century there was diminishing royal control of the coinage and many mints were in the hands of the Church. The hoards reveal a general trend for the currency to be dominated by issues from local mints, with a compact age structure, showing evidence of a requirement for incoming coins to be exchanged at the mints for local types. Silver extracted from the Harz Mountains peaked in *c.* 1025 and diminished rapidly after 1040, leading to a dearth in minting in Saxony, Bavaria, and Poland, in Scandinavia and the Baltic, and west in the Rhineland and Frisia (Spufford 1988b: 95–6). The coinage of France was dominated by large powerful fiefdoms that continued to produce coinage of poor fabric, workmanship, and aesthetic appeal (Grierson 1990: 68–70). With diminished central control, mints were free to debase their issues to such an extent that by the end of the eleventh century the *denier* of Toulouse was equivalent to two *deniers* of Melgueil, and four of Le Puy (Spufford 1988b: 103). In stark contrast to Germany and France, England evolved a closely controlled national coinage of uniform design struck at some seventy mints. A high level of control is visible in the frequent changes of type that were made, to the profit of the king, at about three- to six-year intervals. Under the Norman kings of England the Anglo-Saxon monetary system and coinage was little altered at first, mirroring the Norman preference for flexibility seen in its success in establishing the Norman *Regno* in Sicily and southern Italy. Coin use, as revealed by metal detector finds, was still limited to the principal towns of the kingdom and selected rural areas in eastern and southern England (Kelleher 2015: 59–60).

The Viking Age brought coin production to Ireland for the first time. In *c.* 995 Sihtric Silkenbeard (*c.* 989/95–1036) struck coins at Dublin in his name, and it would be Dublin that was the principal focus for coin use. Beyond the kingdom of Dublin, hoards and single finds show that coinage was uncommon and, like many states on Europe's periphery, was effectively the preserve of a small and urban minority (Woods 2014: 296–312). Likewise, coin use in Viking-Age Scotland was of mixed pedigree and comprised Anglo-Saxon, Norwegian, and Islamic imports. These were limited to the Norse settlements (Williams 2006b: 171). It was only after 1000 that Scandinavian minting took root, most effectively in Denmark, where Anglo-Saxon pennies of Æthelred II were used as a prototype.

Italy was foremost in the use of money, but the picture is unclear, with contradictory evidence for patterns of growth and recession (Spufford 1988b:

97–8). Two systems were in place there: in the north was the German imperial system of silver pennies; while in the south there was a mixture of Byzantine and independent issues with a circulating currency of Arab Sicilian gold and Byzantine copper. The Normans established settlements in southern Italy by the 1050s, which were later legitimized by papal patronage, and conquered Sicily by the end of the century. The mints they inherited continued to strike the same coins as before; copper *folles* in Capua and Salerno, gold *tareni* at Salerno, Amalfi, and Sicily, and tiny silver *kharubba* in Sicily (Grierson and Travaini 1998: 76–8).

In Eastern Europe, coinage became better established. In Hungary, crudely engraved pennies were struck, while in Bohemia coins were produced in great quantity, although they became lighter in the second half of the century. At the start of the century, monetization in Poland was limited to the *emporia* and ducal and royal courts, but in the second half of the century, local markets were more frequent users of coin, in particular imports—principally German—of which at least 50,000 are known as single finds (Bogucki 2011: 147). The drying up of silver in Germany after 1040 was mirrored in the Islamic lands with the decline in the mines of Central Asia. This had the knock-on effect of sharply reducing the Byzantine silver coinage after 1000, which was abandoned altogether in the 1092 reform of Alexius I (1081–1118). One's experience of money in the eleventh century was contingent on geographical and social factors. The fragmentation of coins into smaller sums and the import of foreign coins suggest a shifting dynamic of use, but as yet supply and demand were not in equilibrium.

## COINAGE AND CURRENCY IN THE TWELFTH–FOURTEENTH CENTURIES

Paradoxically, twelfth-century Europe experienced an increase in trade activity and greater demand for coin, while at the same time suffering a continuing shortage of bullion (Grierson 1991: 81). In the three major coinage areas (Germany, France, and England) this dynamic was felt in different ways, often, but not exclusively, resulting in debasement and weight reductions. Gold coins remained largely the preserve of Byzantium or those states bordering, or reconquered from, the Islamic World. Germany remained the most powerful European state despite the setbacks of the previous century, particularly under Frederick I Barbarossa (1152–90) and Henry VI (1190–7). However, minting was in the hands of bishops and archbishops, as well as the emperor, and although Frederick revived or established new mints, there was by no means a standard imperial coinage throughout the empire. In fact, the coinage generally diverged significantly along geographical lines; smaller flan silver pennies were the norm in some areas, but large flan bracteates became common in others. In

France, the coinages of the great feudatories, such as Champagne and Melgueil, circulated widely, and eclipsed those of the crown in quality. However, the resurgent monarchy, under Philip II Augustus (1180–1223), would begin the process of reclaiming royal control of the coinage. In the twelfth century, the patchwork of local princely coinages in the Angevin territories of Henry of Anjou was brought together in a more closely integrated system, which after 1180 was fixed to the English sterling (Cook 2006: 671).

In England, royal control was maintained and debasement generally avoided, although during the civil war of Stephen's reign a number of magnates, as well as Matilda and her Angevin allies struck coins (Blackburn 1994; Allen 2016). The currency circulating when Henry II (1154–89) assumed the throne was soon replaced by a wholesale recoinage in 1158 which abandoned the centuries-old *renovatio* system. A second recoinage in 1180 replaced the Cross and Crosslets coins with the Short Cross type, which would endure in immobilized form across four reigns and 80 years (Figure 4.3). The 1180 recoinage significantly increased the productivity of the mints and the size of the currency (Allen 2007: 273).

The minting of Scotland's first coins was made possible when David I invaded Cumbria and took the English mint of Carlisle. Pennies of English-style were struck in small numbers in Carlisle and Edinburgh but these are rare as finds. As in much of northern and western England, regular engagement with money was still some way off. What, then, of Ireland? Prince John's investment as lord of Ireland in 1185 saw the resumption of minting at Dublin, and the production of light weight pennies. In the 1190s a second coinage of pennies and halfpennies was issued. Pennies and halfpennies were also struck by the Ulster baron John de Courcy.

FIGURE 4.3: Silver Short Cross penny, struck at York by the moneyer Isaac © Fitzwilliam Museum, Cambridge.

The two most commercially advanced areas were the Low Countries and Italy. In northern Italy, new mints were opened but the three main monetary areas of Pavia, Verona, and Lucca that had emerged following the Carolingian collapse continued to be dominant (Saccocci 1999: 41–2; Day *et al.* 2016). In the south the Norman mix of coins was replaced in 1140 by a new monetary system. Byzantine and Islamic elements were still visible in the four denominations (one of copper, two of silver and one of gold) and two monies of account, while still allowing local traditions on the mainland (Travaini 2001: 184). The coins of the Low Countries assumed a distinctive character, diverging from the imperial or French types of previous centuries. Small *petit deniers* were struck widely under municipal and comital authority. Danish coins were the most important in Scandinavia. The Danish hoards are dominated by local coins, except at the edges of the kingdom where German influence is seen. The Kampinge hoard of small bracteates, for example, is linked to the Scanian fairs (Steen Jensen 1999: 314).

The First Crusade of 1096–9 saw the establishment of four new states in the Levant. Like Norman Sicily they were at the center of a complex mix of cultural influences from the Latin homeland, the Byzantine Empire, and local Islamic traditions. In the Latin East, the northern states of Edessa and Antioch adopted coinages that drew heavily on the Byzantine model. However, the extent to which such coins were adopted by local populations is debatable, at least for Edessa. The few excavated sites of the period have produced few Edessene coins. At frontier settlements like Gritille in the Upper Euphrates, coin finds are scarce, and those recovered are typically Frankish silver *deniers* or local Islamic copper *fulus* (Redford 1998). Antioch was richer, more powerful, and much longer-lived than Edessa and developed a large coinage of billon *deniers* beyond the initial phase of copper *folles* (Metcalf 1995). The proliferation of the billon coins of Antioch, particularly those of Bohemond III (1163–1201) suggests a coinage used extensively in the major towns, but how far they penetrated beyond the hinterland awaits further excavation and synthesis. This is not the case for the Kingdom of Jerusalem, where the planned *villeneuve* settlements, for Frankish colonists at Parva Mahumeria and Bethgibelin, have provided a fascinating insight into the use of money in the rural communities servicing Jerusalem, Tyre, and Acre (Kool 2007). Excavations at Parva found a total of nearly 100 coins in 50 percent of the dwellings excavated, including a small gold hoard. The single finds were a mixture of coins of Jerusalem, Antioch, Tripoli, feudal France, and Byzantium. The everyday use of money at this site was diverse, and charter evidence from *Castellum Regis* (a town north of Acre) shows that low-value coins (half a *denier*) were required for the use of the communal bath (Kool 2007: 139–47). The local coinage would meet the demand for low-value denominations needed for transactions involving most everyday services. Developments in the twelfth century laid the foundations for the fundamental shifts of the thirteenth. Already by the 1170s the use of coin was extending downward socially, but a dramatic increase in Europe's silver supply would be required to make money an everyday object.

The thirteenth century was one of significant advancement in the "ordinary" use of money, particularly in the second half of the century. Pennies were minted in increasing quantities, while the introduction of large silver coins, and the return of the minting of gold, facilitated large-scale trade and fueled the "Commercial Revolution." Growth would not have been possible without a surge in newly mined silver, which came early in the century from the prolific areas of Friesach in Meissen. Gold was largely derived from the Islamic world; but mines in Silesia, Hungary, and Transylvania were locally important (Grierson 1991: 105). In France, royal control was extended against the feudatories throughout the century, limiting the circulation of non-royal *deniers* to their areas of issue, and placing royal *deniers tournois* and *parisis* (and their fractions) at the forefront of the currency (Grierson 1991: 113–14). In 1266 Louis IX established the *gros tournois* of 12 *deniers*, which proved immediately successful and was widely imitated (Figure 4.4). The monetary innovations seen elsewhere in Europe failed to materialize in Germany, where silver Pfennige continued to be used in eastern and southern areas.

England's sterling coinage became one of the most important in Europe in this century. A huge increase in mint output, coupled with the recoinages of 1247 and 1279, cemented royal control over the profits of coin production and the centralized activity of ever fewer mints (Allen 2012, especially Chapter 2). A gold penny was introduced and quickly abandoned in the 1250s, and new silver denominations appeared at the close of the century, successfully in the case of penny fractions, but not so with the groat. The lack of low-value

FIGURE 4.4: Silver *gros tournois*, © Fitzwilliam Museum, Cambridge.

denominations in England before the last quarter of the thirteenth century provides a puzzle for our understanding of the English economy. In recent years, metal detectorists have partly provided an answer to this through finds of thousands of pennies deliberately cut into halfpennies and farthings. Their distribution provides strong evidence for money being used in day-to-day business by those engaged in commercial activities, with many finds coming from rural locations (Kelleher forthcoming). The quality and relative abundance of the sterlings led to their use on the continent, where they occur in many hoards, particularly in France and Germany, but also in the distant Balkans and eastern Mediterranean (Allen 2001: 114–18). An unwelcome consequence of their popularity was their imitation at mints in the Low Countries and northwest Germany, often at a fineness below that of the English standard. This at least was a reason given for the 1299–1300 English recoinage and prohibition against their use (Kent 2005: 18). Hoards and single finds show how widespread these issues became in circulation in England (Mayhew 1983; Kelleher forthcoming). The Scottish and Irish coinages were deeply influenced by the English, through imitation in the former and by tradition in the latter. Large Scottish hoards from Tom A'Bhuraich (Aberdeenshire), Dun Lagaidh (Ross), and Keith (Banffshire) indicate that circulation was dominated by English coins (Bateson 1997: 45), a picture supported by single-find evidence (Holmes 2004: 247). Coining in Ireland was sporadic and limited to three periods of activity in *c*. 1207–11, 1251–4 and 1275–1302. These issues were more for the enrichment of the Anglo-Irish state than for local use, with the great majority of coins pressed into servicing Edward I's military campaigns (Colgan 2003: 27). They are found, and indeed imitated, on the continent in some numbers.

Italian coinage was influential over much of Europe but continued to be defined by the differences between the northern and central states and those of the *Regno* in the south. It was the commercial city-states of Venice, Florence, Genoa, and Pisa that would be most influential, where large *grossi* of good silver, which contrasted starkly with the increasingly debased local *denari*, found use, and became essential for international trade (Grierson 1991: 105). Venice created denominations for specific purposes; *piccoli* for everyday use and *grossi* for long-distance trade (Stahl 2000: 202–12). Gold coins appeared in Genoa and Florence in 1252 and Venice in 1289 and soon came to dominate international trade: florins north of the Alps and ducats in the eastern Mediterranean (Grierson 1991: 110). In the south, gold *tareni* continued to be struck alongside billon *denari* but the reforms of the Angevin Charles I more closely aligned southern Italy with the rest of Europe (Grierson 1991: 112).

The Low Countries also came to commercial prominence in this century, although its coins were influenced by those of its neighbors, and they were in no way consistent across coin-issuing authorities. The *petit denier* gave way to penny coinages in the north Netherlands, and double pennies and *petit gros* in

Hainault (Grierson 1991: 121–2). English sterlings played a significant role, and were tariffed at four Flemish pennies. The *gros tournois* appeared towards the end of the century. In politically unstable Denmark the coinage degenerated spectacularly, and sterlings were used as groat equivalents, as shown by their presence in hoards from Skafterup and Bornholm (Steen Jensen 1999: 315–16). While the coins might have degenerated in fabric their extensive use is revealed by the more than 4,400 single finds found at Tårnborg in Jutland (dated *c*. 1240–*c*. 1341), and more than 170,000 from Denmark (Grinder-Hansen 2000; Gullbekk 2011). In Norway, small groats and sterlings replaced the tiny, inadequate bracteates. This coincided with an increase in monetization, although there was a distinction between the towns, where coins were used, and rural areas, where commodities were more common (Gullbekk 2003). In Sweden, bracteates continued to be used. A study of finds from Swedish churches reveals significant monetization in the second half of the century (Klackenberg 1992).

The coinage of the Iberian Peninsula began to improve; Barcelona was already an important locus in western Mediterranean trade and its *grossi* an important currency. Leon and Castile produced gold *doblas* based on the Almohad double dinar and an abundant billon coinage. In Portugal, there was some gold and poor billon *dinhieros*. States in Eastern Europe experienced differing fortunes; Bohemian coinage declined in fineness, adopting bracteates on the Saxon model, despite the opening of the Jihlava mines in the 1220s (Grierson 1991: 131; Spufford 1988b: 119). In Silesia and Poland, bracteates of varying weight were struck. Hungarian coinage was dominated by Friesacher Pfennige, which appear to have increased the use of coins in the countryside (Spufford 1988b: 134–6). In Serbia, the Balkans, and Cyprus, the currency of copper trachy (in Serbia) and base gold *hyperpyra* (in Cyprus), inspired by Byzantine models, gave way to Venetian *grossi* and their imitations. The Fourth Crusade and the establishment of the Latin Empire stimulated the flow of *deniers* from France and led to their imitation, and rise to dominance, by the mid-century. The remnants of the Crusader states of the Levant at Acre and Tripoli continued to issue gold bezants and silver until their destruction in 1291. The thirteenth century began a new period of the widespread use of coin. Elites and merchants had new gold and silver coins to facilitate business, while coin, emanating from the towns, began to replace customary systems in rural areas. Barter and commodity exchange remained part of the everyday experience, but coinage was now a familiar fixture in rural economies.

The fourteenth century saw the extension of the monetary innovations and trends of the thirteenth. The extension of gold coinage was a principal development, thanks in part to gold available in the Mediterranean through Italian cities trading with Africa, and the discovery of new European sources such as Kremnica (Spufford 1988b: 267–8). The mines at Kutná Hora in Bohemia produced an abundance of silver beginning at the start of the century. Gold coinage spread from Italy and France to Spain, the Low Countries, Hungary, and England by the end of the century. But, like the silver coins, weights and finenesses diverged from state to state (Grierson 1991: 139). The century also witnessed the social upheaval and demographic change wrought by the Black Death, which had a keen impact on coin supply and demand. France was the most powerful state in Europe, with a royal coinage that had become the most important in the kingdom with the reforms of St. Louis. The scourge of debasement continued to dog the currency in the mid-century—largely as a source of finance during the Hundred Years War—although Charles V temporarily remedied the problem in the 1360s (Grierson 1991: 142–3). The great period of Gascon coinage came under Edward III and Edward the Black Prince during the Hundred Years War. The coins, in gold, silver, and base silver, were modeled on the French feudal pieces in circulation in those lands.

England caught up with the rest of Europe with the permanent addition of gold nobles and their fractions, and large silver groats and halfgroats. Sterling was imitated extensively on the continent, with the most common English single finds of these coins being those of Gaucher of Châtillon (1313–22) and John the Blind (1309–46) (Kelleher forthcoming). A mint at Calais was established to convert the profit of the Staple's wool trade into English coins; first in gold and later silver (Allen 2010: 131) with output sometimes equaling that of London (Mayhew 1992: 150). The circulating medium in Scotland, as shown by finds and hoards, was mostly English (Holmes 2004: 158) and the Scottish coinage closely mirrored that of England until the mid-century. After David II (1329–71) was released from English captivity in 1357 he inaugurated a new coinage which added gold nobles and silver groats and their halves to the mix. The silver pieces were underweight, and a further reduction in 1367, and debasement in 1393, led to their prohibition in England. As a result, English coins became less common in Scotland and by the end of the century the silver coinage was dominated by Scottish coins of Robert III (1390–1406) (Bateson 1997: 59). Ireland's coinage followed the reforms seen in England under Edward I, with pennies, halfpennies, and farthings being struck. However, the economic growth of the Anglo-Irish colony in the early century was undermined by the systematic draining out of good silver coin, and by its replacement with sterling imitations, debased continental pieces, *deniers tournois* and lightweight Scottish groats (Colgan 2003: 27–33). Apart from a tiny issue of halfpennies and farthings of Edward III, no coins would be produced in Ireland until the fifteenth century.

North and central Italy made extensive use of gold, particularly Florence, Venice, Genoa, Rome, Bologna, and Milan (Figure 4.5). The silver coinages are very complex and fall within six main monetary zones: Asti and Savoy, Genoa, Milanese currency, Venice and Verona, Aquileia, and Bologna and Ancona.

What is striking is the fact that coin use in these areas was overwhelmingly dominated by the issues of the dominant mints, sometimes with less than 1 percent coming in from neighboring areas (Saccocci 1999: 43). In the fourteenth century, Venice began producing silver *soldini* as a coin for everyday use, with the *tornosello* (three-penny piece) made for export to Greece where it drove out all other coinage (Stahl 2000: 217–25). In the south, gold was replaced by large silver coins, supplemented with poor quality billon *denari*. In the Low Countries, large silver *gros* were struck, alongside coins based on the sterling, and black billon. From the 1330s, gold coins, based on florins or French gold, formed an important part of the currency of this commercially important region (Grierson 1991: 158). Germany lagged behind its neighbors and was late in introducing any large silver or gold coins. Minting was largely now the preserve of cities which formed some of the earliest monetary unions. In the north, a convention agreed between the Hanseatic towns of Lübeck, Wismar, Hamburg, Lüneburg, and others, saw them strike a silver *witten* of related type and weight (Grierson 1991: 164).

The poor native coinage of Denmark led to the import of *gros tournois*, sterlings, and German bracteates. A hoard from Kirial comprised 80,000 of the latter. The *witten* coinages of the Hanseatic towns would replace these after 1365 (Steen Jensen 1999: 316–17; Grierson 1991: 166). The first silver multiples appeared in Sweden and the Baltic towns of Riga, Dorpat, and Reval all began striking coins for the use of the town and its trade. In Bohemia, the rich Kutna Horá mines made the *pragergroschen* the most important currency in central Europe. These were complemented by Hungarian gold coins of Charles Robert. In the eastern Mediterranean, the *grossi* of Cyprus oiled the wheels of trade, as did the *gigliati* of Rhodes and Chios in Asia Minor (Grierson 1991: 174–5).

FIGURE 4.5: Gold florin of Florence © Fitzwilliam Museum, Cambridge.

## AN EVERYDAY EXPERIENCE?

This chapter has surveyed the production and monetization across a broad chronology in search of evidence of the everyday use of money. The traditional view is that between the seventh and twelfth centuries, European coinage was based everywhere on the silver penny and was of limited use to most people. But, from the thirteenth century (or more probably the late twelfth century), increased silver supplies, the minting of large silver coins and gold coins, and the use of bills of exchange and credit transfers, helped to extend the use of money to all levels of society (Spufford 1988b: 378–9). This process was linked to quickening urbanization from the twelfth century, rising populations, and, essential for rural communities, the commutation of customary services into cash rents.

Away from Byzantium, where monetization was fundamental to the workings of the empire, coinage was rare in the early Middle Ages, but for those at the very top of society, coin became an object of the exercise of kingship. It carried prestige and projected identity, allowed access to luxury goods, and played a role in symbolic and religious rituals. This began with the gold of the Merovingians, and later the silver of Francia and England. Weak rulers lost mints, while strong ones controlled minting as a source of revenue and power. As coin became more common from the eleventh century its uses multiplied. For the elitetime coins paid for war, diplomacy and ecclesiastical gifts; funded the foundation of new monasteries and programs of castle building; and maintained the household. One of the most dynamic and active players in stimulating the demand for coin was the merchant (Spufford 2002). Monetary innovations began in the commercially important towns and ports of Europe, first in northern Italy and then in the Low Countries. Experiences of money in the towns differed from those in the countryside, but the differences became more nuanced and subtle from the thirteenth century (see papers in Wilkin *et al.* 2015). Long-distance flows of silver were inter-urban but percolated out to the countryside so that a radical change in the rural as well as urban use of coin took place between the late-twelfth and early-fourteenth century (Spufford 1988b: 143). The medieval town was a large settlement in which most inhabitants made their living from non-agricultural pursuits such as trade, industry, and services. Towns had occupational diversity and multiple economic functions, which coinage was vital in maintaining. The body of a woman excavated from a Black Death cemetery in London provides a tantalizing glimpse of the everyday use of money in an urban context. Two purses totaling 181 coins were recovered, one from the armpit, which contained most of the larger coins, and one from the waist, which held most of the small coins; a clear example of money readily available for daily use (Kelleher *et al.* 2008). Towns were where mints were located. In some cases, the towns operated the mints and could form monetary unions, which formalized and streamlined the use of coin between them. Finally, we turn to the rural population. Peasants were an individually insignificant but collectively vital part of the economy who lived in villages within diverse and complex economic systems varying from place to place. The majority were self-sufficient, relying on seasonal, small-scale barter. But as the provision of coinage grew so did rural engagement with money, which was accrued through sales of surplus and paid as taxes, rents, and fines, and for specialist goods and services. The volume of currency that passed through the English countryside is remarkable (Mayhew 2002) and finds are beginning to flesh out the bones of the documentary record for the period after *c.*1200 (Kelleher forthcoming). The question posed at the start of this chapter about the everyday monetary experience has a multiplicity of answers. Everyday contact with coin depended on the sophistication of the economy and level of society, and when and where one lived.

CHAPTER FIVE

# Money, Art, and Representation

*The Powerful and Pragmatic Faces of Medieval Coinage*

REBECCA R. DARLEY[1]

## INTRODUCTION

A persistent trope in numismatic literature and exhibitions is that coins are art. It is seen, perhaps, as a way of making these small objects more engaging or of asserting their equivalence with other works found in galleries. It is perhaps also a projection onto the Middle Ages of the phenomenon developed in the fifteenth century of the decorative medal as a form of artistic expression. The idea of medieval coins as art, however, faces a twofold problem. First, the concept of "art" in the Middle Ages is contested by historians of visual and material culture because although objects might have been beautifully made in the Middle Ages this was always secondary to and in service of another (non-aesthetic) primary purpose. The concepts of beauty as its own purpose and the artist as individual were absent (Berger 1972; Belting 1994; Kessler 2004). Second, while many medieval coins are attractive and enticing to modern eyes, others challenge even the most culturally relativist viewer to assert with confidence that these objects were created to be admired for their beauty. They were all, however, certainly intended to be tools of representation. Indeed, representation is integral to the identity of a coin. Without designs marking it apart, a lump of metal is not a coin; it is simply a lump of metal, or perhaps an ingot. Marking a coin with a representation to make it recognizable theoretically simplifies transactions, as people are able to just exchange coins in specified amounts rather than having to test the purity and weight of metal themselves or pay somebody else to do so (Kroll 2012: 39–40). In the medieval world this did not always work perfectly in practice, as some examples in this chapter will demonstrate, and the rationale for issuing coins in the Middle Ages was not necessarily exclusively to facilitate transactions. Nevertheless, the aims and consequences of representation are in all cases fundamental to understanding the role of money in the Middle Ages.

Consequently this chapter focuses not on coins as art but on the interactions which made representation on a medieval coin possible and meaningful. These interactions are usually discussed in terms of the connection between the authority which caused a coin to be made and the intended audience for its use, as a top-down communication, which only rarely extended into a visible dialog, for example when an intended audience rejected a coin or a contemporary commentator mentioned some change in design. This dialog is explicit in the documentary record of, for example, King James I of Catalonia-Aragon (r. 1213–76), under whom a council of merchants in Barcelona was given authority to negotiate with the king about coin production (Crusafont *et al.* 2013: 51). The process is visible, even if the details are not, in the account of the so-called Maronite Chronicle compiled in Syria in the seventh century which records that in *c.* 661 the Muslim ruler Mu'awiya, in territories populated mainly by Christians, "minted gold and silver, but it was not accepted because it had no cross on it" (Palmer 1993: 32). Such interpretation is, however, implicitly grounded in the idea of coins as art (or perhaps propaganda—also a problematic term in medieval contexts since it is closely associated with modern ideas about the conscious aim and capacity of states to influence directly and totally the political consciousness of their subjects), in which the authority becomes the artist and minute details or changes in coin design have been read as sensitive barometers revealing the personal feelings and political preferences of kings and emperors (e.g. Füeg 2007: 16; Treadwell 2009: 369; Kotsis 2012). A medieval coin, though, was fundamentally an object of use, created to mediate a range of social contexts, from paying taxes and armies or engaging in commerce to giving religious donations or distributing imperial largesse. Its uses thus all required an audience which both understood and accepted the social role played by that coin.

Therefore, this chapter begins with the intended audience, examining the ways in which people in the Middle Ages encountered coins and what this tells us about the capacity for representation on coins to communicate within, and to create, shared visual contexts. Only then does it turn to the authority, examining how and why issuers of coins decided to situate their representational choices on a spectrum between conservatism and innovation. These choices, however, were not usually enacted by the authorities who ordered coins to be made. The often-overlooked role played by makers of medieval money is considered as a separate and vital component in representation and visual communication. Finally, this chapter turns to unintended audiences. Medieval money traveled, as money has always done, and representation on coins influenced visual culture far beyond the spaces controlled by its issuing authority. Differences in the responses of unintended and intended audiences to medieval money bring us closer to understanding complex landscapes of visual familiarity and foreignness, both during the Middle Ages, as coins traversed space and time, and in the present, where the ultimate unintended audience—the modern viewer, collector, scholar, or curator—responds to representation on medieval coins, but also generates new understandings of it.

When this chapter talks about representation it takes in all of the intentional visual symbols placed on coins by their makers. It includes human images and other complex designs of animals, buildings, or abstract patterns. It also includes smaller, simpler representations, which might be part of these complex images or which might appear beside them. Some of these formed part of the wider visual culture of the coin's intended audience, such as crosses on coinages issued by Christian polities. Crosses could be encountered in multiple contexts, such as in wall paintings, manuscripts, and sculpture, and were probably immediately familiar to most of their viewers. Other images and marks had more esoteric and specific meanings which may have been irrelevant or unknown to many users of these coins, such as mint marks. Other marks, though useful to numismatists today for identifying and seriating coins, are still not always understood and may have had specific meaning or have been purely decorative, such as stars or dots (often termed "pellets") around the main design. Representation on coins can also refer to text in the form of inscriptions making political statements, proclaiming titles and religious views, or naming the maker, the mint or the value or denomination of the coin. The balance of image and word itself became an issue of political representation in the Middle Ages, discussed below.

## THE INTENDED AUDIENCE

The starting assumption with every coin series is that its intended audience consisted of the people subject to the authority issuing it, but this already subsumes a range of complex questions, from the uses people intended to make of coins to the status and social roles of those people. Beginning with the use people intended to make of a coin, to ask whether coinages in the early Middle Ages were primarily used for fiscal purposes (for the payment of employees by the state and of taxation to the state) or whether they were primarily market coinages designed for buying and selling commercially is a simplification, but the crux of a long-standing and still fundamental debate (Grierson 1959; Hendy

1985; Banaji 2001; Metcalf 2006). It also provokes important considerations about how the context in which a coin was received or relinquished might have affected reactions to its representation. While both rich and poor may have been intended audiences for medieval coins, at least in some states, it is also likely that their experiences of coinage would have been very different. Peter Sarris has emphasized, for example, that when the emperor Anastasius I (r. 491–518) reformed Roman base-metal coinage, he was lauded by elite writers for enriching the treasury and reviled by non-elite commentators because these reforms reduced the buying power of the low-value coinage on which the urban poor relied (Sarris 2006: 200–1). By the later Middle Ages, significant commercial and fiscal roles for coinage are both visible but that in no way obviates the question of how each individual encountered a coin (Spufford 1988b). Some coins, moreover, appear to have been created for audiences outside their issuing society, for export or payment of tribute, raising further questions about the possible dialog between creator and intended audience. As in the case of much medieval evidence, however, the responses of elites are usually more visible to us.

A finely wrought gold armband (Figure 5.1 below), probably made in the mid-seventh century and now in the Dumbarton Oaks Museum, Washington DC, features five gold coins set into a decorative panel and hints at such elite responses (Ross 2005 (1965): 44–6, BZ.1938.64M, available online: http://museum.doaks.org/Obj27448?sid=6582&x=54346&port=2607). It was

FIGURE 5.1: A Byzantine armband with framed gold coins, probably made in Constantinople in the seventh century. Image © Dumbarton Oaks, Byzantine collection, Washington DC, BZ.1938.64.

probably made in Constantinople, the capital of the state which is known in modern scholarship as the Byzantine Empire, but which considered itself to be the unbroken continuation of the Roman Empire. The armband has been dated to the seventh century on the basis that the coins set into it are of the emperors Maurice Tiberius (r. 582–602), Phocas (r. 602–10) and Heraclius (r. 610–41). It is, of course, possible that it could have been made at any time later, but if so one might expect coins of later emperors to have been included. Other stylistic features of the armband itself also match other specimens of seventh-century Byzantine gold work. The lavishness of the object makes it likely that the wearer would have been an attendant in some capacity at the imperial court; bearing this in mind, the choice of coins even for a mid-seventh-century date, is perplexing. All five coins are set into frames of beaded gold with the imperial portraits facing outwards when worn. In the middle of the five coins is a *solidus* (the highest gold denomination, also known in Greek as a *nomisma*) of the emperor Phocas. It is surrounded by four lower denomination gold coins, of Maurice, Phocas, and Heraclius. This is curious because Heraclius came to power by deposing Phocas in a violent coup.

Phocas had himself deposed Maurice in 602 in a bloody rebellion which sparked renewed warfare with the Sasanian Persian Empire, the eastern neighbor of the Byzantine state. While the accuracy of accounts which all post-date Phocas's death is hard to judge, he is condemned in surviving sources as an unstable, bloodthirsty nepotist who almost destroyed the state (Turtledove 1982: 1–3). Assuming, therefore, that the armband was made for an attendee at the court of Heraclius, an image of Phocas in its center might be interpreted as either a dramatic and possibly dangerous political statement or an act of extremely ill-judged carelessness. That is, however, only if one assumed that anybody would have noticed or cared. While it is tempting to construct political conspiracies, the presentation of these coins raises the question of what their purpose may have been in this particular visual setting. The mixture of recent, good-quality, and unworn, but not necessarily brand new coins suggests that for the jeweler, and therefore probably the commissioner of this piece, the coins were decorative items, displaying status and access to resources. They represented wealth and were perhaps fashionable within a wider symbolic language of dress *in toto*, of which coins were recognizable but not closely scrutinized components. A late sixth- or early seventh-century Byzantine marriage belt or necklace (Figure 5.2), also in the Dumbarton Oaks collection, and made of twenty-three coin-like circles of metal strung together, suggests the visual impression which small, round, stamped golden shapes were meant to create (Ross 2005 [1965]: 37–9, BZ.1937.33, available online: http://museum.doaks.org/Obj27445?sid=6582&x=3690&port=2607). Thus one of the core intended audiences for Byzantine gold coinage, the elite of the imperial court—the regular recipients of wages and largesse from the emperor, as discussed

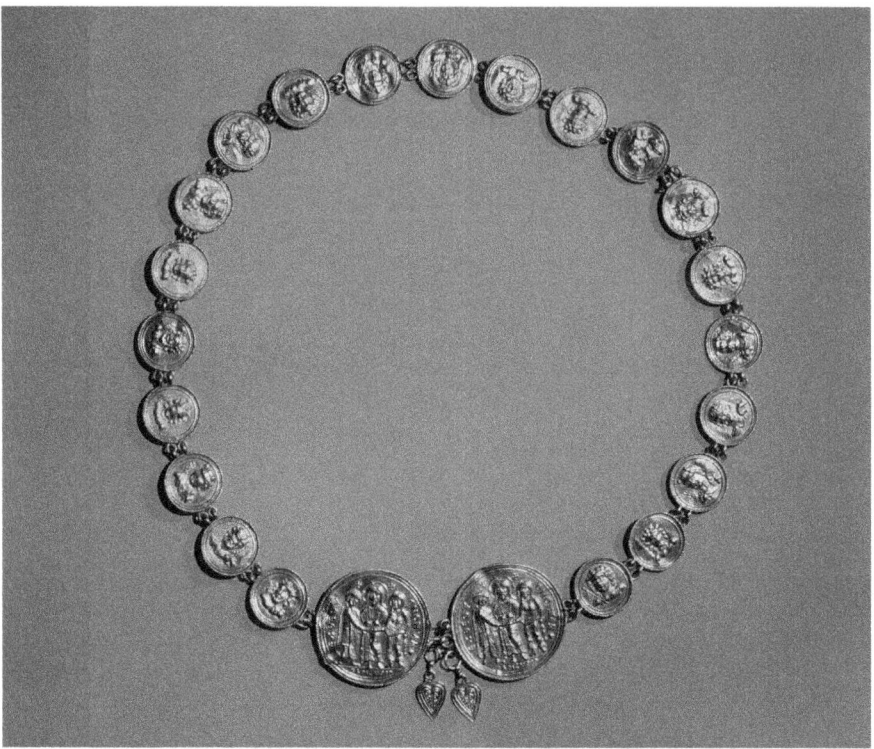

FIGURE 5.2: An early Byzantine marriage belt or necklace with round, coin-like medallions, probably made in Constantinople at an unknown date. Image © Dumbarton Oaks, Byzantine collection, Washington DC, BZ.1937.33.

below—exhibited in these two objects an understanding that gold coins represented recognizable units of value, but this understanding also transcended any particular representation on an individual coin.

Coins used as jewelry or in dress provide a valuable reminder that representation using coins in the Middle Ages was not just a matter of the designs imprinted upon them. Coins were routinely used in spectacles of imperial generosity, and indeed, subjects of the empire expected to receive not just material enrichment but also public recognition and confirmation of status by this means. Liutprand of Cremona, a Western diplomat traveling to Constantinople in the mid-tenth century, graphically described Byzantine court officials receiving from the emperor large sums of money, carefully graded from huge bags laid "on [the recipient's] shoulders, and not into [his] hands," to smaller ones not received directly from the emperor but from his chamberlain, in an annual ceremony held before Easter (Squatriti 2007: 200–2). Liutprand's record of a table "fifteen feet long and six feet broad" being placed at the front of the court, with bags of money labeled with their value placed upon it and then disbursed, "each one receiving a sum proportionate to his office," makes clear the element of spectacle and the affirmation of social hierarchy involved. Coins were also presented at imperial wedding ceremonies and diplomatic visits (Hendy 1985: 269–72). Spectacle, therefore, could play a vital role in the interactions between audiences and money in the Middle Ages and was not restricted to the Byzantine world. The *Life* of the Merovingian saint Eligius (*c.* 588–660) makes reference to Eligius earning the favor of the king, who "turned over to him a huge heap of gold and silver and gems without even weighing them." The reference to heaping up the gold and gems, closely followed by reference to jealousy among other courtiers strongly suggests another context of public reward, simultaneously signifying status, and thus also the participation of the intended audience in this representation of power through wealth (McNamara 2001: 143–4).

If these examples provide a warning not to assume that coins were always read by their intended audiences primarily as vehicles for imagery, they should not imply that intended audiences never responded to the depictions stamped onto coinage. A remarkable Carolingian manuscript (Sankt Gallen Stiftbibliothek MS 731) produced in the monastery of Regensburg, features an image alongside the text of a law code of a *denarius* or *denier* of the king, later emperor, Charlemagne (r. 768–814) (Garipzanov 2016). The image is unusual in using the power of the idea of a coin, on which the inscription *Karolus Rex* (King Charles) is prominently visible, to convey the authority of the king himself. It is also a very detailed and accurate rendition of a coin type which had only recently been introduced, and suggests that for at least one member of the intended audience the visual language of this coin, which proclaimed the king's status in a highly Romanizing fashion, using Latin and a monogram form which had been employed in Roman architecture and on coinage for centuries, had very much the effect intended by the issuing authority. It communicated the power and above all the legitimacy of the king to act as an endorsement of law and order within a Roman tradition. In the context of debates about the nature of Carolingian government, this image is of particular value. Despite the undoubted military power of the Carolingians, the administration of the realm may have been quite light-touch, with governance consisting of repeated acts of participation by largely autonomous magnates who chose to consider themselves part of the empire for the sake of mainly symbolic benefit and unity. The Carolingian Empire was certainly a realm made up of a variety of different peoples, many of whom continued to use their own laws, language, and customs. That they now did so under the aegis of the king, who was militarily powerful but not necessarily unchallengeably so, hints at the importance of shared symbolic languages, visual codes, and accepted narratives of authority which could make everyday difference coexist with a sense of broad-scale inclusion.

*Codex Sangallensis 731* offers just a hint at how monetary representation might have played a role in the dialog which made this possible.

The Byzantine armband and *Codex Sangallensis 731* illustration provide opposite audience reactions to representation on coins, from apparent indifference to detailed examination, but a vast space lay between them in the Middle Ages, which again sometimes emerges in our sources. Francesco Balducci Pegolotti was a fourteenth-century Italian merchant to whom a guide has been attributed to European and especially Mediterranean trade. This includes a list of coins which merchants might encounter. It is an invaluable insight into trading practices and responses to coin imagery in a world in which states issued competing and complementary currencies, and in which merchants were accustomed to using fluctuating coin values to turn a profit. The most commonly used coins are not described at all, except in terms of their weight and fineness. More unusual coins receive a few lines of description. One example refers to imitations by Latin rulers in the eastern Mediterranean of coins of John III Vatatzes (r. 1222–54) of the Empire of Thessaloniki. The type was based on traditional Byzantine coin design and featured imagery which might be considered familiar within a Christian Mediterranean context. On the obverse sits Christ, enthroned, with a halo behind his head containing the mark of the cross. On the reverse, in a slightly more distinctively Byzantine image, the Virgin Mary crowns John III Vatatzes, clothed in Byzantine imperial garb, with abbreviated Greek legends visible to either side (Figure 5.3).

Pegolotti is pragmatic and concise. The coin, he says, may be recognized because on one side it has two figures. One holds a pestle which hangs down between them. On the other side there is a single figure. Above the cross are some small shapes. These are then drawn in the manuscript, and the author remarks that the quality of gold is worse when the coin carries some of these

FIGURE 5.3: Latin imitation of a gold *hyperperon* of John III Vatatzes, probably minted in Constantinople, 4.62g. Photograph courtesy of Barber Institute of Fine Arts (B6088).

signs in comparison to the others (Evans 1936: 288; Leonard Jr 2008: 81). There is, in other words, throughout the text and in this example, a consistent and total lack of interest in what these figures were meant to represent, even when they had been observed quite closely by the author. The appearance of the coin in this context was a key to its identification and thus its value, and denoted to the author's mind only exchangeability.

## THE AUTHORITY

The coin described by Pegolotti provides some insight into the choices available to the authority issuing coins as well as to audience responses. Why were Latin rulers, who in the first half of the thirteenth century controlled the Byzantine Empire from Constantinople, nonetheless issuing copies of coins produced by a ruler in Thessaloniki, who was himself copying earlier Byzantine styles in order to project his claim to be the legitimate, if exiled, emperor of Byzantium? Representation on medieval coinage is often described as highly conservative, or less generously as repetitive and unimaginative, but there were important premiums attached to continuity and consistency for any issuing authority. This authority need not be a state, but in the medieval world usually was. Early Anglo-Saxon and Frisian pennies, also termed *sceattas* in the numismatic literature, may constitute an exception, with current research suggesting that they were produced by merchants who collectively agreed on their fineness and value for mutual convenience (Naismith 2012: 143–4). For the most part, though, money was a creation of states and so, officially, a product of the head of that state. This was frequently denoted by the name of the ruler appearing on coins, often alongside a depiction either of the person or a symbol of their authority. In all cases though, the primary aim of the issuing authority in producing coinage was that the coin be usable, for whatever purpose they required. Usually this seems to have been a mixture of commercial and fiscal payments, and so coinage had to be acceptable to the employees of the state who were paid in it, and to traders wishing to do business with it. It also usually had to be recognizable as the medium by which people returned payments to the state, most obviously through taxation. From this perspective, changing the appearance of coins as little as possible from one issuer to the next within the same system made sense. It preserved familiarity, trust, and therefore usability. As a head of state, placing one's own name on coins which resembled those of previous rulers also seems to have legitimized the most recent ruler by situating him, or more rarely her, in an unbroken line of continuity from earlier rulers (Naismith 2012: 47–68). The speed with which usurpers, rebels, and even legitimate but short-lived rulers produced coins in the medieval world suggests that the ability to produce recognized and accepted coinage was a vital demonstration of political viability, which in most cases seems to have mitigated against innovation. Thus, while changes in design offer the clearest indication of the aims and representational strategies of issuing authorities, conservatism was itself a potentially conscious and effective mode of visual communication. In the example of the Latin imitation of Vatatzes, discussed above, both issuing authorities—the Latin emperors of Constantinople and John of Thessaloniki—made use of continuity and conservatism as statements of political ambition in extremely unstable times.

Another period of instability, marked by innovation rather than conservatism, occurred in the seventh century. This chapter has already touched on the difficulties faced by a succession of Byzantine emperors from Maurice to Heraclius at the turn of the seventh century. From 610, when Heraclius was crowned emperor, war with Persia was followed by the emergence of the first armies fighting in the name of the Prophet Muhammad from the Arabian Peninsula. The year 629 witnessed both the final and definitive conclusion of the Byzantine-Persian War, with Heraclius winning an improbable and hard-fought victory, and the first incursions of armies from Arabia into Syria. Heraclius did not live to see this new power stabilize as the first Islamic Caliphate, but did witness the fall of the Sasanian Persian Empire before it and the loss of almost all Byzantine territory in North Africa, Egypt, and the Levant. By the 690s the Umayyad Caliphate had changed the shape of the Mediterranean and established Muslim rule over most of the Middle and Near East and the southern shores of the Mediterranean (Kennedy 2004). The coins of Heraclius, his grandson Constans II (r. 641–68) and the Umayyad Caliph Abd al-Malik (r. 685–705) reveal particular uses of representation on money as a means for issuing authorities to communicate with their subjects, in a century for which narrative historical sources are extremely thin.

Figure 5.4 depicts a *hexagram* of Heraclius, a coin which demonstrates the use of both innovation and continuity. It communicates a very precise set of

FIGURE 5.4: Byzantine silver *hexagram* of Heraclius, Constantinople, 6.47g. Photograph courtesy of Barber Institute of Fine Arts (B3057).

messages and appears to have specific, as well as general audiences in mind. The *hexagram* was minted in silver at a time when the Byzantine monetary system was based on gold coins with linked copper alloy denominations. This reflected economic necessity at a time when Heraclius's resources were severely depleted by the war with Persia. Making some state payments in silver, while continuing to receive taxes in gold, seems to have been a strategy for eking out the state's limited funds (Kaegi 2003: 90–1). The use of silver may also have carried visual and symbolic weight. It has been argued that one of the reasons the Byzantine state did not regularly issue silver coinage by the seventh century was because by then silver had come to be associated with ecclesiastical use (Leader-Newby 2004). Church ornaments and altar covers were made of silver and so gold became the metal of worldly payments and silver the metal of God. Theophanes, a ninth-century chronicler who provides the only substantial narrative source for Byzantine history in the seventh century, records that Heraclius took silver plate from the churches of Constantinople and melted it to help the treasury (Hendy 1985: 495). The appearance of the *hexagram*, and (perhaps in Constantinople at least) some awareness of the use of church silver in making them, may have been designed to evoke a sense of divine approval of the Christian, coin-issuing emperor, fighting against non-Christian enemies. The remarkable inscription on these coins supports such an interpretation. It read DEVS ADIVTA ROMANIS or "God help the Romans." While the impact of this prayer may have been intended for the Christian population of the empire at large, it seems possible in this case to discern a more particular audience for such representation. It is likely that the army formed a large component of Heraclius's intended audience for the *hexagram* and there is a hint of dialog in the choice of inscription. Heraclius's imperial predecessor-but-one produced a manual on warfare, the *Strategikon* of Maurice, dating to the late sixth or early seventh century, which records a call-and-response, to be used during training as being a valuable morale-booster for troops. In this exercise the officer would shout *adiuta* ("help [us]") and the soldiers would reply *Deus*! ("[oh] God!") (Dennis 1984: 146). The *hexagram* might, therefore, be perceived as both a prayer by the head of a Christian state and a message of solidarity with his troops issued by an emperor who was an active field commander.

The design was not, however, wholly innovative, and its continuities reflect other communications which were considered valuable at a time of crisis and uncertainty. The cross on the reverse had been introduced by Tiberius II (r. 574–82) and became a standard depiction on Byzantine precious metal coinage, a powerful but simple symbol of a Christian empire. The obverse carries an image of Heraclius flanked by his son, Heraclius Constantine, later emperor Constantine III (r. 641). Heraclius Constantine, probably born in 612, shortly after his father became emperor, was almost immediately made co-emperor and depicted alongside his father on coins, presumably to indicate that upon Heraclius's death there would be a smooth transition of rulership, unlike the violent coup that had brought him to power. As the years passed, Heraclius Constantine was presented in varying stages of maturity, starting as a small and chubby-cheeked child alongside a bearded Heraclius, becoming a young man of almost equal size to his father, either beardless or with a fuzz around his chin, and culminating in a portrait of a full-sized and bearded man beside a mature Heraclius, now sporting a lavish, chest-length beard with wide moustaches (Grierson 1982: 84–138; Arnold 2013). These changes, at a time when rulers on medieval coinage were often portrayed in an entirely stereotyped fashion without clear differentiation between individual, age or other aspects of personal identity, have generated suggestions that Heraclius sought to revive "portraiture," in the sense of physical likeness, in order to convey elements of his personal identity. One speculation has tried to connect this to a possible Armenian origin for the emperor's family (Douglas 1992: 141).

Representations of Heraclius and his family, however, are better understood in terms of modern developments in the analysis of medieval portraiture than efforts to match monetary images to personality traits. The modern concept of portraiture, which derives from a Renaissance and post-Renaissance idea of individuality, judges portraits by how closely they represent the physical likeness of the individual, their unique personal characteristics, and perhaps some intangible sense of their personality (West 2004). Research into medieval imagery, however, has shown that this individual likeness was not the primary goal of representation. Instead, portraits were valued for representing the social identity of the individual. The image was not expected to look like the physical body of the person represented but to show to an audience, using socially comprehensible visual codes, the social status and relationships of the individual: their age, sex, employment, social or marital status, and perhaps regional identification. Thus, representation might focus on dress, symbols of maturity or wealth, or images of religiosity. In the context of the coinage of Heraclius, the emphasis on beard length and height focuses on the relative maturity and therefore social status of the figures. The pair of images perhaps also emphasized initially that Heraclius had an heir, and therefore a viable plan for succession, and as time went on projected the growing capability of that heir, as a full adult, to rule meaningfully and independently in his father's stead (Brubaker 2013).

The addition of Heraclius's second son, Constantine Heraclius, usually known as Heraclonas, to the imperial coinage after his birth in 626 operated within the same set of visual symbols but communicated something slightly different, showing the flexibility of even outwardly conservative representation. Heraclonas was the son of Heraclius and his second wife, Martina. Martina, however, was also Heraclius's niece, causing the marriage to be condemned by the Church as incestuous and raising questions about Heraclonas's legitimacy.

Nevertheless, Heraclius elevated Heraclonas to the status of co-emperor and Heraclonas appeared on coinage alongside his father and half-brother with no visible difference except initially in his height and beard length, denoting his youth. Beyond that, the sons are indistinguishable on the coins, both from each other and from their father. All wear and carry the emblems of Christian emperorship and the coins project an unambiguous statement that Heraclonas was to be considered a legitimate and worthy co-heir to Heraclius.

Examining familial representation alongside the *hexagram*, however, suggests that more important for the seventh-century emperors of Byzantium than any particular coin design was communication of their ability to issue a working currency despite crisis. Even when the state had to use silver to make ends meet, it did not give up altogether on gold coinage and its determination to keep the economic structures of the empire going is most apparent in the issue of copper-alloy coinage. Seventh-century base metal coinage is often left out of discussions of representation on coinage, and it is initially easy to see why. Constans II's copper-alloy coinage, like most emperors of the seventh century, is marked by a tendency towards low-quality production, with simple and often poorly executed imagery. The flans or blanks onto which these coins were struck were often hacked out of metal in irregular shapes, and were sometimes not even blank. Coins could be restruck directly over existing coins, leaving the old design showing through and obscuring the new. Nevertheless, the images on these copper coins had to be cut into dies, in a skilled process that will be explored in more detail below. Mint workers had to be employed to strike the coins and people had to receive them. Copper-alloy coinage of the mid-seventh century was not a neglected space of representation, and indeed, how could it be? Just as, at their simplest level, coins are objects of representation, which cannot exist without images, so no coinage, however unprepossessing its appearance, can ever be the result of total neglect.

Making money requires resources, and any coin represents at least a minimum expenditure of effort. It is not clear for whom these coins were struck or why it was at times necessary to produce them sufficiently quickly or with such a lack of resources that the depictions on them are all but incomprehensible, but this perhaps leads us back to the realm of spectacle, to coins as representation, rather than carriers of representation. For urban non-elites, for soldiers receiving regular payment rather than an annual lump sum, or changing their lump sum into something they could spend, or for taxpayers expecting change back from handing gold over to the state, it is possible that the coinage of Constans II simply needed to exist, to be a tangible reminder at the point of disbursement, which might itself have been a moment of governmental theatre—a military parade, a public procession, festival, or communal tax gathering—that the state remained committed to performing the functions of government, and thus providing small change (Figure 5.5).

FIGURE 5.5: Byzantine copper-alloy *follis* of Constans II, Constantinople, 4.38g, overstruck on a coin of Heraclius. Photograph courtesy of Barber Institute of Fine Arts (B3982).

Towards the end of the seventh century the Caliph Abd al-Malik introduced one of the most dramatic innovations in coin representation in the medieval world, but it too was closely connected to this need for rulers to exhibit their capacity to generate and regulate currency. By the 690s the newly formed Islamic polity, now known as the Umayyad Caliphate, was faced with the task of running a single fiscal administration across territories and bureaucracies formed from two entirely different currency systems and visual traditions. The territories of the former Sasanian Empire were accustomed to a silver-based currency system and a repertoire of state imagery derived from Zoroastrianism, while the subjects of the formerly Byzantine regions of North Africa, Egypt, and the Levant operated with a gold-standard currency and a shared visual arena dominated by Christianity (Treadwell 2009). In addition to, or as a result of this difficulty, in the reign of Abd al-Malik the projection by the Umayyad state of a clearly identifiable Muslim identity also became visible for the first time in a range of sources, from the built architecture of the Dome of the Rock to the earliest copies of the text of the Qur'an (Johns 2003). In the case of coinage, some attempt was made just to modify the existing Sasanian and Byzantine systems, but these were ultimately abandoned in favor of an entirely new design (along with new weight standards). This new design rejected all imagery and instead used political and religious inscriptions in Arabic (Heidemann 1998). It in turn subsequently became the basis for consistency, becoming the model for Islamic coinage with little deviation for several hundred years (Figure 5.6).

This inscriptional model was still the default for most Islamic coins by the mid-thirteenth century when the Levant was contested by local Muslim rulers and states set up by western Europeans, who had traveled eastwards on Crusade. It was a situation that gave rise to a rich and sophisticated (as well as violent and

FIGURE 5.6: A gold *dinar* of Abd al-Malik, minted AD 701–2 at an unnamed Middle Eastern mint, 4.27g. Image © Fitzwilliam Museum, Cambridge, CM.PG.8449-2006.

contested) exchange of visual languages. This is especially clear on the coins of the Crusader kingdom of Acre, particularly on one issue of 1251 (Figure 5.7). Minted by the beleaguered Christian kingdom, these coins were anonymous silver dirhams in the style of local Muslim coinage, including a largely aniconic Arabic design. In this case, however, a cross in the center of the obverse suggests hints at innovation by the issuing authority, which is continued in the inscription itself. The Arabic reads "one God alone, one faith alone, one baptism alone," and on the reverse, "Father, Son, Holy Spirit, one Godhead alone" (Malloy *et al.* 1994: 138). While the desire to communicate and the beliefs of the issuing authority are clear—an unequivocal commitment to Christianity, directed towards key points of disagreement between Christian and Muslim belief—the audience is less certain.

FIGURE 5.7: Anonymous Crusader silver dirham of the kingdom of Acre, struck 1251, 2.92g. Photograph courtesy of Barber Institute of Fine Arts (CR014).

There were by 1251 bilingual Christians living in Crusader states like Acre who had grown up in the Levant and spoke Arabic fluently, but Latin or another European language was perhaps a more obvious medium for addressing these people in a way which conveyed religious and cultural solidarity, and a unity that excluded Muslim neighbors. Alternatively, the coins were perhaps intended for Arabic-speaking Muslims in the region, but the hope of converting people via messages on money seems either far-fetched or a sign of desperation. The blending of visual messages on this coinage, layering linguistic, representational, and theological codes into a fascinating but confusing whole, reflects the difficulties the issuing authority faced, both in knowing and communicating effectively with plural audiences in a contested political space. It also hints at the difficulty of trying to read a dialog for which we often only have half of the script.

## THE MAKER

The examples considered so far have addressed the interactions of intended audiences and issuing authorities with representation on money, but representation on coins was not simply a dialog between authority and intended audience, situated on a scale between conservatism and familiarity at one end, and innovation and engagement at the other. We have few indications of how coin design was actually enacted in medieval polities. These imply that coin design was a political pronouncement by the ruling authority, but the same can be said of almost any act made possible or claimed by authority. Kings and emperors built walls (Brubaker and Haldon 2011: 413), supported religious foundations (Jordan 2009), commissioned manuscripts (Hilsdale 2005), led armies (Flori 2006), and made laws (Wormald 1977). We usually do not know what the level of personal involvement in these tasks was any more than we know how far emperors and kings approved their coin designs or whether they were even consulted by officials. It seems plausible to argue that the more a coin broke with expectation and tradition in its design, the more likely it was that increasingly senior voices of a kingdom or empire were consulted or initiated the changes. Thus, when Edward III (r. 1327–77) introduced a gold denomination to the English monetary system in 1344, he personally selected mint masters to oversee its (unsuccessful) development (Allen 2012: 214). When Theudebert of Francia (r. 534–48) had his own name engraved in place of the Roman emperor, it is likely that this development too was approved directly, but we do not know for sure (Grierson and Blackburn 1986: 115–16). The rarity with which sources mention direct guidance about the appearance of coins suggests that it was unusual for authorities to be so prescriptive. In every case, though, after a decision had been made, how was it enacted?

"Maker" is a simple-sounding but tricky category. An initial definition of the maker might be "the moneyer," a term for a figure given responsibility for issuing coinage or "mint master" if the person responsible actually managed a larger team of workers, but these likewise offer little assistance. For most medieval polities we do not know much about these figures, nor even in some cases whether there was one such general overseer at every mint. While mint organization in the Byzantine Empire, for example, was undoubtedly complex with multiple workshops and, at times, multiple mints producing similar designs across the empire, nothing personal is known of any moneyer or overseer. For other places, we know more. In the Merovingian Empire, for example, gold coins were issued in the names of moneyers rather than kings from c. 570–670 and silver until the mid-eighth century, and in some cases we even have documentary sources that provide biographical information about these figures (Jarnut and Strothmann 2013). Nevertheless, being able to attach a name and, more rarely, a story to a moneyer gives an illusion rather than a reality of intimacy, especially when it comes to representation on coins. Maybe, in the case of small-scale coinages, one man was responsible for every stage of production, but probably not for larger operations in which, beneath the term "moneyer," we ought to imagine a whole variety of people responsible for aspects of production. Dies, used for striking most Western and Middle Eastern medieval coins, are complex pieces of technology. They were cut, with the design inverted, into hardened metal (Malkmus 2007). They had a limited lifespan and could either crack and break as a result of wear, or be retired because a design changed or an emperor or king ceased to rule or because demand for coinage or the bullion to make it from waned. Much of what we think of as representation on coins was thus the direct product not of the commissioning authority, nor even the moneyer in the sense of overseer, but of the die cutters.

These were the people who created the images that we see on coins. Their skill, or apparent lack thereof, created many of the fine details which have optimistically been read as insights into the minds of issuing authorities. This can sometimes overlook fairly significant gaps in our knowledge, such as how designs, even if sanctioned by an authority, were transmitted to mints further away for die cutters to engrave. In some cases, for example across most of the Sasanian Empire from the fifth century, it seems that dies were cut centrally and distributed to mints (Schindel 2005: 292). For the Carolingian Empire, the 864 Edict of Pîtres includes a description of the design to be used on imperial coins, though this is sufficiently vague that it could not have been the sole instruction sent out to moneyers (Hill 2013: 101, 104). The edict, however, refers to moneyers coming to the court to receive silver from which to strike coins, while the Domesday Book from eleventh-century England also refers to moneyers coming to court to receive dies (Archibald *et al.* 1995; Naismith 2012: 139), suggesting various models of centralization. From France and the Iberian Peninsula in the high Middle Ages, examples have been found of coin-like

FIGURE 5.8: Silver object found in 2007 in Staffordshire, measuring 20.5mm and weighing 7.19g. It has been identified as a piedfort striking of a coin type of Philip IV, King of France (r. 1285–1314). Image courtesy of the Portable Antiquities Scheme, WMID-47EBE7.

objects (Figure 5.8), known as piedforts (or piéforts), in designs which seem not to have been struck as coins, and which have been tentatively identified as prototypes circulated to mints to demonstrate new designs (Crusafont *et al.* 2013: 152).

In addition to the die cutters, who were almost certainly skilled and valued artisans, the term "maker" included other individuals relevant to the issue of representation. Working through the stages of making a medieval coin highlights a number of processes that might have fallen within the remit of a variable number of people. Somebody had to calculate the metallic composition of the blank flans onto which coins were struck, or decide not to and select an appropriate number of old coins and poorly formed pieces of metal, with serious implications for representation. An even mixture would take a struck design better than a mixture full of different metals. A heavily lead-based copper alloy, for instance, such as that used in a series of coins produced in Sri Lanka during the fifth and sixth centuries (Figure 5.9), limited the design that could be impressed on the coins, as it made the metal friable and likely to crack under pressure (Walburg 2008: 67). It should be remembered, indeed, that the creator of the alloy from which coins were struck may have been a more valued worker to medieval mint masters even than a skilled die cutter. It requires a great deal of technical expertise to create flans of correct metallic composition and weight, and especially in the case of precious metal coinages these characteristics were more likely to determine the success of a coinage than the designs impressed upon them.

Even if the composition of flans was important beyond the designs impressed upon them, it also affected the legibility and extent of designs. Flans of even

FIGURE 5.9: Image of a copper-alloy imitation of a late Roman *nummus* made in Sri Lanka, from the National Archaeology Museum, Colombo. Image by R. Darley, 2011.

thickness would take a design better than one thicker at one end than the other, and it is, of course, easier to strike a more elaborate design onto a larger coin, while thick coins with small diameters limited the space for inscription or image. In the later Byzantine Empire, from the mid-eleventh century, coins were struck on concave flans, involving a complex process of using multiple dies to strike images clearly onto the two curved sides, and so the skill of the maker of the flans and of the person or people physically striking the coins were crucial to the resulting image (Bendall and Sellwood 1973; Sellwood 1980; Bendall 1998). Finally, a host of other, probably increasingly less skilled makers played their part in the appearance of a coin, such as the person or people responsible for placing the flans between the two dies for striking. Whether this was done consistently or accurately affected both the overall appearance of a series of coins and, on each individual coin, how much of the design created by the die cutters was actually visible.

The arrangement of a mint may also have contributed to the results of makers' efforts. Some coinages of apparently "crude" appearance are thought to have been rushed or made in peripatetic mints. This is not impossible, but should provoke some consideration of logistics. Even in a mint moving with a royal court, it seems most likely that the actual acts of die cutting and striking would be done during stopping periods. The idea of a "mint on the move" can sometimes appear in discussions of representation on medieval coins as a kind of fantasy, but should not be overstated (e.g. Göbl 1971: 32). It may be true that a worker in a mobile mint might have had less time to produce a certain quota of coins before moving on, or that the die sinkers may have had to work with a small repertoire of tools that could be easily carried. The Late Roman Empire, however, seems to have had mobile mints, moving with the court of peripatetic emperors, which were capable of producing coins indistinguishable in their quality from those of any other mint, as did Castilian kings of the late fifteenth century (Hendy 1985: 393–4; Crusafont *et al.* 2013: 399–400). As a general rule, the higher the value of the coins, the more likely authorities were to enforce good production standards, whether at a fixed or a mobile mint, but this was not always the case. The efforts of English kings between the tenth and fifteenth centuries to prevent not just forgery but also the passing of poor coin by state moneyers and officials testifies as eloquently to recurring failure as it does to intermittent success (Allen 2012: 368–76). The Artuqid rulers of northern Mesopotamia in the eleventh century onward issued silver only sporadically and mostly minted in copper alloy, but their coins were usually well made, with dies centered accurately on large flans, allowing complex designs to be legibly struck (Hillenbrand 1990; Whelan 2006).

Makers, therefore, played a vital part in the representations we see on coins, and raise important questions about whose work we are reading. Clearly the aims or intentions of authorities are visible but sometimes so are the makers'. The gold coinage of some of the post-Roman states of western Europe, in particular the Merovingian and Visigothic kingdoms, is striking for its use and modification of Roman and Byzantine models. An examination of the metalwork produced within these societies suggests that prominent stylistic differences from the monetary prototypes being used were not just a result of lack of skill (Perea Caveda 2001; James 1988: 80–96). It is very clear in the case of Visigothic and Merovingian coinage that the coinage of the contemporary Roman/Byzantine world was being consciously imitated (Grierson and Blackburn 1986: 39–54, 81–135; Castellanos 2012), but that the end results are visually distinctive may reflect different cultural norms and mores, or the aesthetics of different makers, for whom the images being imitated were translated through a lens of non-Roman image creation and cultural practice.

The Frisian and Anglo-Saxon *sceattas* mentioned previously suggest similar processes. Many of these carry an image resembling a porcupine (Figure 5.10), which evolved from a Late Roman portrait of an emperor, in which the hair became an increasingly prominent crest that eventually replaced a recognizable human bust altogether. Its original meaning and eventually its original appearance faded in importance in comparison to the role of the image as a symbol with a newly constructed set of social meanings.

Analysis of these coins, which are usually well made, carefully struck, and of good silver, suggests that this distinctive visual feature became a focal point because it was recognizable and distinctive, not because the die cutters could do no better. The same might be considered in the case of the Visigothic figure of Victory (Figure 5.11), who to modern Western eyes (eyes trained in the aesthetics of ancient Rome) looks rather lizard-like and in some cases difficult to recognize as humanoid (Grierson and Blackburn 1986: cat. nos 192–208). Rather than a sign of inadequate or inadequately supervised die cutters, however, this might

FIGURE 5.10: Silver penny or *sceatta*, minted in England *c.* 700–50 at an unknown mint, 1.13g. Image © Fitzwilliam Museum, Cambridge, CM.1744–2007.

FIGURE 5.11: Gold *tremissis* of Visigothic rulers of Spain, minted *c.* 507–580, showing on the reverse a standing figure of Victory, 1.44g. Image © Fitzwilliam Museum, Cambridge, CM.PG.10349-2006.

perhaps provide insight into varied cultural "ways of seeing," born out of artisanal practice coming into creative contact with existing models. Makers played a crucial role in the mediation of representation between authority and intended audience, and thereby in the construction of a shared realm of visual symbolism.

## UNINTENDED AUDIENCES

All of the interactions with coin representation considered so far have assumed a shared visual context for audience, authority, and maker, examining coins in their originally constituted social setting, but in the Middle Ages coins did not circulate exclusively within their original context. The final examples considered here lie potentially, and in many cases actually, beyond their original shared realm of visual symbolism, and outside the lines of communication which coin representation was created for. Unintended audiences, both medieval and modern, are useful to compare in their responses to numismatic representation. On the one hand, many unintended audiences ended up being users of medieval coins whose own spheres of representation were affected by them. On the other hand, the reactions of unintended audiences to medieval coins provide insights into the ways in which the ideal triangulation of maker, authority, and intended audience worked in practice. The outside viewer offers a point of comparison and contemplation. Byzantine coins found in India, for example, traveled far beyond their original political and monetary context (Darley 2015). They moved initially by means of long-distance trade but entered a local economic and social context in south India in which they could not easily serve as currency and did not represent a tangible or well-understood political authority. Reactions to the images represented on these coins appear to have been the reverse of that seen in, for example, the armband with which this chapter began. It would appear that in a south Indian context, Byzantine coins were valued primarily as vehicles for the representations they carried. Great care was shown to the images on them, though usually with no indication as to how these were understood. Imitation or partial imitation of coins suggests elements of design which were imbued with particular significance (Figure 5.12). Alternatively coins might be pierced in India, and earlier Roman coins had often had a frame and loop fitted to enable them to be hung from cloth or on a

FIGURE 5.12: Imitation Byzantine gold *solidus* of Theodosius II (r. 408–50) found in Karnataka, south India, as part of the Akki Alur Hoard (Day 2012), with double piercings allowing the imperial portrait to hang upright. Weight and place of minting unknown. Photograph reproduced from original by Peter Berghaus, with permission.

chain, giving an insight into the way in which people oriented the images they saw. In south India, piercings on Byzantine coins invariably left the portrait bust of the emperor upright, and sometimes patterns of wear show that the portrait was probably worn facing outwards, while the reverse received more wear by rubbing against skin or clothing. Imitations also focused on the imperial bust, even when other features, such as inscription or reverse design, were ignored or altered significantly.

In Britain too, where Merovingian coins of the sixth and seventh centuries traveled across the Channel or were copied locally, both original and imitation coins sometimes carry piercings which aligned with certain features to leave them hanging upright (Figure 5.13). Use of money, however, is nothing if not unpredictable. The grave of an elite Anglo-Saxon warrior at Sutton Hoo revealed 37 Merovingian coins deposited with the highly staged ship burial, recalling the element of performance which can be so elusive in our imagining of medieval coins as tools of representation. The burial, however, contains three other coin-like objects, which present a fascinating contrast. They are entirely blank flans or pseudo-coins, in gold, and of similar weight and size to the Merovingian pieces, but nothing could testify more clearly to coins in this instance representing objects of use not as carriers of representation, their imagery apparently irrelevant to the purpose at hand (Bruce-Mitford 1968: 47).

Quite a different interaction with the visual is demonstrated by the coinage of the Artuqids, already mentioned. Artuqid coinage exhibits a promiscuous

FIGURE 5.13: An imitation of a late-sixth or early seventh-century *solidus* type from the mint of Marseille. In this case, the imitation was gold-plated, then pierced for suspension before being broken and lost. It was found in Old Buckenham, Norfolk, England in 2004, 1.8g. Image courtesy of the Portable Antiquity Scheme, SUR-09EA44.

and highly creative use of coin images borrowed and adapted from other coins and visual media. One side almost always carries an epigraphic Arabic design proclaiming the issuing authority and operating within the tradition of Islamic coinage established by Abd al-Malik in the seventh century. The other side, though, might contain images drawn from contemporary Byzantine coins (including the Virgin Mary crowning the Byzantine emperor), from much older coins, including the seventh-century designs of Heraclius and Heraclius Constantine, and even some Roman and older Hellenistic images (Figure 5.14). The precise economic function of Artuqid coinage is mysterious, but it is well-made and the scope and combination of imagery suggests a concern with what was depicted. The coinage perhaps speaks to multi-focal and deeply historicized ideas of authority which must have been swirling around northern Mesopotamia around the time of the Crusades, with the Byzantine Empire claiming the

FIGURE 5.14: Artuqid copper alloy coin of Kutb al-din Ilgazi II (r. 1176–84), possibly minted in Mardin, 12.1g. Beneath it, a prototype for the obverse design, a seventh-century gold *solidus* of Heraclius and Heraclius Constantine, Constantinople, 4.41g. Photographs courtesy of Barber Institute of Fine Arts (TK0033 and B2818).

authority of the Roman Empire, Crusaders claiming the authority of papal Rome, the Seljuks projecting power in an Islamic tradition, and numerous smaller kingdoms all projecting their own claims to identity through a blend of tradition and experimentation.

## CONCLUSION

There are, therefore, no absolute keys to unlocking medieval coin representation. Some intended audiences saw in coins the things we imagine their issuing authorities intended, but many did not, and reactions could differ up and down the social spectrum. Some makers executed representations with care and others badly enough that the images are all but incomprehensible, but this does not necessarily tell us about the sophistication of the issuing state or what was at stake in producing coins. The process alludes to a world of "live performance," now largely lost, but which may have been crucial to how many medieval coins were used as vehicles of representation. Many unintended audiences, too, saw in coins icons of power or meaning in their local context. Sometimes these seem legible to us—western European kings using Roman imagery, for example. In other cases it is harder to know what Indian users saw in Byzantine coin portraiture, or what the people burying the corpse in Mound One at Sutton Hoo thought was conveyed by the Merovingian coins and ingots buried with him. There are some generalities, however, which tentatively emerge.

All coins must carry some representation, but in much of the medieval world the idea of coinage was familiar enough that the content of that representation did not necessarily matter to all issuers or audiences. It could be enough that a coin was recognizable as a coin, and some of the transactions for which money was produced, such as payments to armies and bureaucracies, could be made in staged contexts in which the representation on a coin might either have become a focal point, perhaps echoing a familiar military acclamation, or could have been entirely subsumed, with money being scattered or given out in bags, of which weight and quantity were the uppermost concerns.

Medieval money provides indications of major political statements being played out through coinage, and designs are often complex and tailored in response to particular circumstances. They could also be highly conservative and imitative, however, and the copying or modification of an existing design, by a predecessor, a neighboring power, or a usurped authority, testify to an evolving visual language of statehood and power shared at least across northern Europe, the Mediterranean and the Middle East. It was a shared language constructed as well as communicated by the movement and reception of coins. For makers and moneyers, executing the designs of authorities could be an act of craftsmanship and creativity, reformulating old or foreign symbols, or experimenting with technological innovation. It might at other times and in other places have been a mechanical task to be accomplished, requiring little skill and the ability to produce quickly and with limited resources. Finally, money moves. This meant that coins frequently came into contact with unintended users, for whom the representations they carried might be more significant than for their intended audiences. These coins could become props in new performances of power or piety and might be worn, buried, or imitated and in all of these ways suggest to us how new audiences viewed these coins.

At no point, however, even when coins were used decoratively, is it clear that the term "art" applied in the Middle Ages. It is a label applied to medieval money by perhaps the least intended audience of all—modern viewers. Medieval audiences for coins, however far removed from the original issuer, were dealing not just with interactions of representation but also with realities of interaction with the object and their own social context, whether in the form of diplomatic ties, aggressive neighbors, or the use of the exotic to project power in domestic contexts. Even the Artuqids, using images from centuries before, were doing so to make coins of their own and thereby a performance of statehood.

These unintended audiences did not, as far as we know, theorize, explicate, or debate the meaning of representation on coins. That has been left to academics, collectors, and dealers of the most recent centuries. Due to its imagery appearing "crude" to modern eyes, for a long time medieval coinage stood in the shadow of classical coinage. As its value has been recognized, the meaning of representation on medieval money has been debated and constructed into sometimes overly elaborate "translations." Extensive previous work has enabled this chapter to examine a selection of medieval coin images within their historical and archaeological context, and to leave out hundreds of other examples that might have nuanced, strengthened, or diversified the arguments made. In both cases there is a perhaps unavoidable tendency to discuss representation on medieval coins as if this new forum—constituted from the museum cabinet, the auction catalog, and the journal article or conference paper—is somehow the definitive and the primary arena in which to identify meaning. It is a view which can only be tempered by thinking systematically, as numismatic research increasingly does, about coins as objects with social uses and relationships, embedded into larger material cultural contexts, which shaped representation on money and were in turn modified by that representation.

CHAPTER SIX

# Money and Its Interpretation

*Attitudes to Money in the* Societas Christiana

SVEIN H. GULLBEKK

During the Middle Ages the history of money developed alongside state formation, urbanization, and sweeping changes in society, politics, and religion. Describing developments in the eleventh century, the historian Alexander Murray observed that: "The entry of money into the European economy was such a radical change in the environment. It brought in new possibilities; and with them new goals, activities, and habits" (Murray 1992: 59). The rise of money economies forms part of what is usually called the "Commercial Revolution" of the eleventh, twelfth, and thirteenth centuries (Lopez 1971). Within medieval Europe many of the developments associated with this period already had a long history behind them, and progressed in fits and starts. In Alan of Lille's (*c.* 1120–1202) work *De planctu naturae*, the poet's heavenly visitor lamented the state of the world where "cash conquers, cash rules, cash gives orders to all" (cited by Langholm 2015: 96). Recent scholarship has placed more emphasis on interpreting money in cultural history, especially in religious contexts. The Church was integrated into earthly society, dealing with these evolving social and economic conditions (Jasper 2012).

As a consequence of reform in the eleventh century, the Church would construct a singular identity for the Latin West, that of the *societas Christiana*, reaching a zenith in the thirteenth century. The question of what a Christian society should be was continually debated in the Middle Ages. In the fourteenth century, political theorists increasingly acknowledged the complexity of Christianity, rulership, and society. In the wake of the Reformation, the dissolution of Christendom as one *societas Christiana* represented a watershed in European history. In modern scholarship the idea of the universal society has been refined and nuanced from scholars within a wide range of subjects. With the expansion of Christendom, the impact of Church Reform, and as the idea of eternal suffering or salvation became a common denominator in the lives of Christians everywhere (discussed below), the values and expectations of the *societas Christiana* or Christian society increasingly shaped the daily lives of Europeans, including how they used and thought about money.

Within the remit of Christian learning and culture, the status of money would take many different shades and forms, and as Rory Naismith has observed, "These shifts played out differently across Christian Europe" (Naismith 2015: 19). Attitudes towards money and monetary cultures would be shaped by Christian doctrine and learning in ways that influenced not only attitudes to money, but also how coins and coinages were designed and used. The adoption of monetary concepts, standards, and not least ideas, were particularly important to the history of money and will constitute the central focus of this chapter. It will contribute to the broader discussions about the use of money and attitudes towards money, focusing in particular on Northern Europe in the tenth to the fifteenth centuries, where the impact of both the increased availability of money and of the *societas Christiana* emerge most clearly.

## THE IDEA OF MONEY AND COINAGE

The sociologist Max Weber wrote that "Money is the most abstract and impersonal element that exists in personal life" (Weber 1958: 331). This impersonal medium of exchange, which even a stranger is willing to receive in exchange for goods they give others or services they render others, is widely held to constitute the vital fluid of the urban and commercial organism. One of the most impressive aspects of money is the force with which it penetrated societies of different religious, cultural, and socio-political denominations. Money provided a technology of exchange and communication that proved more effective, more flexible, and more adaptive than any other tangible social instrument. The nature of what is designated as money in a society is often compared with basic conventions that determine standards of time, the development of language, or the side of the road for passing (Tobin 1992: 770–8). In short, what is important and universal is that something is chosen, not what is chosen (Tobin 1992: 771). Hence, the forms of money in world history constitute a large and varied collection of artifacts and commodities.

The concept of coinage gained increased prominence in the Latin West in the tenth to fifteenth centuries (Spufford 1988b: 74–263; Bolton 2012: 19–43 and 113–38). The Roman Empire had functioned on cash, but initially the post-Roman West did not. A sophisticated monetary system continued in the Byzantine Empire from late Roman times until the thirteenth century, however, and the monetary reform of Abd al-Malik in CE 698 would form the basis for the enormously successful Islamic currency which built on the riches of the Caliphate and influenced monetary systems beyond its own borders. The silver penny had been the universal standard for coinage in the West from the eighth century. When the borders of Christianity expanded, coinage followed swiftly. In the thirteenth century, the monetary scene in western Europe took a big leap forward, beginning to resemble Roman monetary culture in the first to the third century AD. The introduction of a multiple silver penny—the *gros tournois*—in France under Louix IX (the Pious) in 1266 paved the way for the groat and the *Groschen*. At the same time gold coinages were reintroduced in the northern Italian city-states of Florence, Genoa, and Venice. These florins and ducats were of great significance given their extensive geographic distribution and long continuation (the Venetian ducat, the longest standing of these, was minted with the same types until Napoleon Bonaparte's conquest of Venice in 1797), and would nurture the development of gold coinages in northern Europe.

The history of money and monetary culture in the Middle Ages was much more than coins, however. As Peter Spufford observed,

> In most parts of late medieval Europe ... a dichotomy existed in the functions of money. On the one hand, money of account was the measure of value, whilst on the other, the actual coin was the medium of exchange and the store of wealth. Money of account derived its name from its function. As a measure of value it was used almost exclusively for accounting purposes. Most financial transactions were first determined and expressed in money of account, although payments were naturally made subsequently in coin, or surprisingly often in other goods.
> 
> —Spufford 1988b: 411

In many cases and many regions of Europe, commodities were used for the purpose of payment and accepted on monetary terms with set standards of value, very much in the same way as currency. Commodities serving as units of value included swine in Anglo-Saxon England, cattle and butter in medieval Spain, Scotland, and Scandinavia, *vaðmal* (cloth) in Iceland, walrus ivory in

Greenland, salt in Tibet, iron in Congo, silk in the Caliphate, and cowrie shells in coastal areas of south east Asia and regions of China.[1]

Precious metals were universally accepted as valuables and formed the basis for money as we know it, in their capacity as currencies and coins. Some regions depended heavily on silver, such as Europe in the period *c.* 800–1200, while the Byzantine Empire would prefer gold and copper and the Islamic Caliphate gold and silver. Movable wealth transformed into currency would eventually be money of universal status with an international catchment area.

The idea of money being intangible or merely a representation of value was still in its infancy even in the northern Italian city-states in the 1290s. In medieval China the monetary system was operated and administered as fiat currency. For several centuries paper money was a common feature of the Chinese economy. In his travel accounts the Venetian explorer Marco Polo provides telling insights into the different ways money was conceived in medieval Chinese society and culture compared with the West:

> It is in the city of Khanbalik that the Great Khan possesses his Mint . . . In fact, paper money is made there from the sapwood of the mulberry tree, whose leaves feed the silkworm . . . The method of issue is very formal, as if the substance were pure gold or silver. On each sheet that was made into paper money, officials would sign and affix their seal. When this work has been done in accordance with the rules, the chief impregnates his seal with pigment and affixes his vermilion mark at the top of the sheet. That makes the note authentic. This paper currency is circulated in every part of the Great Khan's dominions, nor dares any person, at the peril of his life, refuse to accept it in payment.
>
> —Marco Polo, *Travels in the Land of Kubilai Khan*, ch. 18; Polo 2005

Marco Polo was amused at the thought that whereas the alchemists had struggled vainly for centuries to turn base metals into gold, the Chinese emperors had very simply turned paper into money (Schefold 2016: 366). Hence, the Italian nobles presented with these valuable pieces of paper were reluctant to accept their status. Their reluctance is revealing, as it indicates what was considered acceptable money in some of the most advanced economic regions within the *societas Christiana*. Paper money, as we know it, was first introduced into the European economy in Stockholm in Sweden in 1661. In contrast to the Chinese, Europeans would continue to emphasize trust in tangible artifacts with intrinsic values, either currency or commodities, for centuries. The second half of the chapter will return to the impact of these ideas of value; first, however, the chapter will address how the Church thought about and used money.

# MONEY, THE CHURCH, AND THE *SOCIETAS CHRISTIANA*

The concept of money is closely linked to its social and cultural contexts, which for Europe in this period primarily meant the context of the *societas Christiana*. Money was prominent in the Bible, in positive and negative contexts. Commentators such as the Archbishop of Tours, Hildebert of Lavardin (*c.* 1055–1133), echoed the Bible in writing that "Wrongdoing today all stems from love of money," but the Gospels also included examples of money used fruitfully, from the parable of the talents to the gift of the widow's mite (Hildebert of Lavardin, *De Nummo*; ed. Migne 1844–64, vol. 171, col. 1403C). As Rory Naismith has pointed out:

> To speak simply of "the Church" as a monolithic entity is, therefore, gravely misleading. When it came to attitudes to wealth there was no single Church line. This was a period of adaptation and polarization: ideas and practices separated, collided, and reconverged in kaleidoscopic fashion. Ambiguity in attitudes to wealth was to be expected. Money and coin was just one component of this, and one which had played a part throughout Christian history thanks to its prominence in the Bible.
>
> —Naismith 2015: 19

In the conduct of Christendom, the concern was never that money was evil *per se*. The motivation and intent with which money was used, however, would always be a matter of scrutiny in the *societas Christiana*.

The earliest Christian author to explore the close connection between the physical aspects of coins and their spiritual meaning was the early ascetic writer John Cassian (d. 435). For Cassian, every believer has to constantly examine the thoughts that emerge in his heart in order to ascertain their origin and true nature. Accordingly, every Christian needs to become a spiritual money changer by scrutinizing his heart in the same way that a secular money changer determines the value of the coins in the marketplace. First, he makes sure that the coin (*nomisma*) is made of purest gold (*aurum purissimum*) and is not a common brass *denarius*. Then the money changer should verify the image on the coin and assess whether its weight is correct; coins that do not weigh enough have to be refused (John Cassian, *Conferences* I.20–2, trans. Ramsey 1997: 59–63).[2]

St. Gregory the Great (Pope 590–604) also used the coin as a metaphor in a series of analogies where Christians were urged to weigh the quality of their prayers in their hearts as money changers test the quality of gold coins. One should test the intentions of man like a money changer tests the metal content of a coin, and determine if a man's character matches his outward appearance, just like a money changer observes the designs of a coin. One should test the quality of a man's deeds in the same way that a money changer tests whether coins are of proper weight (St. Gregory the Great, *Morals on the Book of Job*, III.2; ed. Adriaen 1979–85). There was a long-standing Christian tradition that saw the work of money changers as comparable to the weighing of souls (Welch Williams 1993: 137). The process of sorting the good from the bad was the very core of a money changer's task. The many different currencies and the nature of medieval monetary regimes that produced ever-changing coinages distributed locally, regionally, and internationally, demanded a vast and up-to-date knowledge of the current state of the market.

For Archbishop Anselm of Canterbury (1096–1109), one of the most influential medieval thinkers, money and possessions were not in themselves good or bad, only in so far as they acted as the agency for sin or for charity. Anselm did think about money, and he did use money. It did not, however, represent for him the root of *all* evil. In his capacity as archbishop and abbot in Canterbury, Anselm was in charge of minting, exchange, and the administration of financial affairs, including the collection of taxes and dues, land rents, and the oversight of building projects and offerings, to mention but a few.[3] Thus Anselm would have found nothing objectionable in the definition of money proposed by Thomas Aquinas: "money . . . was invented chiefly for exchanges to be made, so the prime and proper use of money is its use and disbursement in the way of ordinary transactions" (Thomas Aquinas, *Summa theologica*, Iia, Iiae, q. 78, art. 1; Aquinas 1920).

The reformed Church of the eleventh century operated in a society where minting rights and ecclesiastical institutions went hand in hand, with many archbishoprics, bishoprics, and monastic houses issuing coins across Europe. For example, there were more ecclesiastical mints than secular mints in eleventh-century Salian Germany (Steinbach 2007). Indeed, papal minting in partnership with the local secular authorities had commenced already in the late seventh and early eighth century, during the papacy of Adrian I (772–95) (Grierson and Blackburn 1986: 262–3). Ecclesiastical minting commenced in Denmark during the reign of Sven Estridsen (1047–74), and Danish bishops had a share in the income from the mints in every diocese (Hauberg 1900: 61 ff.). In 1293 a conflict arose between the bishop in Roskilde and the king's moneyer, who had made extra income on the king's behalf by outmaneuvering the bishop's moneyer in the preparations for a recoinage. According to the bishop, the Church lost the lion's share of its annual income from the mint (Hauberg 1884: 219–20). A few years later in the Norwegian town of Stavanger, a Bishop Arne stood trial concerning the rights to the income from an offering box at the main altar in the cathedral. The bishop lost and had to pay court costs amounting to fifteen marks of Norwegian money (Lange *et al.* 1847–2011, IV, 25). Both these conflicts involved members of the ecclesiastical elite dealing directly with monetary issues, but neither was, as far as we know, anything approaching a principled discourse on money as the product of evil. Dealing in money was a natural part of important ecclesiastical offices that often included management of minting, and involved issues of both moral and practical significance.

Sometimes the clergy would use the income from offerings in ways considered immoral: Peter Abelard in Paris (d. 1142) commented critically on the habit of clergy of his day rewarding minstrels and jugglers heavily with money taken from the benefices and offerings of the poor (Murray 1967: 30–1). Hincmar, Archbishop of Reims from 845 and advisor of Charles the Bald, provides an early account of individual clergy handling monetary earnings. Hincmar records that men of the cloth kept coins in envelopes made from the leaves of old books, and were doing so out of love for money (*Vita Remigii*, preface, (ed. Krusch 1896: 251–2), cited by Nelson 1987: 28).

Money was always a universal currency for the Church in its worldly dealings. Money became the preferred medium and concept with which the Church administered its finances, both locally and internationally. In 1308, Pope Clement V proclaimed the price of pardoning a year's worth of sins to be the contribution of one penny, Tours currency, to the Crusade against the Muslims (Lunt 1934: II, 458). Financing Crusades was an arduous task for the medieval Church, which levied recurring taxes for the purpose. These efforts to manage the increasing demand for funds to support large-scale building projects, Crusades, and ostentatious display for the honor of Christ, would have unintended consequences of monetization in that members of congregations in the smallest parishes in remote corners of Christendom would need to produce cash for the purpose of fulfilling demands of the Church.

The Papal See in Rome was the heart of the largest financial operation in medieval Europe. Money was transferred from the smallest parish church to the diocese, to archbishoprics and on to Rome (and Avignon). The records are overwhelming for institutions and individuals transferring sums of money from all parts of the Latin West to mother monasteries and the Papal See.[4] While the tithe belonged to the parish, a sophisticated catalog of taxes, dues, and donations ensured a steady stream of money in the direction of Rome.

The theological and moral concern regarding money lay in its potential to become a distraction in the battle to perfect one's spiritual life (Newhauser 2014: 3). The crusade against depravity of money reached a zenith in the early thirteenth century with St. Francis of Assisi: Francis is synonymous with poverty and its radical adoption in the mendicant way of religious life (for a general introduction to St. Francis, see Robson 2011). St. Francis detested money and sought to protect his friars from the contamination of money and coins. In the *Regula bullata* of 1223 he prohibited his friars from accepting coins and money in all forms (*denarios vel pecuniam non recipient*) (Merlo 2009). This was slightly modified for those procuring clothes and necessities for the sick (Coleman 1987: 80–1; see also Lambert 1961). The constitutions of the mendicant order expressly forbade the collection of money on the occasion of preaching or for friars to store money (Lawrence 1994: 186).[5] The Franciscan order produced a doctrine of poverty that spread out from thirteenth-century Italy and became widespread and influential. A monastic movement of mendicants including Franciscans, Benedictines, Dominicans, and a few minor orders such as the Friars of the Sack became part of the cityscape in Europe in the thirteenth and fourteenth centuries and influenced the way in which people thought about the temptations of money and property (for a discussion, see Andrews 2015: 189–90). St. Francis told his followers to have extreme caution in their attitudes and practical encounters with money: "If we should find coins anywhere, let us pay no more attention to them than to the dust which we tread under our feet" (Lambert 1961: 39–40).[6]

The poverty movement that developed significantly from the late eleventh century was a reaction to the marked increase in commercialization and monetization in the tenth and eleventh centuries. Being a good Christian in an increasingly monetized society was complex. As urbanization and specialization became the way of life for large numbers of people, a range of services within the medieval city and town would, by default, be contrary to the canon of Catholic learning. One such issue was lending money and demanding interest. At the end of the twelfth century, Peter Cantor in Paris noted that a merchant had little choice between going to hell for usury, or falling into beggary by respecting the Church's prohibition (ed. Migne 1844–64, vol. 205, col. 263, cf. col. 145–6, 149, 157–8).[7] Money and its commercial use were in essential respects at odds with Christian teaching. Like ecclesiastical attitudes towards money, the question of usury was vigorously debated, not only within Christianity, but also within Islam.

The traditional notion that usury was "shameful profit" was abandoned when Archbishop Anselm of Canterbury equated usury with theft in his Homilies and Exhortations in the late eleventh century (ed. Migne 1844–64, vol. 158, col. 659. Abulafia 2002: 35). Thomas Aquinas asked: "Is it a sin to make a charge for lending money, which is what usury is?" The reply states clearly that usurious theft is a sin against justice in the thirteenth century: "Making a charge for lending money is unjust in itself, for one party sells the other something non-existent, and this obviously sets up an inequality which is contrary to justice" (*Summa theologica*, Iia, Iiae, q. 78, 20; Aquinas 1920). As Thomas Aquinas made clear in another connection: "Money does not reproduce itself."

In the case of usury, more than money was at stake. Medieval theologians developed increasingly refined arguments in the discourse on usury; a thirteenth-century manuscript, the *Tabula exemplorum* in the Bibliothèque Nationale at

Paris, reads: "Every man stops working on holidays, but the oxen of usury work unceasingly and thus offend God and all the saints, and since usury is an endless sin, it should in like manner be endlessly punished" (ed. Welter 1926: 83, no. 306). When time had a price—interest on a debt calculated in accordance with the passage of months and years—it strained the mind and the moral sense because time was God's exclusive property. If time had a price, if time were a thing that could have a numeric value, then what about other unsegmented imponderables, like heat or velocity or love (Crosby 1997: 71)?

The issue of usury was not about money as such, but in the context of monetary culture within a *societas Christiana* the concerns were how money could be made to conform with Christian learning and eventually also with worldly transactions. In some ecclesiastical circles the attitudes towards lending money and charging interest softened in the thirteenth century, when the Bishop of Saragossa in 1232 openly remitted capital plus 10 percent interest to the Temple (Goudsmit 2004: "International banking + Templars."), while others' attitudes towards usury changed remarkably little in the late Middle Ages and early years of the Renaissance (Geisst 2013: 58). However, in the secular world the necessities of getting a return on capital made political authorities establish maximum legal limits above which the interest was to be declared usury and therefore illegal. In thirteenth-century Italy the level of interest on loans would fluctuate between 10 and 50 percent (Cipolla 1963: 404–5).

One alternative was, of course, to use money for good causes, and almsgiving was generally accepted as a significant virtue within the *societas Christiana*. The principle of charity manifested through coin extended to all levels of society. The message was that good deeds were rewarded, almsgiving especially. A twelfth-century book of Homilies from Norway contains a text *Om dydene og lastene* ("On vice and virtue") originally authored by Alcuin at the court of Charlemagne in the ninth century (ed. Salvesen 1971: 18–45).[8] One of the virtues held in high regard by Alcuin is almsgiving, and of all the virtues, almsgiving and fasting were the most powerful in the battle against sin (ed. Salvesen 1971: ch.17). An eyewitness account by a group of Danish pilgrims who visited the Norwegian town of Bergen in 1191 described the many travelers and commodities available in the town. Their observations of the locals were ambiguous, but nevertheless they acknowledged that "the Norwegians were generous when it came to offering alms, but they were heavy drinkers" (ed. Salvesen 1969: ch.11).

Many would see money as a natural opportunity to secure salvation for themselves and their families. As Sir Richard Southern noted, dying with a penance incomplete or without having made provisions for its completion was of all things on earth the most to be dreaded. No man could be saved until his debt was paid. A great man could either pay the stipulated sum or engage other men to undertake the penance for him (Southern 1990: 227). The numbers of records of donations and bequests left to churches and monasteries within the medieval church is enormous. For people with capital, money would buy burials within a consecrated place closer to the saints and Christ, preferably in the chancel of a church. Prayers could be purchased through the services of priests and monks, for many years at a time. In this way the Church became the largest landowner in Europe.

However, the relationship between being a good Christian and money was not simple and straightforward in the sense that giving more money would ensure a safer and faster journey to heaven. The "Topography of Ireland" *(Topographia Hibernica)* composed by Gerald of Wales in around 1188 indicates the importance of the spiritual quality of the gift. Soon after the Norman incursion into Ireland, after the fall of Dublin (1171), a bowman wanted to offer a penny at the cross, in the Cathedral of the Holy Trinity (Christ Church), but, as he turned, the penny hit him on the back. He took it and offered it again, but the penny came back again on him, leaving everybody astonished. The bowman, ashamed, had to confess publicly that he had plundered the archbishop's palace. He was asked to return all he had taken; having done so, he offered the penny again, with devotion and fear, and the penny remained at the bottom of the cross. The story is a striking reminder that in religious exchanges, purity of the metal is not enough; purity of the heart is essential for the efficacy of the religious transaction (Gerald of Wales, *The History and Topography of Ireland*, ch. 75 (trans. O'Meara 1982: 86–7)).

This sentiment resonated long after the end of the Middle Ages: the Italian traveler Pietro Della Valle in a letter from Isphahan of 24 August 1619 recorded that the King of Persia used special coins to offer as alms; to each of the poor he gave three sequins but not just ordinary ones. The sequins had been purchased from the Armenians because, so he wrote, their coins were reputed to be earned with justice and hard work, and therefore most appreciated by God (Della Valle 1843: II, 42. Cited in Travaini 2009: 242).

Within the borders of Christendom, money offerings were an established custom from the first century. Records of this practice are abundant in both historical and archaeological sources. In *c.* 870 Archbishop Wulfad of Bourges wrote to the influential laity of his diocese: "Hasten to it [the Church] with your offerings and ask there to be prayed for" (ed. Dümmler 1925: 188–92, no. 27; cited by Nelson 1987: 28). In this case offerings were exchanged for prayers. People all over Western Christendom were expected to make donations, giving vast sums for the purpose of honoring Christ, helping the needy, and providing funds to maintain the church and provide pastoral care. Already in the thirteenth century it was widely acknowledged that a good priest would need financial assets to be able to fulfill his duties of pastoral care satisfactorily, and at the same time ensure the upkeep of his church and develop his parish (Hoskin 2014).

Initially voluntary offerings became compulsory for the parishioner through immemorial customs which had the strict force of law (Coulton 1925: 289).

In their search for eternal salvation, peasants, townspeople, and members of aristocracy all over Western Christendom flocked to Mass and to place their offerings on altars, in offering trunks, boxes, and bags. In David Ganz's words:

> The Christian altar became a privileged setting for gifts to God and to His Church, because it was also the setting for the commemoration of God's gift to mankind: The sacrifice of the body of Christ which He had enjoined all believers to share in and which defined the membership of His Church, the Eucharistic experience of the reciprocity of giving, the constant and necessary repetition of giving, and the spiritual dimensions of giving, were fundamental.
> —Ganz 2010: 18

Over the centuries this universal tradition would account for the enormous sums that found their way into church and cathedral coffers every Sunday and on major feast days. The practice encompassed a large part of the population dwelling within Western Christendom. Nevertheless the evidence for this religious practice is rarely more than passing references in documentary sources, sometimes sermons, saints' lives, and literary texts, at other times in canons, laws, and court cases. The individual experience of religious practice in making these offerings was significant in the devotional lives of Christians everywhere. Archaeological evidence allows a better understanding of the aims and rationale of the religious practice, and how, where and when it was carried out, though there is still much to be learned.

In-depth studies of Scandinavian and Swiss churches such as Bunge on Gotland, Høre stavechurch in Norway and Jomala church in the Åland Islands in Finland and Steffisburg church in Bern in Switzerland have produced patterns of coin finds related to focus points such as the high altar, the chancel arch, side altars, entrances, with coins being distributed randomly within the nave (Kilger forthcoming; Jonsson forthcoming; Risvaag forthcoming; Schmutz and Koenig 2003). The topography of coin finds in churches changes with the Reformation, after which the coin finds are more often found scattered within the nave, and less so related to particular altars and other focal points (Tveito 2015).

In early fourteenth-century Norway, the church accounts of the monastery of St. John in Bergen detail substantial sums in sterlings, *gros tournois* and Swedish and Gotlandic currency, given in offerings to St. Olav's altar in the monastic Church. The money was kept in bags containing separate currencies: 61 marks by weight in *gros tournois*, 40 marks and 12 oras and 53½ marks weight in English sterlings, 88 marks and 104½ marks weight in Swedish, Gotlandic and other currencies, all locked up in a chest that was to be moved on King Håkon's instructions for the purposes of security and reorganization in the absence of an archbishop, and due to the monastery's severe financial and disciplinary problems, involving accusations of simony (Lange et al. (eds.), 1847–2011: II, 96; I, 107; IX, 78). The elements of foreign currency from the offerings in Bergen stand in stark contrast to the coins current in parish churches in rural societies, where the collections almost always would consist of local currency, and almost solely of small change when a choice of currencies was available.

Archaeological investigations and excavations in Scandinavian churches have produced more than 60,000 medieval stray finds of coins. These show clearly that coins were the customary form of offering among the people of Norway from the second half of the twelfth century, and probably also earlier, reflecting universal practice within Western Christendom. Christian donations of coins replaced the offerings of animals and fodder of pagan times after the eleventh-century Christianization of the Norwegian realm.

Of the enormous numbers of stray finds of coins produced by Church archaeology, small change makes up over 90 percent of the total. The quality and size of the offerings was seldom based on monetary value. In this context the New Testament parable of the poor widow's mite should be recalled: her two small coins (*duo minuta*), were more valuable than all the coins offered by the rich (Mark 12:41–44, and Luke 21:1–4; on this subject see Travaini 2004: 173). The numerous stray finds from the Norwegian stave churches provide a rare insight into the practice rather than the theory on the matter. The emphasis on ritual rather than value is indicated clearly in the archaeological evidence. In the period between 1263 and 1320, pennies, halfpennies, farthings, and bracteates (the smallest coins produced and weighing *c.* 0.15 to 0.2 grams) were issued. More than 4,000 finds of these coins have been made in churches all over the realm, with the following denominational ratios: 62 percent bracteates, 19 percent farthings, 12 percent halfpennies, and 8 percent pennies (Gullbekk 2009: 269–73). The breakdown reveals that 81 percent of the coins weighed less than 0.25 grams. These low denomination coins reflected the amount that a farmer or wage earner could afford to give. But the size of the offering was less significant than the ritual exercise of the liturgical drama. In France the smallest coins in circulation were called *deniers de l'aumosnerie* in the fourteenth century, and in November 1421 a Parisian made a note in his diary that the limited availability of small change made it difficult for poor people to receive alms (Spufford 1988b: 330–1; for a discussion of the subject, see Courtnay 1972–3; and Murray 1977).

The low value of these offerings became a dilemma for local clergy and the ecclesiastical administrators responsible for the Church's finances. While they should confine their pecuniary activities within the framework of biblical texts, the parable of the widow's mite would not support their obligations towards society in a monetary culture. On 1 June 1424 the town council in Visby on Gotland ordered that women in particular who made offerings in Danish currency that was no longer valid anywhere, should not continue this practice (Galster 1972: 20, n. 70a; Jensen (ed.), 1989: no. 670).[9] The reason was, of course, that the income from offerings formed an essential part of parish finances for carrying out the tasks expected of them such as pastoral care and the upkeep of local churches. The metropolitan see of Uppsala decided not to collect Peter's Pence in 1363 because the peasants would only make contributions in poor currency. When monetary conditions became difficult, people would often take advantage and make use of their poorest pennies via institutional channels such as church offerings, taxation, and alms (*Diplomatarium Suecorum* no. 7108).

Times of crisis, however, might also prompt generosity by the Church. The devastating earthquake in Constantinople in 557 gave rise to a wave of rumors that the world was nearly at its end. Within the Christian narrative the Apocalypse had an important place, and faced with apocalyptic signs, people would put their trust in the Church. Agathias, a lawyer in the city, remarked how people changed their lives and attitudes confronted with these signs: "suddenly all men were honest in their business dealings" as even public officials put aside their greed. An increase in religious behavior was widespread, people lived better lives, and gifts were given to the Church (Agathias, *Historiae*, V.5, ed. Keydell 1967: 169–70, quoted in Palmer 2014: 1). Agathias observed a universal response to crises. People become unsettled and seek comfort in something greater than themselves; in sixth-century Constantinople and medieval Europe religion was an obvious option. When the Black Death spread throughout Europe, a rise in money offerings in churches can be observed through the archaeological finds in churches in many places (for Norway and Finland, see Gullbekk 2009; and Jonsson forthcoming).

Documents and hoards associated with pilgrimage have also provided insight into the movement of money across the European continent that in other contexts would have been highly unlikely. Pilgrimage connected Rome monetarily with Anglo-Saxon England in the tenth century and Norway in the twelfth (Metcalf 1992; Schive 1867: 276; Skaare 1995: I, 58). In the tenth century, for example, the *Vita Oswaldi* described how Oswald traveled to Rome to receive his pallium and become a bishop in 972, and his generous gifts during his journey. He gave large sums in silver pennies to churches, monasteries, and civic communities along the way, just as Bishop Coenwald of Worcester had done in 929 (Keynes 1985: 198–9; Leyser 1994: 96).

We know that travelers visited Rome in their millions during the Middle Ages and tangible evidence for pilgrims leaving monetary offerings is plentiful in the archaeological remains of the tombs of St. Peter and St. Paul (Alteri 2009). As many as 2,400 stray finds of coins from the tomb of St. Peter date from the first to the fifteenth century, with a significant number originating in Northern Europe. In this case documentary records from the Great Jubilee in the year 1300 and the archaeological evidence reinforce each other. Papal accounts recording offerings at the altars of St. Peter and St. Paul during the year have values in the range of 30,000 and 20,000 gold florins respectively, all made in large numbers of petty local coins of all provinces (counted in millions!) (Fedele 1934: 7–25; cited by Travaini 2004: 174).

In the history of pilgrims and their use of money, the accounts for Bishop Wolfger of Passau's (1191–1204; and later patriarch of Aquileia, 1204–18) travels to Rome provide valuable information on the major routes crossing the Alps and the economy of those journeys (Zingerle 1877; see also Birch 1998: 64–5). Wolfger changed silver ingots of different values into local coins as he and his party traveled southwards. The development of numerous different monetary regimes on the European continent made it necessary for travelers to adapt to and use a number of different local currencies. Arriving in Tarvis at the border with Italy, he exchanged three marks of silver, in Padua one mark, in Ferrara eight marks and in Florence five, while in Bologna and Siena he exchanged unknown weights in silver, and on arriving in Rome he exchanged a total of 44 marks of silver before heading back. Bishop Wolfger's travel accounts also give an insight into some of the costs incurred during his travels. For example, in Viterbo he paid out 23 *solidi* for bread and 20 *solidi* for wine, all in local currency (Jesse (ed.) 1924: 251, no. 370). As a traveler en route to Rome with an extensive retinue, the use of silver in the form of ingots made perfect sense as meta-currency, exchangeable into local currency along the route.

In towns, at markets, and ecclesiastical centers, the trade of a money changer was highly specialized. In Toulouse in 1198 a statute issued by Raymond, Count of Toulouse and the councilors of St. Giles granted permission to money changers to lawfully change money for pilgrims provided that they weighed their gold, silver, or coin and correctly counted their pennies without deception. Money changing should not take place at inns or shops, but be carried out in the House of the Hospitallers, of the Knights of the Temple, or in the Cloister of St. Giles (Webb 2001: 98). By 1337 Toulouse had eighty money changers in operation (Chevalier 1973: 153–60). Famous shrines would attract devotees and cash in significant sums. At Chartres in France one of the streets leading up to the cathedral was where the money changers would pursue their activities. In Chartres the mutual benefits to the Church and the money changers resulted in the Guild sponsoring a set of windows depicting money changers at work in the cathedral, thereby making a fine contribution to the cathedral display and legitimating their activity and close relationship with the Church (Welch Williams 1993: 103 ff.).

In a complex monetary landscape the money changer was a familiar figure throughout Europe, though hard to find in surviving records. The challenges involved in dealing with an ever-changing money market are best illustrated

FIGURE 6.1: Caricature cartoon of Jews, money, and greed on an Exchequer Roll (London, The National Archives, E 401/1565) from 1233 listing Jewish taxpayers in Norwich. Image © The National Archives, UK.

through the writings of Francesco Pegolotti in his handbook *Pratica della Mercatura* from the beginning of the fourteenth century as manager of the business house of Bardi in Antwerp (1315–17), London (1317–21), and Famagusta in Cyprus (Grierson 1957; Spufford 1988b: 143). In medieval Europe the Jews represent a special chapter in the history of money, especially in their capacity as moneylenders, money changers, and administrators of business, but were rarely involved in minting. In thirteenth-century Hungary there is charter evidence of Jews being directly involved in minting, and also royal issues marked with Jewish letter-symbols (Berend 2001: 124). As outsiders to the *societas Christiana*, Jews were both invaluable, especially to rulers, and highly vulnerable (Figure 6.1). Even though the Church as an entity was the single largest contributor to the medieval economy, the majority of economic activity would be carried out by secular entrepreneurs, although within the framework of the *societas Christiana*. It is to the understanding of value and trust in this secular world that the chapter now turns.

## KINGS, MONEY, VALUE, AND TRUST IN SECULAR TRANSACTIONS

The relationship between God and king was of utmost importance in medieval society. The ostentatious display of wealth and royal submission to Christ was paramount in the medieval theatre of rulership, and also expressed in coinage. Coins were artifacts of mass production in a pre-industrial age. The possibility of furnishing coinage with political, religious, and personal messages meant that anyone in charge of minting could reach more people in society than anyone else. Royal taxation and monetary policy also had far-reaching impacts upon contemporary society, and are particularly revealing for the ideas of value and trust that prevailed in the *societas Christiana* (for a discussion of trust in medieval society, see Reynolds 2012).

Far down the Sognefjord in western Norway in 1318, we encounter the first court case dealing with counterfeit money recorded in Norway. The accused was a woman by the name of Gudrun who came from Jostedalen, in the province of Sogn og Fjordane in the inner part of Sognefjorden in western Norway. Gudrun stood trial for having put tubers in the butter that was paid in land rent to the king (Lange *et al.* (eds.) 1847–2011: I, 432). The punishment

FIGURE 6.2: A well-preserved robe made from so-called "Greenland vaðmal" dated *c*. 1250–1400, found at the Norse settlement Herjolfsnes on Greenland. Image © The National Museum, Copenhagen, mus.nr. D10584.

for counterfeiting money was severe: the penalty for tampering with money within the realm was outlawry under the land law of 1274 (*Magnus Lagabøtes Landslov* ch. X, 2 (ed. Taranger 1970)). In this case Gudrun had not made counterfeit coins, but counterfeit currency which she had used to pay the annual tax to the king. Thereby she had tried to deceive the authorities' tax collector and ultimately the king. The outcome of the trial is unknown to us, but the rationale behind Gudrun's bold undertaking was presumably financial rather than political: either she was unable to meet the burdens of royal taxation, as a result of the great famine that ravaged Northern Europe and caused crop failure and emergency situations at that time, or she disapproved of the sums involved (Jordan 1996). Gudrun's case opens up some of the concerns and challenges of value in an economy that used commodity money, as well as the relationship between kings and their tax-paying subjects.

People adopt standards of value that are known to them and available in the perspective of tradition and custom. The commodities adopted as a standard of value, such as cattle in the Scottish Highlands, western Norway, and northern Spain, pigs (swine) in England and *vaðmal* (cloth) in Iceland (Figure 6.2), reflect the main focus of agriculture locally. These key commodities would be made standard units of value and means of exchange (Mayhew and Gemmill 1995; Jarrett 2014). In societies where commodities and monetary means of exchange were used side by side, the complexity of economic business should not be underestimated. Still, despite its complexity, this system would ensure that currencies and commodities were interchangeable and thereby provide a society with means of exchange that had many of the qualities that a monetary economy could offer.

Valuation was one aspect where the practice of using commodities as means of exchange in a transaction would produce a different set of concerns. The standard value of a cow in thirteenth-century Norway was one-third of a burnt mark of silver (*c.* 71 grams) or one mark of currency in the 1270s. In Norway a standard cow was carefully defined in the Gulathing law written down in the mid-twelfth century, as no more than eight years old and pregnant with at least her second calf, without unsightly exterior faults, and so forth (Gulathing law §223: for discussion see Lunden 1978: 56–62). Haggling over the value of cows must have been a recurrent situation in these societies. Indeed, legal provisions suggest that the parties engaged in transactions would sometimes view the quality and value of their payment differently from each other. This was an obvious obstacle for commerce and a potential source of conflict; a fact that is reflected in old Icelandic laws that include provisions for assessment of payments. Each party in a transaction was "to select his man as a lawful valuer and lawful viewer. And if they do not agree, then they are to draw lots and the one who draws the lot is to value it on oath" (Grágás §246, trans. Dennis, Foote and Perkins 1980–2006). In the case of disagreement the valuation became a responsibility of honor. A just valuation was required to avoid dishonor as witness and assessor in Viking society.

Contrasting frames of reference for value in coin and commodity also explain Halldórr the Icelander's strong reaction to King Harald of Norway's debased silver coin. After returning from Constantinople in the 1040s the Norwegian Viking Harald Sigurdsson, later to obtain the epithet Hardrade (hard ruler) as King of Norway (1047–66), introduced a national currency containing one-third silver, the rest copper. A passage in the *Morkinskinna* version of the *Heimskringla*, the Norwegian King's sagas authored by the Icelandic chieftain snorri sturluson in the 1220s or 1230s, described how one of his fellow Icelanders responded to the debasement:

> On the eighth day after Christmas the men were given their pay. This was called the Haraldsslátta being mostly of copper. At its best it was half silver. It goes with this story that when Halldórr [Snorrason] received his pay, he held the money in a fold in his mantle and gazed upon it. The silver did not look fine. He struck his fist with his other hand so that all the money fell down on the floor.
>
> —*Morkinskinna*, ch. 30, trans. Andersson and Gade 2000: 190.
> Discussed and translated by Skaare 1976: 9–11 (Figure 6.3)

King Harald naturally regarded this as an insult. But the saga portrays the Islandic Halldórr as a man of great integrity, who says: "I don't think I have

FIGURE 6.3: Harald Hardrade (1047–1066), penny, struck in Nidarnes (Trondheim), Norway, *c.* 1050. The obverse legend reads HARALD REX NO and the reverse legend VLF ON NIDARNE. This coin belongs to a group of early issues struck from good quality silver and with legible legends that constitute less than 10 percent of the total coinage of Harald Hardrade that has survived today. Image © Museum of Cultural History, University of Oslo.

been so treacherous when following King Harald, as he was in paying me." Halldórr had been a loyal follower of King Harald for many years. They had fought in the Varangian Guard together, been imprisoned by the Byzantine Emperor in Constantinople together, and eventually returned to Norway where Harald was made king. At this point in life Halldorr wanted to return to Iceland and settle down. The money being offered to him was surely accepted and appreciated as currency within the Norwegian realm, but not equally so on Iceland. Halldorr was reluctant because when he moved to Iceland the value of the King's coinage would be gauged from the silver as a commodity rather than King Harald's authority.[10] In its usual style the saga provides a glimpse into the drama of strong versus weak money on a personal level exemplified through a conflict, and the debasement in question has been confirmed by modern metrological analysis (Skaare 1976: 79–85 and 191–206).

Conflicts between people and governments were nothing new in the history of money, nor was this something particular to the scheme of Christianity. Secular conflicts over money were often related to value. In 538/9 the Byzantine Emperor Justinian introduced a lightweight *solidus*. The historian Procopius of Caesarea described this as Justinian "cutting off a seventh part of the value of every gold coin . . . from all men," and thereby increasing his revenues on a grand scale (Dewing (ed. and trans.) 1935: 297). He was far from the only ruler to use the coinage as a source of revenue, leading to popular discontent and threatening public trust in the currency.

In the Saga of Olaf Haraldsson, the narrative provides an insight into the question of trust in a society without a national currency to rely upon. Thrand, a landowner with royal privileges, had been gathering tribute from the Faroe Islands in the 1020s. At the Thing he was asked by a royal representative called Leif, who collected the tribute on behalf of the king, how he had managed over the silver. Thrand answered:

> "Here is a purse, Leif, which you should have, and it is full of silver." Then Leif poured out the silver onto his shield, stirred it about with his hand and called his companion Karl to look at it. They examined it and Karl asked Leif what he thought of the silver, and he said: "It is my opinion that every single bad coin in the Northern Isles has got here . . . I will not deliver this money to the king."

A fight almost broke out, but finally Thrand offered money which he said his own tenants had brought. At this Leif remarked, "No need to look long at this silver, each coin here is better than the last. This money we will accept" (Heimskringla, *St. Olaf's saga*, ch.143, trans. Laing 1964).

Leif's understanding of trust was not related to any authority guaranteeing the quality or value of the currency. The question of trust was paired with distrust, and the tax collector's response to the payment he was offered was to examine the currency. His dismissal of one group of coins, but only after careful examination, suggests that he was experienced in the business. As a royal representative, Leif and his companion Karl provide a fair explanation for their position when the first bag of coins is turned down; the king, in this case Olaf Haraldsson (1015–28, 1030), who was later to become St. Olaf, will never accept poor quality currency.

Indeed, the majority of coins from hoards and finds from the first half of the eleventh century in Scandinavia offer tangible evidence of a widespread practice of testing the quality of coins.[11] In the late Viking Age, silver *Pfennigs* struck in the Holy Roman Empire at mints along the Rhine and in the Goslar region were exported to Scandinavia in massive quantities, in significantly larger numbers than contemporary Anglo-Saxon pennies. When these pennies left their homelands they also left the jurisdiction within which they were issued. On arriving in the lands of the Vikings, there was no longer any authority to back this currency. Thus people would see its value differently as it was transformed from currency to silver as a commodity. The silver in these currencies would frequently be tested by people in the Viking world who made peck marks or test marks into the surface of individual coins. German tenth- and eleventh-century *Pfennigs* found in Scandinavia often have quite substantial numbers of peck marks. A comparison between German and Anglo-Saxon silver pennies in Scandinavian finds indicate that German coins were tested much more intensely than the English (Figure 6.4). While the German coinages often were carelessly struck and minted in a large number of different types and designs, the English were carefully struck and produced with one type at all mints in the realm. The patterns of peck marks strongly suggest that the Vikings had more confidence in the English than the German currency.

The custom of pecking was not confined to foreign coins, but is also observed on ingots, hacksilver, silver rings, and jewelry. The practice is described in the

FIGURE 6.4: An Anglo-Saxon silver penny of Æthelred II (978–1016) found in the Årstad hoard, Norway (now in the collection of the University of Oslo) (Screen 2013, no. 568; © Sylloge of Coins of the British Isles).

Islandic Law Book *Grágás* from *c.* 1100 where it is referred to as *hvitr i skór* (Grágás Ia, 141, Grágás Ia, 248 and Grágás II, 214, trans. Dennis, Foote and Perkins 1980–2006). When it was taken up in Icelandic law, the practice had long ended in Denmark and Norway. When the Norwegian King Harald Hardrade established a national coinage in the late 1040s, the custom of testing coins disappeared almost immediately. The coins in circulation were no longer a commodity, but a specific currency issued by the crown. The distribution of the national currency in hoards and as stray finds provides evidence that they were accepted into the economy; the material evidence for test marks ceasing reveals people trusted the new currency, even when each coin was heavily debased.

The question of trust was concerned with quality and value. There was also a question of reputation involved. A prince who debases the coinage takes wealth from the community and thereby loses the community's trust (Farber 2006: 35). In medieval thinking this was a subject of importance in scholastic scholarship, in particular for Nicholas Oresme in the fourteenth century (b. *c.* 1320). Few, if any, have expressed more clearly their opinion upon monetary matters and the nature of money in medieval Europe than this French bishop and scholastic philosopher, who stated in his thesis *De Moneta* written in the 1350s that coinage belonged to the people, not the prince (Johnson (ed.) 1956; cf. Hokenson and Munson 2014: 42–4). It should not be up to the prince to decide upon the quality of the currency. Thereby the sovereign had no right to alter the coinage without consent from the people. Oresme was writing after some of the most severe debasements in medieval monetary history. In France the Crown was in desperate need of resources to finance expensive wars with the English over Gascony in the southwest of France and Flanders in the north. King Philip IV the Fair (1285–1314) took extraordinary measures such as seizing Jewish property and extracting large incomes from debasement of the coinage. When Philip IV and Edward I signed the Treaty of Paris in 1303 the value of the French currency had fallen by two-thirds. The inflationary effects of debasement in France in the years prior to 1422 led to a twelve-fold increase in prices. The rise in prices caused by the royal currency policies was far greater than the largest increase in agricultural prices brought about by bad harvests (Spufford 2015: 63–4).

As observed by Peter Spufford, debasement was, of course, generally a by-product of war (Spufford 1988b: 289). A downward spiral would lead to reduced confidence in the coinage and thereby incur problems for the government. Nobles, merchants, and ordinary people became reluctant to accept the currency at face value. Its value would fall and as a consequence the government's earnings from minting would dwindle. To restore confidence and trust in the currency, restoration of the coinage was necessary. When the value was restored, the strengthening of the coinage would produce different problems: the return to strong money could also be a heavy burden (Allen 2016: 41–52, esp. 49). In Paris, social unrest increased as a consequence of improvement of the coinage. The commoners in towns, including fullers, weavers, innkeepers, and others, refused to accept the terms and in January 1307 they attacked and destroyed the manor of one of the members of the *bourgeois*—Étienne Barbette, also called *La Courtille Barbette*—who insisted upon full payment in the new coinage, de facto imposing a rise in rents caused by the alterations to the coinage. The mob then moved towards the palace of the Knights Templar where the king was. The following day the king ordered twenty-eight men to be hanged from the gallows at the various gates leading into Paris (Cohn 2004: 30–2). When the currency was strengthened after the Treaty of Troyes in December 1420, a rise in rents in Paris made poor people riot, and many then abandoned their tenements and left the city (Spufford 1988b: 309). In these cases we meet large numbers of people that left little or no trace in the historical sources, who raised their voices and protested against monetary regimes they found unacceptable and which had a real influence on their lives and wellbeing. Monetary measures that created unstable economic conditions and unpredictable situations would sometimes cause serious effects. The response from the public on unstable monetary policies seems to be unanimously negative.

In popular culture, Dante Alighieri, the Italian poet responsible for one of the most influential vernacular books in the Middle Ages, *La Divina commedia* (*The Divine Comedy*, written between 1308 and 1322), made a clear statement on the question of debasement at a time when this scourge made the lives of millions of people difficult. Dante placed the French king Philip the Fair in the *Inferno* (Figure 6.5) to suffer eternally for his corrupted monetary policies (Canto 19, trans. Hollander and Hollander 2000). The French king became a symbol for hundreds, if not thousands, of other rulers who debased the quality of the currency, including emperors, kings, noblemen, city councils, and men of the cloth. The number of French feudal lords running debasements at their mints in the tenth to the thirteenth centuries can be counted in hundreds alone. Many rulers in French and Iberian territories would demand extraordinary taxes for not debasing the coinage (Bisson 1979). The Danish currency was debased into pure copper during the civil wars in the period 1241 to 1340 (Grinder-Hansen 2000). The Norwegian kings Harald Hardrade (1047–66), Sverre Sigurdsson (1177–1202), Eirik Magnusson (1280–99), and Håkon V (1299–1319) likewise would have been good candidates for Dante's *Inferno*, together with rulers from Aragon and Castile and German nobility in the late Middle Ages, who were all involved in the dubious art of heavy debasements (Skaare 1976; Gullbekk 2009).

French kings went down the slippery slope of recurring debasements that inspired social unrest and even riots. In French monetary tradition, debasement was the rule rather than the exception in the feudal period. In contrast the

MONEY AND ITS INTERPRETATION 147

FIGURE 6.5: An illustrated folio from an early manuscript copy Dante, *Inferno* (Paris, Bibliothéque Nationale, It. 74, f. 1v). Image © Wikipedia Commons, Creative Commons license.

English crown kept a more or less stable coinage from the Viking Age onward, choosing recoinage over debasement as their method in the pursuit of revenue. Replacing the currency in circulation would provide ample income from the payment of seignorage, a traditional due paid when coins were produced. A recoinage could be called on a regular basis or on the grounds that the currency was in a bad state. The chronicler Matthew Paris observed that in 1247 the merchant communities complained about the coinage due to wear and tear. Early in that year an inspection of the coin in circulation in England concluded that they were so deteriorated that it was necessary to replace them with new ones. Old and worn coins were called in, melted down and restruck. Matthew Paris explains the introduction of the new Long Cross design as a measure to try to control the widespread clipping of coins. In this connection he drew the reverse side of the sterling to show the long arms of the voided cross in contrast to the Short Cross-type that had prevailed until then (Figure 6.6). In 1247 the Short Cross-sterling had been issued since the 1180s. Many coins were characterized by wear and clipping. Matthew Paris put the blame on the Jews

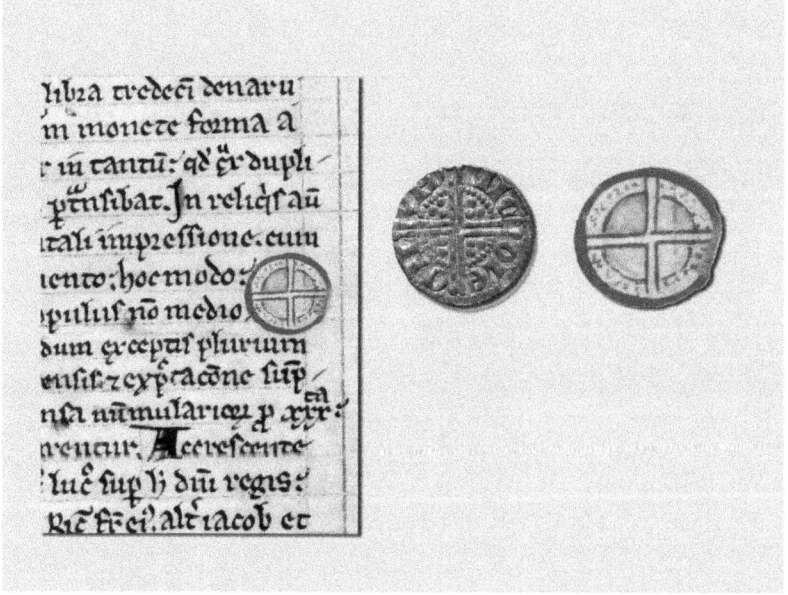

FIGURE 6.6: Matthew Paris, who describes the recoinage in his *Chronica Majora*, explains the introduction of the new Long Cross design as a measure to try to control the widespread clipping of coins. In this connection he drew the reverse side of the sterling to show the long arms of the voided cross on the new issue in contrast to the Short Cross-type that had prevailed until then. The thought was that the long arms of the cross would prevent further cutting of the coins. As far as we know this is the oldest drawing of a coin type in existence. Image © The Master and Fellows of Corpus Christi College, Cambridge.

for this fraud: "the coins were circumcised by circumcised men" (Vaughan 1993: 15).

Even though replacing old and worn coins with new ones sounds good, it led to considerable costs for most people. First of all, the king demanded a recoinage tax of six pence for each pound of reminted coins. In addition, the old coins were weighed when they were delivered, so a trader who brought ten pounds in old coins might receive nine pounds back if his coins were worn or cut. It is unsurprising that people complained. The contemporary chronicler Matthew Paris wrote that: "One barely received twenty new shillings for thirty old ones at the coin exchange." This was probably an exaggeration, but it expressed popular dissatisfaction with the recoinage (Vaughan 1993: 62). When Henry III's successor Edward I (1272–1307) reformed the coinage in 1279, it had not been recoined since 1247. King Edward could introduce his own portrait on the coinage and ensure extraordinary income. By the end of 1281 the mint accounts provide evidence for earnings at £18,219 (Prestwich 1988: 247). Still, retaining the sterling as a currency of international standing from the Cycladic Islands to northern Norway, as is witnessed through archaeology, provided English merchants with a strong advantage in foreign markets.

## THE CHURCH DRIVING FORCE FOR MONETIZATION

In the tenth to fifteenth centuries, the concept of money became ubiquitous. From theologians to money changers, people concerned themselves with questions of value and trust raised by money, and the spiritual value of that money. The Church was the largest individual player in the medieval economy, and its demands and ideas shaped use and ideas of money significantly. Everywhere concerns about moral issues surrounding the uses of money were disseminated through sermons, saints' lives, and medieval literature. The cardinal sins defined by Christianity were pride, greed, lust, envy, gluttony, wrath, and sloth which would form the basis for acts of wrongdoing, many of which would be related to the use of money. In medieval society the Church's view on money would put limitations on its use. While mendicant orders would exclude its members from involvement with money in general, the Church would use monetary arguments to stigmatize Jews in medieval society. However, in spite of the many dilemmas related to the use of money, ecclesiastical attitudes towards money in the secular world were kaleidoscopic. A monetary culture developed where money was embedded in all walks of life, and encountered by all classes from paupers to kings, and thereby influenced how people thought about money, value, and measures in society.

As Peter Spufford has pointed out, "The availability of adequate and regular money incomes allowed for a revolution in the government of states" (Spufford

1988b: 247). The Church Reform instigated in the second half of the eleventh century took advantage of the increasing level of monetization and output of coinage from monetary regimes of growing sophistication. Availability of money allowed for the rise of a Church organization as the most sophisticated administrative and economic entity in the Middle Ages. Within Western Christendom a uniform doctrine was promulgated with basic features that stuck in the minds of most people. Rules were adopted for the observance of Christianity that created a common pattern of behavior everywhere from Jerusalem to Greenland. Even in the most remote areas of Christendom the incorporation of the Church did succeed, to a very considerable degree, in bringing into effect the external forms of a European and Catholic Christianity during the high Middle Ages.

The way in which the Church was able to organize itself as a hierarchical network of papacy, metropolitan sees, and parishes encompassing a vast geographical area from the eleventh century onward, would not only take advantage of monetary technology, but also serve as a driving force for introducing it into every corner of Western Christendom. In that way the Church Reform became the major contributor for monetization and the rise of money economy in the West. In the north and northeast it seems like coinage followed in the footsteps of Christianization. In many ways the Church became the most prominent driving force for monetization within the Latin West.

CHAPTER SEVEN

# Money and the Issues of the Age

*The Plurality of Money*

RORY NAISMITH

In Florence in the 1290s, the Dominican scholar and preacher Remigio dei Girolami (d. 1319) told one of his audiences how their fair city had been endowed by God with seven gifts. Two of these, the first and second, derived from the city's money (Florence, Biblioteca Nazionale Centrale di Firenze, Conventi Soppressi G.4.936 (s. xiv), ff. 89v–90r (quoted in Davis 1960: 668)).

> For God has conferred on this city seven unique gifts by which a man may be blinded if (as often happens) he abuses them, or enlightened if he uses them properly. They are: the abundance of coin, the nobility of the money, the volume of people, the civility of life, the industry of wool, the craft of arms, and dominance of the countryside (in the county or district) . . . Concerning the first, it must be noted that money can blind a man with greed, if he uses it greedily. About the second, note that the nobility of money is apparent in three respects: from material, in that the gold of the *tari* is good and the gold of the *augustale* better but the gold of the florin is the best; from design, since on one side it has the blessed John the Baptist about whom the Lord spoke in Matthew 11 . . . and on the other a lily, which is a thing of great excellence, such that Christ and his mother are compared to the lily in Song of Solomon [5:13]; and from circulation, since it circulates

through almost the whole world, and even among the Saracens. By such nobility a proud and vainglorious man is thus blinded.[1]

Remigio's comments on these gifts contain a contradiction. The volume of money leads him to a dire warning about the perils of greed. But it is followed by extended praise of Florence's money as an institution, which excels others in its purity, appearance, and popularity. Florence's currency was one of the cornerstones of the city's reputation. This combination of features—personal risk coupled with collective pride—provides an appropriate point of entry into some of the central and most paradoxical features of medieval money, which I have termed the plurality of money. With this title I have sought to pin down some of the major issues which affected medieval money. Money at this time could mean many things. Readers of Isidore of Seville's (d. 636) *Etymologiae*, an encyclopaedic text which was widely read for centuries, would have found money (*pecunia*) categorized under gold in book 16. Isidore noted that the Latin name for money derived from cattle (*pecus*), in his view because early coins had been made from leather, but ultimately cleaved to the view that money meant coined units of metal (Isidore, *Etymologiae*, XVI.xviii (ed. Lindsay 1911 II.212–14; trans. Barney *et al.* 2006: 329–30).[2] Juggling the ideal of a general and dependable means of exchange with the actuality of what was essentially a commodity money, dependent to some degree on its precious metal content, was to be one of the perennial problems of medieval money.

A second form of plurality, complementing the first, can be identified in the relationship between money and authority. Medieval money derived from that of the Roman Empire, and elements of this Roman heritage had enormous staying power: the pounds (£ or *librae*), shillings (s. or *solidi*), and pence (d. or *denarii*) of medieval and pre-decimal modern money have their roots in Roman denominations. But the unity that characterized late Roman currency dissolved in the early Middle Ages, and in many areas the issue of money became atomized to an extreme degree. The result was that individual cities and principalities across Europe operated their own currency. These ran the gamut from large and centralized territories with a single and relatively stable coinage, such as England, through to areas like the Low Countries and northern Italy which each saw a vast number of distinct coinages emerge.

A third and final form of plurality is to be found at the juncture between medieval uses of coin and modern interpretation of them. Coined money was, as Remigio dei Girolami stressed, a powerfully symbolic phenomenon. It provided not just a means of exchange and a store of value, but a physical embodiment of abstract value in terms of both a system of account and broader notions of worth. Medieval Christians knew well the New Testament story of how a poor widow's gift of two *minuta* ("mites") to the Temple represented a much greater and more meaningful sacrifice than a large offering from a wealthy donor (Mark 12:41–4; Luke 21:1–4). In other words, although coins always had an economic role, they are also a window into how medieval people negotiated ideas of value with the world around them, sometimes in startling ways. Coins might be deliberately folded and discarded to secure the support of God and His saints, put into the ground to sanctify a church dedication, or used in elaborate rituals in courts or churches. Most individual finds of coins do not of course give any indication of whether they ever factored into such uses, and they could easily slip back and forth between sacred and profane contexts—but the possibility of such wide-ranging uses, socially and symbolically as well as commercially driven, is one of the most fascinating features of medieval money.

## THE FORMS OF MONEY

Medieval sources tend, if taken at face value, to maximize the extent of monetary circulation. Systems of monetary account grounded in gold and silver coins—most famously the late Merovingian/Carolingian reckoning of twelve pennies to the shilling, with twenty shillings (i.e. 240 pennies) to the pound, which survived in the UK until 1971—were ubiquitous. This, however, is a case in point of systems of account becoming divorced from actual circulation of corresponding coins as a means of exchange. The vast majority of coins which did change hands under this system were pennies, supplemented (and for high-value transactions replaced) by gold and larger silver pieces in the thirteenth century and after, but often coins did not change hands at all. It was commonplace to make payments using commodities valued in the standard system of account, sometimes specified as *res valentes* ("articles of [equivalent] value") (Bloch 1939). A colorful example is provided by a charter from seventh-century England: an abbot paid a king 500 *solidi* for a piece of land, with an explanation that these *solidi* consisted of twelve beds (with ornate pillows and sheets), two slaves, a gold brooch and two horses with two saddles (Kelly 2009: no. 4c. See further Naismith 2012).

The relationship between monetary thought in terms of units of account, and monetary action through the circulation of means of exchange, was a complex one. Limitations in the range and quantity of coined money, and the influence of quite different traditions of exchange, meant that coins were by no means the only medium which could be thought of in terms of money. Indeed, it is often debatable whether a commodity valued in monetary terms as part of an exchange represents just that, or a form of money in itself, and the frequently terse sources are not able to provide full clarity.

Difficulties are most acute for the immediately post-Roman centuries. Already there was a strong sense of money as a system of account, inherited from Roman tradition and based on the gold *solidus*. The high-value *solidus* did exist as a coin, although it was increasingly outnumbered by *tremisses*, each worth a third of a *solidus*—the lowest gold denomination in the traditional framework. Gravitation towards the *tremissis* was the principal concession towards practicality that can be detected in this period. Yet its shortcomings were still considerable: a *tremissis* in the fifth century would buy about 30kg of pork (based on *Codex Theodosianus: Novellae* XIII.4 (Valentinian III, 445) (ed. Mommsen and Meyer 1905 II: 95–6), in which a *solidus* is the value given for 200lb (*c*. 90.7kg) of pork). Lower-value denominations were not well represented in the post-Roman period. Copper-alloy coins which had formed the basis of day-to-day coin use under Roman rule withered swiftly in Britain, Gaul, and Spain; they persisted on a significantly reduced level in north Africa and Italy under barbarian and later Byzantine rule. Only in the eastern Mediterranean did a functional base-metal coinage weather the early Middle Ages, and even there tenuously. Circulation of gold coin, to judge by corpora of modern finds, actually remained quite buoyant from the fourth to the seventh century (e.g. Naismith 2014a: 281–3 on Gaul). The persistence of gold was tied to its place in systems of account and taxation, and although by default gold pieces found some degree of use in other forms of exchange, such as payment of rents and high-value or bulk commerce, there is no doubt that the monetary system of the early medieval West was severely restricted. How people reacted is far from clear. Systems of distribution and exchange, together with the wealth and scope of local elites, did contract in the aftermath of Roman rule, but began to recover well before the end of the gold-dominated phase of currency (Wickham 2008; Banaji 2009). Forms and flows of money had little discernible impact, and at this time monetary transactions must simply have been a relatively small component of the economy as a whole. Coins were not essential and probably did not factor into most acts of exchange. Forms of favor-swapping, credit, and in-kind transactions must have been commonplace, though are rarely recognized in surviving records. Old Roman copper-alloy coins might have been pressed back into service under some circumstances to facilitate relatively low-value exchange. Some of these coins were even marked with new values in Roman numerals (Grierson and Blackburn 1986: 28–31). But this measure would not have been sustainable.

It is worth stressing that for the rural bulk of the population, engaged in agricultural production, this was probably not a major change from earlier conditions. Coin had always been rarer in the Roman countryside, and payments involving cash were generally few, seasonal and imposed from above, by landlords or agents of the state. The restricted economic resources of post-Roman elites simply meant less extraction of surplus in any form (Wickham 2008: 23–4). As landowners in Gaul and Spain came gradually to demand more from their tenants, local agents set about bridging the gap created by the contracted monetary system by gathering and redistributing agricultural produce in sufficient bulk to make commutation into gold an option (Naismith 2014a: 298–9).

FIGURE 7.1: A hoard of Migration Age (fifth- or sixth-century) gold coins and bracteates, deposited in a rolled silver disk. Fuglesang, Denmark. Image © National Museum, Copenhagen.

The appearance of the silver penny in the late seventh century alleviated this basic problem of early medieval currency. Each individual coin had significantly less buying power, and at some times and places between the seventh and twelfth centuries silver pennies were available in large quantity. But the penny only went so far in alleviating the difficulty: a single denomination of relatively high value still predominated. Alternatives to coined money were restricted to a few preferred media. Gold and silver in uncoined form—whether as objects, ingots, or hacked-up objects—were a special case right through the Middle Ages. They served as a portable, prestigious, and high-value means of both storing and exchanging value, albeit only to a large degree among the elite and wealthy merchants. Europe beyond the boundaries of the former Roman Empire in the early Middle Ages (i.e. Ireland, Scotland, Scandinavia, most of Germany, and areas further east, down into the northern Balkans) did not have close familiarity with a system of state-sponsored coined money, and hence gold and silver had largely circulated in a ceremonial and/or bullion context. Hoards of hack-metal and ingots have been found in these areas, as well as within the bounds of the Empire (Hunter and Painter 2013) (Figure 7.1). Scandinavia in the Viking Age is the area best known for its focus on precious metal as bullion rather than coin. Its distinct bullion-based element of exchange became most substantial when inflows of Islamic silver coins picked up steam around 800, and lasted until the establishment of Western-modeled monetary economies in the eleventh and twelfth centuries (Kilger 2007; Skre 2007; Williams 2011b) (Figure 7.2). Coinage was thus by no means the norm, and neither did it always become inextricably embedded in societies. Some simply lost the practice of using it. In post-Roman Britain, use of coin seems to have quickly collapsed. Gildas, a writer of about the early sixth century, thought of coined money as an unwelcome Roman imposition of earlier times, and Brittonic/Welsh sources of the early Middle Ages largely eschew traditional Roman monetary terminology in favor of weights for precious metals, and more often livestock (Naismith 2017: 28). Northern Spain was also distinct for the presence of pseudo-monetary standardized livestock—the *bovo soldare* ("*solidus* cow") and its counterparts. It is unlikely that a single "*solidus* cow" measure ever existed; the idea was a malleable ideal, suitable for rural societies

FIGURE 7.2: A late Viking Age (tenth- or eleventh-century) hoard of coins and hack-metal, with the pot in which it was discovered. Image © National Museum, Copenhagen.

in which animals were as effective a unit of value as (largely imaginary) gold and silver (Jarrett 2014). Early medieval Ireland's copious legal texts reveal a system which was similar in some respects. Cattle of different forms were a central unit of value, together with slaves (Kelly 1997: 587–99). This system was of deep antiquity, and indicates something about the commodities which early Irish society prized most highly. But by the early Middle Ages, cattle and slaves were not being led in droves across the countryside. Rather, these had become established as measures of value which might be exchanged using several different media, including gold and silver (Breatnach 2014).

In practice, few if any medieval societies were completely dominated by a single form of money. There was some gold and silver—and some of that in coined form—in early medieval Wales, while Viking-Age Scandinavia had locallymade coins which circulated alongside bullion, as well as extensive exchange in commodities such as cloth, butter, and animal hides. All such societies, together with those that had a tradition of thinking in terms of coin-based systems of account, stood to benefit from a versatile approach to units of account, which was characteristic of the Middle Ages. In the post-Roman centuries, old units were updated and also supplemented with new ones. Pounds and *solidi* survived from the late Roman system, reckoned in relation to silver pennies (*denarii* in Latin) after these were introduced in Francia around 700 (e.g. *Concilium Liftinense* ch. 2, ed. Werminghoff 1906-8: I, 7—one of the earliest dated texts (743) recording the new system). The Anglo-Saxon kingdoms also developed new reckonings of the shilling and pound with reference to pennies around this time (Naismith 2017: 361–5). They used the same Latin terminology as the Franks, as well as a set of corresponding vernacular terms closely related to those of other Germanic-speakers in what is now Germany. *Libra* was *pund*; *solidus* was *scilling*; *denarius* was *pæning* or (more rarely, and generally only in early texts) *sceat*, to use Old English examples. Cognates exist in early texts in Old Saxon, Old High German, and other languages from the seventh and eighth centuries (Schröder 1918). The nature of the earliest sources, which consist mostly of glosses, does not make them amenable to close dating or contextualization. But a common vocabulary for money, Latin and Germanic, clearly existed in the early medieval North Sea area. Some sense of the rapidity with which monetary words and ideas could spread is provided by a completely new unit known as the *mancus* or *mancosus* which between the 770s and 790s traveled from central and northern Italy across Francia and England (McCormick 2001: 323–42; Prigent 2014). Deriving either from Arabic or from a colloquial reference to debased Byzantine *solidi*, the *mancus* initially related specifically to gold pieces, and on the basis of their metrology and value in relation to silver came to be assessed at 30d. each. It was also used for corresponding weights of gold, hinting at the essentially bullion-based way in which gold was viewed at the time, and later also as a general unit of 30d.

The spread of the mark was similar in many respects. This unit became a mainstay of central medieval account systems, rated as two-thirds of a pound (160d., or 13s. 4d.), sometimes divided into eight or ten oras. The mark and ora are thought to have emerged in connection with the Vikings, being associated with the taste for silver and gold in uncoined form which grew up in Scandinavia (Williams 2011b: 342–50). Oras are mentioned in an early runic inscription on an iron ring from northern Sweden, while marks first occur in Scandinavia on stones which are probably of late Viking date (see the runestones Jungner and Svardström 1940–70: no. 4; and Brate and Wessén 1924–36: no. 11, with Liestøl 1979 for the Forsa ring), but appear earlier in a treaty made in England between Alfred the Great (871–99) and the Viking ruler Guthrum (Alfred-Guthrum treaty, ch. 2, ed. Liebermann 1903–16: I, 126–7). During the tenth century, marks and oras could be found in texts from parts of eastern England settled by Vikings, but by the beginning of the eleventh century they had reached London and other parts of the kingdom. It was also in the opening decades of the eleventh century that the mark began to be used in northwest Germany (the area with which it was to be most strongly associated later in the Middle Ages). It could have arrived from either England or perhaps Scandinavia: Cologne and other cities of the area had trading connections with both. The mark thus moved from its Scandinavian homeland to England with Vikings, and a few generations later was transferred across the North Sea again. In both cases there was also movement of silver, but it was the terminology—thought in terms of money—which stuck.

The quantity of cash in circulation expanded exponentially from the later twelfth century as new mines entered production and new mint places opened en masse. Italy, for instance, went from having about sixteen known mint places in *c.* 1050 to almost seventy in 1300 (Travaini 2011: 57). In England, the number of mints remained more stable (and in fact shrank) but the supply of money exploded nonetheless: it has been estimated that there were about 1–4 pennies per capita in circulation in Britain and Ireland around 1158, compared to 40–53 in 1290 (Allen 2016: 13; cf. Mayhew 1995). Money, and especially coined money, undoubtedly came to play a larger part in people's lives after about 1200. New monetary instruments were created, mostly with the intention of facilitating higher-value transactions. These were particularly attractive in areas such as Italy which had experienced debasement of the penny, rendering it less practical for large-scale payments. Larger, purer silver pieces appeared early in the thirteenth century, first with the *grosso* at Venice in 1203, and gold pieces followed in the 1250s at Florence and Genoa. Complex and multi-tiered monetary systems were coming into being, both with regard to systems of account and to actual coin in circulation. Coins included three main levels: gold, good silver, and debased silver (the latter two sometimes known as "white" and "black" money) (Spufford 1988b: 319–35). These interlocked in diverse ways. Good silver and gold in particular could circulate well beyond their home territory, along with ingots of silver. Their popularity and flow varied depending on the fluctuating rates which would be charged for coining across Europe and western Asia (Spufford 1999). Merchants using cash internationally on a large scale needed to be alive to these constant ebbs and flows in exchange rates, and produced handbooks of exchange to help navigate them (Spufford 2008). Low-value coins, on the other hand, tended to be more localized in circulation, typically just to the home city or region, with some exceptions such as low-value Venetian coins which filled a niche in England (e.g. Stahl 1999; Cook 1999).

Systems of account embraced all of these difficulties and more. Fundamentally, the same arrangement of pounds, shillings, and pence prevailed across much of medieval Europe, but the accommodation of many new types of coin (and changes to them) added layers of complexity. The underlying problem was how to handle the variable intrinsic value of precious metal coins. In Florence and Venice, there were separate reckonings of account for each individual coin, so that one could have a pound of *grossi* or of *soldini* or of gold, which were reckoned at 240 of the respective coin. Even more confusingly, the value of the coin itself could fluctuate in terms of its corresponding system of account, to allow for debasement and shifts in demand for gold and silver (somewhat like modern "bullion coins" such as the Krugerrand): thus the real coin of variable value existed alongside a more stable unit of account of the same name (Sargent and Velde 2002: 82–3 and 149–85). Money and "money" therefore had an elastic relationship; a reminder that coin, even precious-metal coin, did not always reign supreme or bring stability.

It was on the basis of systems of account that bills of exchange and more widespread access to credit grew up in the later Middle Ages. Italian merchants in the thirteenth century spearheaded the use of bills of exchange to facilitate movement of money between Italian cities, the Champagne fairs, and other commercial centers without the expensive and risky need to carry hard cash over long distances (Spufford 2002: 16–46; Spufford 2008). Credit seems to have grown as an extension of the money supply, and in the Middle Ages was still tied to creditors' expectation of being repaid in cash. Nonetheless, it became far more widely available in the later Middle Ages, even to peasants (Nightingale 2004; Briggs 2009; cf. Bolton 2012: 191–6 and 274–93). The possibilities of what one meant by "money" continued to evolve, in response to the shortcomings of what had been essentially a commodity-based currency.

## THE AUTHORITY OF MONEY

The relationship between money and power was always close but often indirect. Medieval Europe inherited from classical tradition a strong link between ruling authority and money. Emperors had been named and portrayed on coins, and their legislation had enforced proper use of those coins. In the aftermath of Roman rule, western Europe was ruled by a number of barbarian peoples. Their separate kingdoms preserved many aspects of the local infrastructure, and in most cases this included coinage; generally, as discussed above, gold coinage. Yet for the most part these did not name the local ruler. Rather, the mints of post-Roman Europe still placed the name of an emperor on *solidi* and *tremisses*; whether the emperor was current or not depended on a variety of factors, including how familiar his coins were and how politically acceptable he was. This reluctance to name the kings and even mint places responsible for post-Roman gold coins meant that they could still circulate relatively freely as long as they were of good weight and fineness. It also makes the attribution of surviving specimens notoriously difficult, though it is apparent that contemporaries could identify issues of particular kings, areas and mints, as demonstrated by a law issued in Burgundy at the beginning of the sixth century which stipulated which forms of *solidi* were unacceptable (*Constitutiones extravagantes* ch. 21.7, ed. de Salis 1892: 120). Copper-alloy and silver coins, made on a very small scale outside Italy and north Africa, were more flexible, and expressed royal and (in the case of Rome, Ravenna, and Carthage) municipal authority instead. Gold, however, retained a strong association with imperial authority. Procopius famously expressed this when he reported with shock the rumours of a Merovingian Frankish ruler (Theodebert I (534–48)) who had had the temerity to put his name and image on gold coins (Procopius, *History of the Wars* VII.33.5–6, ed. and trans. Dewing 1914–40: IV, 438–9) (Figure 7.3).

There could thus be many layers to the assertion of power through money. New and more overt signals of the profoundly different structures behind

FIGURE 7.3: Gold *solidus* of Theodebert I (534–48). Image: Wikipedia Commons 35517.

western European money appeared in the later sixth and seventh centuries. This was an age of distinction, in which separate spheres and patterns of money became apparent. They generally resulted in more circumscribed circulation, at least of Western-made coins (Carlà 2010). In Visigothic Spain, the king began to be named and shown on all gold pieces from the time of Leovigild (568–86) onward, minted mostly at leading cities (Pliego Vázquez 2009). When gold and occasionally silver coins of secure attribution were minted in Lombard Italy later in the seventh century, they followed a broadly similar pattern (Grierson and Blackburn 1986, 62–6). Merovingian Francia presented a very different mechanism. Coins were made at a plethora of locations; about 800 in total, normally named on the coin. The inscriptions on most coins do not refer directly to either king or emperor, but tend to name the man who made the coin (usually referred to as a "moneyer"). The points of reference in this coinage were profoundly different from those of the Roman period, or even of adjacent kingdoms. Moneyer and mint place were not named out of pride or propaganda as such, but as a means of recourse for those who received false or defective coin. There probably was some form of royal oversight of Merovingian coinage, but the extreme atomization and emphasis on the local mint place and agent responsible are perhaps best understood as a result of devolution in the demand and mechanisms for minting, concentrated in the hands of rural elites drawing income from estates all over the kingdom (Naismith 2014a: 289–300). It is likely that this complex system was influential on the fledgling currency of England and Frisia in the seventh and eighth centuries.

The mid-eighth century saw a firmer imprint of royal authority in northern Europe, apparently beginning in northern England (Naismith 2012a). In southern England and Francia, this process accompanied the adoption of a broader, thinner form of silver coin. Kingdoms on both sides of the Channel placed much more overt emphasis on the king, but differed in how his authority was articulated. The Carolingian kingdom established by Pippin III in 751 named mint places on its coins, generally towns, and occasionally individuals identifiable with powerful magnates. Later legal texts reveal that the key agent responsible for mediating between the king and production of coin was the count: a powerful local authority charged with executing royal commands and upholding the king's justice (Lafaurie 1980; Naismith 2012a: 314–16). England, by contrast, seems to have had a relatively smaller number of mint places, concentrated in important towns (mostly on the coast), which supported a number of moneyers. Like their Merovingian counterparts these moneyers were the prime point of reference for coined money; unlike Merovingian moneyers, however, there was evidently a close relationship between Anglo-Saxon moneyers and the king, probably stemming from their comparatively restricted distribution when kings started to play a larger role in the mid-eighth century (Naismith 2012b: 128–45).

These two distinct systems laid the foundation for developments extending down to the tenth and eleventh centuries and beyond. The spread of the Carolingian-style silver penny or *denier* into new areas was driven in the first instance by political rather than economic incentives: this was the coinage of the Frankish realm, and new additions to that realm had to adhere to it. The high watermark of Carolingian coinage came in the 820s and 830s when Emperor Louis the Pious (814–40) established a new coinage which did away with all reference to local places of production in favor of inscriptions expressing Christian devotion (Coupland 1990: 35–45). This remarkable coinage formed part of the emperor's effort to strengthen the moral fabric of his realm, but Louis's sons returned to the practice of naming mint places. Portions of the empire which they and their successors ruled had very different experiences in the management of minting authority. In central and northern Italy, where the coinage had been largely restricted to cities with a long tradition of minting, it remained a royal and imperial prerogative down to the twelfth century when the rise of city-based government and expansion of the money supply opened up opportunities for other cities and rulers (Dumas 1991; Travaini 2011). Spain saw more sustained royal (and, in early years, comital) involvement in minting and coinage when production revived on a significant scale in the eleventh and twelfth centuries (Crusafont, Balaguer, and Grierson 2013: 66–108). The bond between moneyers and king in England also persisted (with a much expanded network of mint places from the early tenth to late twelfth centuries) and formed the basis of the strong, closely controlled royal currency for which England was known throughout the Middle Ages (Naismith n.d.). Western Europe north of the Alps, however, saw the power dynamic of money become extremely complicated. In the tenth century, counts and other local agents (including bishops and abbots) charged with management of the coinage on behalf of the king gradually began to assert their own authority. Their encroachment was part of a larger process of reification of magnate rights in post-Carolingian Europe (West 2013). This was no means always adversarial, and could take place with royal permission. Many new mints, especially in the east Frankish kingdom, were set up on the initiative of local magnates with the written sanction of the king (Kluge 1991:101–4). In the West Frankish kingdom, recognition of the current king gradually retreated during the tenth century, so that by the time of the last Carolingian king (Louis V (986–7)), there was only one mint place actually issuing coins in his name (Grierson 1991: 51). Other locations were either producing coins in the name of local rulers, or in the name of a former king.

The upshot of this process was the emergence of what has often been called "feudal" coinages: hundreds of separate and interlocking local currencies. They were grounded in a growing economy fueled by expanding towns and increasing levels of exchange and productivity, but the nexus between money and political authority meant that the form this monetary expansion took was highly complex. The range of currencies available in central and later medieval Europe meant that users frequently had several options available to them. If there was no compulsion to use a particular currency, a sort of inversion of Gresham's Law ensued: people would choose the money which they deemed most reliable, in terms of its retention of value and acceptability. Individual coinages thus rose and fell in popularity based on factors including intrinsic quality and availability. Politics, however, was also a major force. Money was closely identified with the success of states. Expansion of French royal power in the thirteenth century brought with it reassertion of royal rights, including over the coinage (Grierson 1991: 113–16). The strength of English currency meant that it was targeted for profitable imitation in the late thirteenth and early fourteenth centuries, when so-called "crockards" and "pollards" of lower fineness made in the Netherlands entered England in bulk and threatened to overwhelm the local coinage (Desan 2014: 138–50). Competition and prestige were important forces: as Domenico di Girolami stressed, a good coinage reflected well on Florence, and when Venice's Council of Forty approved production of the gold ducat in October 1284, it stipulated that the resultant coin should be "of gold as fine and pure, or better, than that of the florin" (Quoted in Stahl 2000: 31 n. 20).

Great profits and prestige could ensue from a successful coinage which became internationally successful, so there was an impetus to keep the currency stable. But the temptation to capitalize on money through debasement was strong for rulers who found themselves short on income and had a coinage at their disposal. Between the eleventh and thirteenth centuries, some kings, dukes, and counts even demanded a tax from their subjects in order to offset income lost by *not* debasing the coin (Bisson 1979). Those who did engage in manipulation of the coinage for profit could do so in several ways. Purity might be retained but the weight reduced. More common, however, was to use less precious metal. A ruler who did so could raise significant sums in the short term. In the longer term, debasement could prove highly disruptive by driving down the value of the coinage and pushing prices up. This tended to benefit those who owed fixed payments such as rents, while those who expected to profit from such rents (including landowners) suffered. Medieval rulers hence found themselves stuck between a rock and a hard place: debasement would bring an injection of cash, but maintaining it would not only destabilize the local economy but also harm their own income from land and anger the landowning elite. The practice also had moral dimensions, for a ruler charged with production of money for all was expected to think more and more of the common good as well as his own need. French debasements of the fourteenth century stimulated some of the most sophisticated medieval discourse on the exercise of monarchical rule over money. Nicholas Oresme (*c.* 1320–82), drawing on earlier fourteenth-century scholars and on Aristotelian and Augustinian thought, asserted in his landmark text *Tractatus de origine et natura, jure et mutationibus monetarum* that ultimate responsibility for coinage, including its debasement, lay with the community rather than the prince (Langholm 1983; Spufford 2000: 62–75); in his words, "although it is the duty of the prince to put his stamp on the money for the common good, he is not the lord or owner of the money current in his principality, for money is a balancing instrument for the exchange of natural wealth ... it is therefore the property of those who possess such wealth" (Nicholas Oresme, *De moneta*, ch. 6, ed. and trans. (with adaptations) Johnson 1956: 10). Oresme's tract (of which he made a French translation) was aimed squarely at the ruling regime of France in the late 1350s, with which Oresme was in close contact, and probably had some influence in discouraging further debasement or clipping (Nederman 2000: 5). Control over money undoubtedly did bring kings power, but to push the coinage to breaking point through debasement was to risk undermining that same power.

There is little question in modern Western society that money is power. In the sense that control over the dispensation of money, and having access to a healthy supply of it, constitutes power, this was also true of the Middle Ages. But the equation held more loosely with regard to the *creation* of money. Although "virtual" money did exist in the form of units of account, these still presupposed eventual repayment in coin (or at least precious metal). As such, attention focused on coin as a symbol of authority and as an economic tool. This was both the strength and potential undoing of medieval power exercised through money. Issuers could win approval by producing coins of familiar form, or make a statement by diverging from tradition. They could likewise see to the production of coins of consistent quality with a range of denominations to suit the needs of different constituencies in society. But the variables which affected medieval coinage—supply of bullion, actions of neighbors, other factors impacting on prices, and so on—meant that the relationship between money and power was always being renegotiated.

## USING MONEY

Medieval money is usually thought of as first and foremost an instrument of commerce: a means of buying and selling. But it had other roles too. These have been at the forefront of discussion of money—particularly coined money—in relation to earlier periods such as the pre-Roman Iron Age of northern Europe, to the extent that "ritual" and other non-commercial explanations for deposition of both hoards and individual coins now loom very large (e.g. Haselgrove and Webley 2016). It is entirely possible that much of the currency of this period was made with the expectation of predominantly symbolic and ceremonial uses.

There was undoubtedly a great deal of difference between Iron-Age and medieval money in terms of the context, balance, and variety of usage, but there is just as clearly a major disjuncture in how modern scholars approach the two. In the context of medieval finds, the general assumption is that individual coins represent casual loss during circulation, while hoards are typically considered to be gatherings of wealth hidden for temporary safekeeping.[3] Yet it is worth addressing other possibilities, and the evidence in favor of them. There has been a turn towards the significance of ritual in research on medieval society in recent decades, leading to stronger appreciation among scholars of the otherness of the period and how it was structured with gestures and acts (Buc 2001; Arnold 2008: 88–94). There is likewise a strong tradition of thinking about some medieval coins (particularly early gold coins) as part of the world of gift-giving (Grierson 1959), even if this has been qualified in more recent evaluations (Naismith 2012b: 252–76). A more open approach to medieval money and its uses is needed; one which takes account of the specific characteristics which made medieval currency different from its predecessors, but which also allows for the full richness of how these objects moved through society in commercial and non-commercial ways.

Of necessity, the focus here will fall largely on coins. Coins have the distinction of being made with some sort of monetary role in mind (though there are some items which lie on the borderline of this definition, adopting the form of a coin but not apparently being intended for this purpose), and while other commodities could and did serve as money, it is usually the transactional context that allows them to be identified as such. In other words, there is no way to distinguish fabric which once served a monetary role in Iceland when it occurs in an archaeological excavation, or in a text outside the context of exchange. Even with finds of coined money it is often impossible to identify a background to deposition. Those occurring in graves are a special case. Coins found in burials can normally be viewed as deliberate and meaningful additions to the assemblage (though a few examples from plague cemeteries and similar contexts may have been unnoticed as part of the apparel the corpse was buried in: Sloane 2011: 98). What exactly coins were meant to signify alongside the body, its adornments, other items, and the unknown ceremonial that accompanied the burial is a matter of speculation. In the case of early Anglo-Saxon England, coins, along with scales, have sometimes been read as a metonym for control over movable wealth, or the freedom to do business independently (Scull 1990). One of the most famous archaeological finds of coins in an Anglo-Saxon grave—the thirty-seven gold coins (along with two ingots and three blanks) found in an ornate gold purse in the magnificent ship burial of Mound 1 at Sutton Hoo, Suffolk—has been read as payment for ghostly oarsmen who would row the king to the afterlife, or perhaps as part of a diplomatic gift which carried special meaning for the deceased and his community (Grierson 1970;

Carver 1998: 169). Coins in burials are rarer in most areas from the central and later Middle Ages, but do occur under specific circumstances. A single silver bracteate depicting Albert the Bear, Margrave of Brandenburg (1124–70), and his wife was found in the Margrave's sarcophagus; being a specimen of the only one of his many issues to show both the margrave and margravine together (produced more than a decade before his death), it must have been picked out deliberately, quite plausibly to underscore the bond between the margrave and his wife (whose tomb lay adjacent to his) (Travaini 2015: 213). Tombs of saints also attracted deposits of coins, left by visitors as (in Lucia Travaini's words) "an act of devotion, a tactile act, and a personal encounter with the saint"—a way of leaving a lasting signal of one's own presence in contact with a revered saint. Coins might also serve as a kind of time capsule when a saint's tomb was opened. Travaini cites the example of the grave of St. Geminiano in Modena, opened for inspection (and, in one case, relocation) in 1109 and 1184; groups of coins datable to these two years have been found inside (Travaini 2015: 211–12 and 216).

Beyond graves, only a handful of medieval coin finds have an identifiable context of use. Those which have been turned into other objects (usually brooches or ornaments) hold considerable symbolic interest but had presumably ceased to function in a monetary context before deposition. Throughout the Middle Ages and after, adaptation of this kind took place: Sir Walter Scott's *The Talisman* was inspired by the Lee Penny, a fifteenth-century English groat adorned with a red stone (Hall 2016: 142–3); and there was a vibrant tradition of adapting coins for wearing as pendants (Figure 7.4). It is considerably rarer, however, for finds of unmodified coins to have clear evidence of use. One remarkable exception is a hoard of mostly English pennies buried beneath the House of the Vestal Virgins in Rome in the 940s which included a pair of silver fasteners with an inscription identifying the assemblage as a donation to Pope Marinus II (942–6). Various other features of the hoard suggest that it may have been brought to Rome by Theodred, Bishop of London (d. 951 × 953) (Naismith and Tinti 2016). But this case highlights two central obstacles. First, finds only indicate the *final* use of a coin. It is likely that coins circulated before being deposited (deliberately or otherwise) or modified to become an ornament (Williams 2006a: 161–4). Some coins in the Forum hoard were fifty or 100 years old: it is highly improbable that all of them had always been intended for this gift. Moreover, it is unclear whether the Forum hoard actually fulfilled its intended purpose. A donation of cash given to the pope would presumably have been spent, probably through distribution among the churches of Rome like the numerous donations of gold and silver recorded in the *Liber pontificalis*. Either the Forum hoard never reached the pope, or if it did it was immediately concealed. It is unlikely, however, that the hoard's concealment was meant to be permanent.

FIGURE 7.4: A penny of Edward I of England (1272–1307), gilded on one face and mounted with a pin on the reverse (PAS DOR-403D81). Image: Portable Antiquities Scheme.

Pre-Christian beliefs may well have included the idea that that which was buried on earth would be available in the hereafter. Although only preserved in later times, it is thought that some echo of earlier pagan thought can be detected in the famous "law of Odin" recorded in the thirteenth-century *Heimskringla* which states that dead men should be burned, and that anything burned with them, or buried by them in the earth before death, would be enjoyed in Valhalla (*Ynglingasaga*, ch. 8 (trans. Finlay and Faulkes 2011: 11)). Conversely, Matthew 6:19–21 commanded "lay not up for yourselves treasures upon earth . . . but lay up for yourselves treasures in heaven . . . for where your treasure is, there will your heart be also" (Reuter 2000: 11–13). Money or other goods hoarded in life might be fit for earthly purposes, but would do no good for one's soul after death. The establishment of Christianity as the predominant religion in medieval Europe hence strongly discouraged the deposition of wealth as such on a permanent basis. This is one reason why medieval hoards in particular are traditionally interpreted as "failed hoards:" assemblages which were meant to be recovered, but for whatever reason were not (Reece 1987: 47).

A gap always existed between principle and practice, however, and there were many other reasons for hoarding and abandoning money besides a wish for enrichment in the afterlife. The ninth-century writer of the *Anglo-Saxon Chronicle* commented that, in 418, "the Romans collected all the treasures which were in Britain, and hid some under the ground, so that no one could find them afterwards, and took some with them to Gaul" (*Anglo-Saxon Chronicle* s.a. 418, ed. Plummer 1892: I, 10; trans. Whitelock 1979: 152). Denying treasure to an enemy might prompt concealment with no intent of recovery. Specific coins could also have been discarded if owners found them to be forged or defective in any other way, and did not wish to risk the penalties that came with trying to pass them on. "Ritual" deposit of coin also extended to a great deal more than expectation of heavenly recovery. Indeed, placement of coins could reflect religious devotion or apotropaic practices accepted within Christianity (Thomas and Ottaway 2008: 383–93; Lauwers 2009). Conceptualizing hoards as "structured deposits," as prehistoric archaeologists now do, encourages stronger appreciation of an assemblage's place within a geographical, imaginary, and social landscape; not just buried at a convenient point, memorable and out of sight of prying eyes, when a group of ruffians with torches and pitchforks (or the equivalent) appeared on the horizon. Hoards have been found in the immediate vicinity of churches from Britain and Ireland, in part because churches in the early Middle Ages were often important focal points for distribution and exchange, but also probably because of the air of sanctity that surrounded them (Woods 2013: I, 331–2). It was, in addition, commonplace to hand over collections of coin in religious ceremonies. In 929, Koenwald, Bishop of Worcester (928 × 929–957 × 958), undertook a mission on behalf of the Anglo-Saxon King Æthelstan to various kingdoms and monasteries in continental Europe, among them St. Gall in modern Switzerland. A short narrative tells how Koenwald arrived bearing silver sent as a donation from the king. On the day after his arrival he entered the church and placed some money on the altar and donated some for the use of the monks before being ceremonially inducted into the monastic community (Keynes 1985: 198–9). It is entirely possible that the Forum hoard was given (or at least was expected to be given) in a similar setting, for there is good evidence that eminent visitors to Rome could expect a personal audience with the pope (Naismith 2016b: 38–9). Once handed over, a gift to a church could meet with many fates, but alms-giving to the poor was a favored use (Figure 7.5). A will from ninth-century Canterbury records how a wealthy priest wished 26 pence to be given to 21 *pauperes* every year so that they could buy clothes, and in addition for another 1,200 *pauperes* to receive one penny plus some bread and cheese or butter on the anniversary of his death every year (Brooks and Kelly (eds.) 2013: no. 64). Almsgiving of this form was much greater in breadth than depth, but could be formidable in scale, and the expectation was that it would intermesh with other ways of using money.

All of these examples relate to what would be classed as hoards if found today. Handling of individual coins was a significantly different exercise. These had a token character which meant religious concerns about the abandonment of wealth did not carry the same weight. There was a lively tradition of adapting coins for all kinds of roles. One remarkable Arabic dirham—minted with Muslim religious formulations in Arabic—was inscribed in Scandinavia with a Christian invocation in Latin, written out in runes: the alphabet used in northern Europe since long before the coming of Christianity. Three different

FIGURE 7.5: A scene of almsgiving from the Utrecht Psalter (Utrecht, Universiteitsbibliotheek, MS Bibl. Rhenotraiectinae I Nr 32) (Rheims, s. ix), folio 65v, illustrating Psalm 111. Image: Universiteit Utrecht.

traditions come together on this one coin, which must have served as a tiny and highly personalized expression and reminder of faith (Figure 7.6). Bending a coin in half was one means of invoking the protection of a saint, for example. When William Cragh was captured and held before execution in Hereford in 1290, he bent a penny in the name of St. Thomas de Cantilupe, and concealed it in his belt for safekeeping. William's remarkable survival of two attempts at hanging prompted the enquiries of a papal mission seeking to establish the sainthood of St. Thomas (Richter 1998: 202; Bartlett 2004). Such stories, from the twelfth century onwards, are numerous in miracle collections (Finucane 1977). Finds of coins provide material corroboration for the custom (Kelleher 2012) (Figure 7.7).

Coins were also sometimes used as foundational deposits. Like coins placed in saints' graves, they served to mark an occasion rather than as a deposit of wealth. Foundation deposits are best known from churches (prominent in both the archaeological and written record), though one (from the eleventh century) has been found beneath a French castle (Mouton 2008: 34). Several written accounts survive of coins being placed beneath new churches. One of the earliest instances recounts how the Bishop of Constance put a gold coin beneath each of the four corners of a new abbey church at Petershausen, Germany, in 983 (*Casus monasterii Petrishusensis*, I, 16, ed. Feger 1956: 54–5). Prestigious gold pieces were perhaps especially suitable for this role, and among the few

FIGURE 7.6: Dirham minted CE 885–96, and inscribed (probably in the eleventh- or twelfth-century) with runes which can be transliterated as ". . . Iesus Christus filius dei vivi. In nomina patris et filii . . . et spiritus [sic]" (". . . Jesus Christ, son of the living God. In the name of the Father, the Son . . ."); the inscription continues on the reverse. Found at an unknown location on the island of Bornholm, Denmark, 1770. Image © The National Museum, Copenhagen.

FIGURE 7.7: A groat of Henry VII of England (1485–1509), found at Fulford, Yorkshire (Portable Antiquities Scheme SWYOR-4F7776). It was discovered folded in half, with the illustrated piece of fabric enclosed within. Image: Portable Antiquities Scheme.

possible cases of an actual find from such a context is one which was discovered during the demolition of St. Clement's Church at Worcester in the 1820s (Blackburn 2007b: no. B8; Baker and Holt 2004: 208–10). A later find from Italy is undoubtedly of foundational character, but in an ecclesiastical setting stands out as quite bizarre, and perhaps deliberately archaic. Beneath a mid-fifteenth-century church at Caronno in Lombardy, archaeologists found the remains of a young cow, kneeling across the nave with its head turned towards the altar, and with a 200-year-old coin of Emperor Frederick II (1220–50) in its mouth (Travaini 2015: 220–1).

Finally, the "ritual" character of coined money could be entirely situational—a function of where and how they were used. Ecclesiastical and other gifts represented by hoards have been mentioned above, but there were also mass individual donations. Some 1,500 medieval coins including specimens from most countries of Europe were found in the *confessio* of St. Peter's in Rome during twentieth-century excavations (Serafini 1951). These coins, found in an alcove within the heart of one of the most celebrated churches in Christendom, are difficult to interpret as anything other than the deposits of generations of pilgrims; the same is true of the tens of thousands of medieval coins discovered beneath the floors of churches in Scandinavia and certain other parts of northern Europe (Sortland 2006). At other sites, pinning down coins as the residue of monetary gifts offered to clergy or shrines is more problematic, especially at wealthy institutions which might have drawn in money and its use for other purposes. An array of Anglo-Saxon coins found in the vicinity of the important church site at Whithorn, Dumfries and Galloway, for instance, could well be linked to pilgrims and worshippers depositing coins, deliberately or otherwise, as offerings, but the case remains debatable (Hill 1997; Hall 2016: 138–9).

Churches—highly visible sites of devotion and ritual—are the best known setting for "special" assemblages and depositions of coin, but far from the only possible one. Payments for land in Anglo-Saxon England were consistently framed as gifts, commonly including cash. Those involved in the transaction may have known that it was essentially a purchase, but it was a purchase of a very special commodity that evoked archaic ideas of the dynamic between "buyer" and "seller," turning them into givers of gifts and counter-gifts. This distinction, artificial though it may have been, persevered in solemn diplomas right down to the eleventh century (Naismith 2016a).

At lower levels of society, handovers of assemblages of coin could also take varied forms. One of the most vivid comes in Wipo's *Gesta Chuonradi imperatoris* (ch. 13, ed. Bresslau 1915: 35), in which King (soon to be Emperor) Conrad II (1024–39) rewards a soldier who lost his leg fighting for his master's cause in Italy with a piece of leg armour filled with coins. A long-lived tradition linked money to liberty in Frankish manumissions—bestowals of freedom on slaves—between the seventh and early twelfth centuries (Kano 2013). The basic idea was that casting a coin before a slave, or out of his hand, in the presence of the king made him a free man. It is never made clear exactly what the coin was supposed to signify, and neither did the gesture necessarily remain stable in meaning. The most recent assessment cautiously identifies the practice as a renunciation of rights over the slave, symbolized by a single penny's worth of tribute. Initially, it was the freeing master who cast the coin, but from about 800 the king took a more involved role by knocking one or more coins from the slave's outstretched hand. In the most lively description (from eleventh-century Italy) it is said that "the king puts the coins in the hand of the boy or man, and afterwards strikes it with his own hand, so that the coins bounce out of the hand and over the head" (*Liber Papiensis*, ed. Boretius 1868: 353).

## CONCLUSION

Stubbornly persisting for some four centuries, this practice gives a small window into the symbolism and layers of meaning which adhered to money. As an embodiment of abstract value, coin is a perfect vehicle for tracing the range of ways in which material wealth might be expended. In an important sense all such uses were therefore part of the economy, taken in its largest sense of how people allocated their resources, and so discriminating between economic and non-economic uses of coin is not always helpful. A more constructive approach is to consider different kinds of meaning and logic (economic or otherwise) laced into acts of coin use, and how they could interlock in parallel or opposition. One might think of commercial versus non-commercial, the two bleeding into each other more often than is sometimes allowed for; of private versus public, with the concomitant possibility that giver, receiver, and different observers might have interpreted the same event in different ways; and of deliberate versus accidental in relation to finds of coins, with an eye to the ways in which cases might be read differently depending on individual circumstances. It is, all things considered, likely that a high proportion of medieval single finds did come to rest in the ground through circulation rather than deliberate deposition; it is also likely that commercial exchange, itself factoring in social and moral as well as strictly economic concerns, played an important part in the to and fro of medieval currency. But to focus simply on the bottom line is to miss the small print, which reveals the nuances of the medieval monetary economy in all its glorious complexity.

# NOTES

## Chapter 1

1. As the former Minorite monk and metal expert Burkhard Waldis put it in a memorandum on monetary policies he compiled for the master of the Teutonic Order in Livonia in 1532: "Whenever they may mint more than one type of coin, they mint that one most which allows them to make the best profit" (Arbusow (ed.) 1910: 799).

## Chapter 2

\* This chapter was translated into English by Marina Starik.
1. There are numerous examples of this in Beaucage 1982. See also legal disputes over excess salary payments in the context of the enforcement of the Ordinance of Labourers in 1349, for example: Kinball (1962: 32–3). A classic commentary on wages in a rural setting can be found in Duby 1961. On these questions, see Bernardi, Beck and Feller 2013.
2. In this regard, Despy (Despy 1968) should be credited for having stressed, contrary to the commonly held view, the importance of local trade in the accumulation of wealth and the process of economic development in the early Middle Ages. His demonstration was amply confirmed in the 1980s in the case of Italy by Pierre Toubert (Toubert 1983).
3. On payments in ingots, see Van Werweke 1932 and Kruse 1988. On the Gniezno bronze doors: Gieysztor 1959.
4. Ibid. *et fist erraument faire mehailles d'argent per doner as maistres la sodee et que ils desservoient, que les petites que ils avoient ne lor venoient enci a eise.* ("And straightaway, [he] had new silver coins made to be given to the masters as a payment they deserved, since the small ones they had did not befit them.")
5. See, for example, Boccaccio, *The Decameron*, the eighth day, second novella, whose very title is a description of these objects: "The parish priest of Varlungo lieth with

Mistress Belcolore and leaveth her a cloak of his in pledge; then, borrowing a mortar of her, he sendeth it back to her, demanding in return the cloak left by way of token, which the good woman grudgingly giveth him back." Indeed, the cloak serves as payment for a chargeable sexual service: Belcolore, desiring to recover a dress and a belt given as a pledge to a moneylender, asks her seducer for money, which he does not have. Therefore, he leaves her his *tabard* (a short cloak) as compensation for the obtained sexual gratification.

6. On Petrarch's lending of the book: Gioanni 2015: 325–7. On another non-returned book loan because the latter was pawned, see also: Sibon 2013.

## *Chapter 3*

1. Honorius of Autun (*Gemma animae* I 35): Migne ed. 1844–64, vol. 172, col. 555B: "*De forma panis*. Panis vero ideo in modum denarii formatur, quia panis vitae Christus pro denariorum numero tradebatur qui verus denarius in vinea laborantibus in proemio dabitur. Ideo imago Domini cum litteris in boc pane exprimitur, quia et in denario imago et nomen imperatoris scribitur, et per hunc panem imago Dei in nobis reparatur, et nomen nostrum in libro vitae notatur."
2. Augustine, *In Psalmum 21. Enarratio II, Sermo ad plebem*, 28: "Ecce Christus passus est, ecce mercator ostendit mercedem, ecce pretium quod dedit, sanguis eius fusus est. In sacco ferebat pretium nostrum: percussus est lancea, fusus est saccus, et manavit pretium orbis terrarum."
3. Ambrose of Milan 1985a: *De Tobia*, 19, 64: "pecuniam habent et non habent, quia usum eius ignorant, pretium eius nesciunt, figuram eius et formam non cognouerunt."
4. *Pirqe Avot*: 21–2 (Brauner 2013).
5. The key reference for this development was a passage in the Gospel of Matthew: "Tunc impletum est quod dictum est per Ieremiam prophetam dicentem: Et acceperunt triginta argenteos, pretium appretiati quem appretiaverunt a filiis Israel, et dederunt eos in agrum Figuli, sicut constituit mihi Dominus" (Matthew 27:9). See Isidore of Seville, 1911, VII 9, 20 (d. 636): "Judas Iscariotes, vel a vico, in quo ortus est, vel ex tribu Issachar vocabulum sumpsit, quodam praesagio futuri in condemnationem sui. Issachar enim interpretatur merces, ut significaretur pretium proditoris, quo vendidit Dominum, sicut scriptum est: Et acceperunt mercedem meam, triginta argenteos, pretium quo appretiatus sum ab eis (Matthew 27:9)." The origin of Matthew's passage was in the Vulgate, Prophecy of Zacharias, 11: 12–13: "Et dixi ad eos: Si bonum est in oculis vestris, afferte mercedem meam: et si non, quiescite. Et appenderunt mercedem meam triginta argenteos. Et dixit Dominus ad me: Projice illud ad statuarium, decorum pretium quo appretiatus sum ab eis. Et tuli triginta argenteos, et projeci illos in domum Domini, ad statuarium."
6. Ambrose of Milan 1985b: 10. 52: "Puteus enim, si nihil haurias, inerti otio et degeneri situ facile corrumpitur, exercitus autem nitescit ad speciem, dulcescit ad potum. Ita et aceruus diuitiarum cumulo harenosus, speciosus est usu, otio autem inutilis habetur."
7. Bernard of Pavia, 1956, III 11: 75–7.

8. *Decretum Gratiani* 1959: C. X q. 2 (c. 2: Imperator).
9. *Corpus Iuris Civilis* 1870–95. *Codex*, 1, 2, 14; 1, 2, 21; *Novellae*, 7, I ff.; *Decretum Gratiani* 1959. 618 ff. (C. X, q. 2, c. 2). On the historical genesis of the *Decretum*, see Winroth 2000.
10. *Decretum Gratiani* 1959. C. XII, q. 2, cc. 1 ff.: 687 ff.
11. Ambrose of Milan 2000. II, 28, 137. See *Decretum Gratiani* C. XII, q. 2, c. 70 (Friedberg ed., 710).
12. Bernardus Papiensis, *Summa Decretalium*, III 11 (*Precaria, commodatum, depositum, emptio/venditio, permutatio, pignus*).
13. *Decretales Gregorii IX* 1959, l. III, t. XIX, c. VI.
14. Henry of Segusio, 1574: 1019 ff.
15. Henry of Segusio, 1574: Lib. 5, ch. 19, 7. I used with some modification the English translation in www.hetwebsite.net/het/profiles/hostiensis.htm; see Cornell 2006: 13 ff., 20.

## Chapter 4

1. I am grateful to Martin Allen, Svein Harald Gullbekk, and Rory Naismith for reading and commenting on a draft of this chapter. Any errors remain the author's own.
2. Corpus of Early Medieval Coin-Finds (www-cm.fitzmuseum.cam.ac.uk/emc/); the Portable Antiquities Scheme (https://finds.org.uk/), and Numis (https://nnc.dnb.nl/dnb-nnc-ontsluiting-frontend/#/numis/).

## Chapter 5

1. This article could not have been written without conversations had as a member of the Bilderfahrzeuge Research Project (2014–15), based at the Warburg Institute, London. My thanks go to the group, and especially to Johannes von Müller. It would not have been written without invitation from Rory Naismith, to whom thanks are due not just for the opportunity but for valuable and constructive feedback during the writing process. I would also like to thank Maria Vrij at the Barber Institute of Fine Arts for help with images. Finally, my thanks to Jonathan Jarrett and Daniel Reynolds, who both read and commented on draft versions and vastly improved the finished product. All errors, of course, remain my own.

## Chapter 6

1. The scholarly literature on the anthropology of money provides us with numerous studies of general and particular focus. An influential figure in this field has been Karl Polanyi, whose relevant studies are collected in Polanyi 1968. For the Middle Ages, non-monetary means of payment are discussed in depth from legal perspectives in Geva 2011.
2. For a discussion of Cassian's writings on coins, see Dinkova-Bruun 2015: 78–80.
3. For a discussion on Anselm and his attitudes towards money, see Gasper and Gullbekk 2012.

4. For the Papal See, see Lunt 1934. For Sweden, see Brilioth 1915; and Norway, see Storm 1897. A detailed study of the finances of a monastic economy is provided in King 1985.
5. The varying attitudes among different monastic orders from the later eleventh to the mid-twelfth century is discussed in Gasper 2015: 44–52.
6. For an interesting discussion of St. Francis and how he came so to detest the power of money with references to contemporary society in Italy and to biblical texts, see Stark 1966–72: III, 286–7.
7. The concern was repeated by the Italian historian Benvenuto da Imola at Bologna *c.* 1350 (Coulton 1925: 327). On usury and theories on money, see Kaye 1998.
8. Alcuin's closest friendship seems to have been with King Offa's daughter Ethelburh, who was an abbess. When she was unable to undertake a pilgrimage, probably to Rome, Alcuin urged her instead to use the money to care for the poor (Dales 2012: 58). The virtue of almsgiving was a recurring theme in the works of Alcuin (Smith 2003: 64).
9. Galster 1972: 20, n. 70a; Jensen (ed.), 1989: no. 670.
10. In the case of this famous saga, with references to money in the time of King Harald Hardrade it should be noted that the saga was authored in the 1220s or 1230s. The essence of its monetary significance has been proven as reliable fact by modern scientific investigations: The pennies that are described as debased in the Morkinskinna was merely one-third silver. Several hundred Norwegian pennies from the second half of the eleventh century have been analyzed using state-of-the-art technology. The saga story in question does not only give factual records of the quality of the coinage, it also provides an insight into attitudes towards the nature of money in the 1050s.
11. For discussion on testing coins in Viking Age Scandinavia, see Malmer 1985: 51; Archibald 1990; Gullbekk 1991; Archibald 2011: 51–64.

## Chapter 7

1. Unless otherwise stated, this and other translations are my own.
2. Modern scholarship inclines more towards the idea that early money *was* cattle, or vice versa: cf. Marcos Casquero 2005.
3. Some older scholarship tends to associate hoards with specific military events, on the understanding that these would have prevented the owner from returning to reclaim the hoard. However, this interpretation is no longer accepted so readily: Armstrong 1998; Curta and Gândilă 2012: 45–7.

# BIBLIOGRAPHY

Abdy, Richard. 2006. "After Patching: Imported and recycled coinage in fifth- and sixth-century Britain." In Barrie Cook and Gareth Williams (eds.), *Coinage and History in the North Sea World c. 500–1250. Essays in Honour of Marion Archibald*. Leiden and Boston: Brill.

Abel, Wilhelm. 1986. *Agricultural Fluctuations in Europe: From the Thirteenth to the Twentieth Centuries*. London: Methuen.

Abulafia, Anna Sapir. 2002. "Theology and the Commercial Revolution: Guibert of Nogent, St. Anselm and the Jews in Northern France." In David Abulafia, Michael J. Franklin and Miri Rubin (eds.), *Church and City, 1000–1500: Essays in Honour of Christopher Brooke*. Cambridge: Cambridge University Press.

Adriaen, Marcus (ed.). 1979–85. *S. Gregorii Magni Moralia in Iob*. Turnhout: Brepols.

Allen, Robert C. 2000. "Economic Structure and Agricultural Productivity in Europe, 1300–1800." *European Review of Economic History* 4: 1–26.

Allen, Martin. 2001. "Hoards and the circulation of the Short Cross coinage." In Jeffrey P. Mass, *English Short Cross Coins 1180–1247*. Oxford: Oxford University Press.

Allen, Martin. 2007. "Henry II and the English coinage." In Christopher Harper-Bill and Nicholas Vincent (eds.), *Henry II. New interpretations*. Woodbridge: Boydell.

Allen, Martin. 2010. "The output and profits of the Calais mint, 1349–1450." *British Numismatic Journal* 80: 131–9.

Allen, Martin. 2012. *Mints and Money in Medieval England*. Cambridge: Cambridge University Press.

Allen, Martin. 2016. "Currency Depreciation and Debasements in Medieval Europe." In David Fox and Wolfgang Ernst (eds.), *Money in the Western Legal Tradition: Middle Ages to Bretton Woods*. Oxford: Oxford University Press.

Allen, Martin. 2016. "The First Sterling Area." *Economic History Review* (published online 2016): 1–22.

Allen, Martin. 2016. "The York local coinage of the reign of Stephen (1135–54)." *Numismatic Chronicle* 176: 283–318.

Alteri, Giancarlo. 2009. *Monete offerte dai pellegrini a san Paolo fuori le mura*. Rome: Ist. Poligrafico dello Stato.

Ambrose of Milan. 1985a. *De Tobia*, in Ambrogio di Milano, *Opere*, vol. VI. Milan-Rome: Città Nuova.

Ambrose of Milan. 1985b. *De Nabuthae*, in Ambrogio di Milano, *Opere*, vol. VI. Milan-Rome: Città Nuova.

Ambrose of Milan. 2000. *De officiis ministrorum*, ed. Testard (Corpus Christianorum, s. l., XV). Turnhout: Brepols.

Anderson, Gary A. 2009. *Sin: A History*. New Haven: Yale University Press.

Andersson, Theodore M. and Gade, Kari Ellen (trans.). 2000. *Morkinnskinna. The Earliest Icelandic Chronicle of the Norwegian Kings (1030–1157)*. Ithaca: Cornell University Press.

Andrews, Frances. 2015. *The Other Friars: the Carmelite, Augustinian, Sack and Pied Friars in the Middle Ages*. Woodbridge: Boydell and Brewer.

Anon. 1553. *Baierische Landtsordnung*. Ingolstadt.

Aquinas, Thomas. 1920. *St. Thomas Aquinas: Summa Theologica*. 5 vols. London: Burns, Oates and Washbourne.

Arbusow, Leonid (ed.). 1910. *Akten und Recesse der livländischen Ständetage, Vol. 3 (1494–1535)*. Riga: Deubner.

Archibald, Marion M. 1990. "Pecking and Bending: the Evidence of British Finds." In Kenneth Jonsson and Brita Malmer (eds.), *Sigtuna Papers, Proceedings of the Sigtuna Symposium on Viking-Age Coinage 1–4 June 1989*. Stockholm: Kungl. Vitterhets Historie och Antikvitets Akademien.

Archibald, Marion M. 2011. "The Cuerdale Coins: Testing." In James Graham-Campbell (ed.), *The Cuerdale Hoard and related Viking-Age Silver and Gold from Britain and Ireland in the British Museum*. London: the British Museum.

Archibald, Marion, Lang, J. and Milne, G. 1995. "Four Early Medieval Coin Dies from the London Waterfront." *Numismatic Chronicle*, 155: 163–200.

Armstrong, Lawrin. 2003. *Usury and Public Debt in Early Renaissance Florence: Lorenzo Ridolfi on the Monte Comune*. Toronto: Pontifical Institute of Mediaeval Studies.

Armstrong, Simon. 1998. "Carolingian Coin Hoards and the Impact of the Viking Raids in the Ninth Century." *Numismatic Chronicle*, 158: 131–64.

Arnold, John H. 2013. "Theoderic's Invincible Moustache." *Journal of Late Antiquity*, 6: 152–83.

Arnold, John. 2008. *What is Medieval History?* Cambridge: Polity.

Augustine of Hippo. 2000. *Expositions of the Psalms*, translation and notes by Maria Boulding. New York: New City Press.

Baker, Nigel and Holt, Richard. 2004. *Urban Growth and the Medieval Church: Gloucester and Worcester*. Aldershot: Ashgate.

Baldwin, James W. 1959. *The Medieval Theories of the Just Price: Romanists, Canonists and Theologians in the 12. and 13. Centuries*. Philadelphia: American Philosophical Society.

Banaji, Jairus. 2001. *Agrarian Change in Late Antiquity: Gold, Labour and Aristocratic Dominance*. Oxford: Oxford University Press.

Banaji, Jairus. 2009. "Aristocracies, Peasantries and the Framing of the Early Middle Ages." *Journal of Agrarian Change*, 9(1): 59–91.

Barney, Stephen A., Lewis, W.J., Beach, J.A. and Berghof, Oliver (trans.). 2006. *The Etymologies of Isidore of Seville*. Cambridge: Cambridge University Press.

Bartels, Christopher. 2000. "Zur Bergbaukrise des Spätmittelalters." In C. Bartels and M.A. Denzel (eds.), *Konjunkturen im europäischen Bergbau in vorindustrieller Zeit: Festschrift für Ekkehard Westermann zum 60. Geburtstag*. Stuttgart: Steiner.

Bartlett, Robert. 1993. *The Making of Europe: Conquest, Colonization and Cultural Change, 950–1350*. London: BCA.
Bartlett, Robert. 2004. *The Hanged Man: a Story of Miracle, Memory, and Colonialism in the Middle Ages*. Princeton: Princeton University Press.
Bateson, Donal. 1997. *Coinage in Scotland*. London: Spink.
Beaucage, Benoît (ed.). 1982. *Visites générales des commanderies de l'ordre des hospitaliers dépendantes du grand prieuré de Saint-Gilles (1338)*. Aix-en-Provence: Université de Provence.
Beck, Patrice, Bernardi, Philippe and Feller, Laurent (eds.). 2013. *Rémunérer le travail au Moyen Âge. Pour une histoire sociale du salariat*. Paris: Picard.
Bedos-Rezak, Brigitte M. 2000. "Medieval Identity: A Sign and a Concept." *American Historical Review*, 105(5): 1489–1533.
Belting, Hans. 1994. *Likeness and Presence: a History of the Image before the Era of Art*. Chicago: University of Chicago Press.
Bendall, Simon. 1998. "The Double Striking of Late Byzantine Scyphate Coins." *Celator*, 12(6): 20–3.
Bendall, Simon and Sellwood, David. 1973. "The Method of Striking Scyphate Coins Using Two Obverse Dies In the Light of an Early Thirteenth Century Hoard." *Numismatic Chronicle*, 18: 93–104.
Berend, Nora. 2001. *At the Gate of Christendom: Jews, Muslims and 'pagans' in medieval Hungary c.1000–c.1300*. Cambridge: Cambridge University Press.
Berger, John. 1972. *Ways of Seeing*. London: Penguin and BBC.
Berghaus, Peter. 1965. "Umlauf und Nachprägung des Florentiner Guldens nördlich der Alpen." In *Congresso Internazionale di Numismatica, Roma 11–16 settembre 1961, Vol. 2: Atti*. Rome: Commision Internationale de Numismatique.
Bériou, Nicole and Chiffoleau, Jacques (eds.). 2009. *Economie et religion. L'expérience des ordres mendiants (XIVe–XVe siècle)*. Lyon: Presses universitaires de Lyon.
Bernard of Pavia. [1860] 1956. *Summa Decretalium*, ed. Ernst A. Laspeyres. Graz: Akademische Druck- u. Verlagsanstalt.
Bernardino da Siena. 1956. *Quadragesimale de evangelio aeterno. Sermones XXXII–XLV (De contractibus et usuris)*, in *Bernardini Senensis Opera*, Vol. IV. Firenze: Quaracchi.
Berschin, Walter and Häse, Angelika. 1993. *Vita Sancti Uodalrici: die älteste Lebensbeschreibung des heiligen Ulrich*. Heidelberg: Universitätsverlag C. Winter.
Biel, Gabriel. 1930. *Treatise on the Power and Utility of Moneys*. Philadelphia: University of Pennsylvania Press.
Birch, Debra J. 1998. *Pilgrimage to Rome in the Middle Ages*. Woodbridge: Boydell Press.
Bisson, Thomas N. 1979. *Conservation of Coinage: Monetary Exploitation and its Restraint in France, Catalonia and Aragon (c. AD 1000–1225)*. Oxford: Clarendon Press.
Blackburn, Mark A.S. 1989. "The Ashdon (Essex) Hoard and the Currency of the Southern Danelaw in the Late Ninth Century." *British Numismatic Journal* 59: 13–38.
Blackburn, Mark. 1993. "Coin Circulation in Germany during the Early Middle Ages: the Evidence of Single-Finds." In Bernd Kluge (ed.), *Fernhandel and Geldwirtschaft: Beiträge zum deutschen Münzwesen in sächsischer und salischer Zeit. Ergebnisse des Dannenberg-Kolloquiums 1990*. Sigmaringen: Thorbecke.
Blackburn, Mark. 1994. "Coinage and Currency." In Edmund King (ed.), *The Anarchy of King Stephen's Reign*. Oxford: Clarendon Press.

Blackburn, Mark. 1995. "Money and Coinage." In Rosamond McKitterick (ed.), *The New Cambridge Medieval History, Vol. II c.700–c.900*. Cambridge: Cambridge University Press.
Blackburn, Mark. 2003. "'Productive' Sites and the Pattern of Coin Loss in England (600–1180)." In Tim Pestell and Katharina Ulmschneider (eds.), *Markets in Early Medieval Europe: Trading and 'Productive' Sites*. Macclesfield: Windgather Press.
Blackburn, Mark. 2005a. "Coin Finds as Primary Historical Evidence for Medieval Europe." In Shinichi Sakuraki (ed.), *Kaheinimiru Dynamism: Ou Chu Nichi Hikakuno Shitenkara (Dynamism in Coinage: Europe, China and Japan, Comparative Viewpoints), Dai 12 kai Shutsudosenkakenkyukai Houkokuyoushi in Fukuoka 2005 (Proceedings of the 12th Conference of the Coin Finds Research Group held in Fukuoka 2005)*. Fukuoka: Coin Finds Research Group.
Blackburn, Mark. 2005b. "Money and coinage." In Paul Fouracre (ed.), *The New Cambridge Medieval History, Vol. I c.500–c.700*. Cambridge: Cambridge University Press.
Blackburn, Mark. 2007a. "The Coin-finds." In Dagfinn Skre (ed.), *Means of Exchange: Dealing with Silver in the Viking Age*. Aarhus: Aarhus University Press.
Blackburn, Mark. 2007b. "Gold in England during the 'Age of Silver' (Eighth–Eleventh Centuries)." In James Graham-Campbell and Gareth Williams (eds.), *Silver Economy in the Viking Age*. Walnut Creek: Left Coast Press.
Blanchet, Jules-Adrien and Dieudonné, Adolf. 1916. *Manuel de numismatique Française, Vol. 2: Monnaies royales Françaises depuis Hugues Capet jusqu'a la Révolution*. Paris: Picard.
Bloch, Marc. 1939. "Économie-nature ou économie-argent: un pseudo-dilemme." *Annales d'histoire sociale*, 1(1): 7–16.
Bloch, Maurice and Parry, Jonathan. 1989. "Introduction: money and the morality of exchange." In Jonathan Parry and Maurice Bloch (eds.), *Money and the Morality of Exchange*. Cambridge: Cambridge University Press.
Blockmans, Frans and Blockmans, Wim P. 1979. "Devaluation, Coinage and Seignorage under Louis de Nevers and Louis de Male, Counts of Flanders, 1330–84." In N.J. Mayhew (ed.), *Coinage in the Low Countries (880–1500): the Third Oxford Symposium on Coinage and Monetary History*. Oxford: Archaeopress.
Bode, W.J.L. 1847. *Das ältere Münzwesen der Staaten und Städte Niedersachsens*. Braunschweig: Viehweg and Sohn.
Bogaert, Raymond. 1973. "Changeurs et banquiers chez les Pères de l'Eglise." *Ancient Society*, 4: 239–70.
Bogucki, Mateusz. 2011. "The Use of Money in the Slavic Lands from the Ninth to the Eleventh Century: the Archaeological/Numismatic Evidence." In James A. Graham-Campbell, Søren Michael Sindbaek, and Gareth Williams (eds.), *Silver economies, monetisation and society in Scandinavia, AD 800–1100*. Aarhus: Aarhus University Press.
Bolton, James. 2004. "What is Money? What is a Money Economy? When did a Money Economy Emerge in Medieval England?" In Diana Wood (ed.), *Medieval Money Matters*. Oxford: Oxbow.
Bolton, J.L. 2012. *Money in the Medieval English Economy: 973–1489*. Manchester: Manchester University Press.
Bonnassie, Pierre. 1975–6. *La Catalogne du milieu du Xe à la fin du XIe siècle. Croissance et mutations d'une société*. Toulouse: Association des publications de l'Université de Toulouse-Le Mirail.

Bonnassie, Pierre. 1978. "La monnaie et les échanges en Auvergne et en Rouergue aux IXe-XIe siècles, d'après les sources hagiographiques." *Annales du Midi*, 90: 275–89 [reprinted in Bonnassie 2001: 199–213].
Bonnassie, Pierre. 1990. *La Catalogne au tournant de l'an Mil*. Paris: Albin Michel.
Bonnassie, Pierre. 2001. *Les sociétés de l'an mil. Un monde entre deux âges*. Bruxelles: De Boeck Université.
Boretius, Alfred (ed.). 1868. "Liber legis Langobardorum Papiensis." In Georg Heinrich Pertz (ed.), *Monumenta Germaniae Historica: Legum tomus III*. Hanover: Hahn.
Bosl, Karl and Weis, Eberhard. 1976. *Die Gesellschaft in Deutschland I: Von der fränkischen Zeit bis 1848*. Munich: Martin Lurz.
Bote, H. 1880. "Von der pagemunte." In *Chroniken der niedersächsischen Städte: Braunschweig, Vol. 2*. Leipzig: S. Hirzel.
Bougard, François. 2010. "Le crédit dans l'Occident du haut Moyen Âge: documentation et pratique." In Régine Le Jan, Laurent Feller and Jean-Pierre Devroey (eds.), Les élites et la richesse au Haut Moyen Âge. Turnhout: Brepols.
Bourin, Monique. 2009. "Propos de conclusion: conversions, commutations et raisonnement économique." In Laurent Feller (ed), *Calculs et rationalités dans la seigneurie médiévale: les conversions de redevances entre XIe et XVe siècles*. Paris: Publications de la Sorbonne.
Brate, Erik and Wessén, Elias. 1924–36. *Södermanlands runinskrifter*. 4 vols. Stockholm: Wahlström and Widstrand.
Braudel, Fernand. 1979. *Civilisation matérielle, économie et capitalisme, XVe-XVIIIe siècle, Vol. 2: Les jeux de l'échange*. Paris: Armand Colin.
Brauner, Reuven. 2013. *Pirqe Avot (The Sayings of the Fathers)*. Ranaana: Reuven Brauner.
Breatnach, Liam. 2014. "Forms of Payment in the Early Irish Law Tracts." *Cambrian Medieval Celtic Studies*, 68: 1–20.
Bredero, Adriaan H. 1971. "Cluny et Cîteaux au XIIème siècle: les origines de la controverse." *Studi Medievali*, 12: 135–75.
Bresslau, Harry (ed.). 1915. *Die Werke Wipos*. Monumenta Germaniae Historica: Scriptores rerum Germanicarum in usum scholarum ex Monumentis Germaniae Historicis recusi 61. Hanover: Hahn.
Brett, Martin. 2012. "The *De Corpore et Sanguine Domini* of Ernulph of Canterbury." In Uta-Renate Blumenthal, Anders Winroth and Peter Landau (eds.), *Canon Law, Religion, and Politics: Liber Amicorum Robert Somerville*. Washington DC: Catholic University of America Press.
Briggs, Chris. 2009. *Credit and Village Society in Fourteenth-Century England*. Oxford: Oxford University Press.
Brilioth, Yngve. 1915. *Den påfliga beskattningen af Sverige intil den stora schismen*. Uppsala: Appelberg.
Britnell, Richard H. 1995. "Commercialisation and Economic Development in England, 1000–1300." In Richard H. Britnell, and Bruce M.S. Campbell (eds.), *A Commercialising Economy. England 1086 to c.1300*. Manchester: Manchester University Press.
Britnell, Richard. 2004. *Britain and Ireland 1050–1530. Economy and Society*. Oxford: Oxford University Press.
Brittain Bouchard, Constance. 1991. *Holy Entrepreneurs: Cistercians, Knights, and Economic Exchange in Twelfth-Century Burgundy*. Ithaca-London: Cornell University Press.

Broadberry, Stephen, Campbell, Bruce M. S., Klein, Alexander, Overton, Mark and Van Leeuwen, Baas 2015. *British Economic Growth 1270–1870*. Cambridge: Cambridge University Press.

Brooks, N.P. and Kelly, S.E. (eds.). 2013. *Charters of Christ Church Canterbury*. 2 vols. Anglo-Saxon Charters 17–18. Oxford: Oxford University Press.

Browe, Peter. 1933. *Die Verehrung der Eucharistie im Mittelalter*. Munich: Herder.

Browe, Peter. 1938. *Die Eucharistischen Wunder des Mittelalters*. Breslau: Verlag Mueller & Seiffert.

Brown, Peter. 2012. *Through the Eye of a Needle: Wealth, the Fall of Rome, and the Making of Christianity in the West, 350–550 AD*. Princeton: Princeton University Press.

Brown, Peter. 2015. *The Ransom of the Soul: Afterlife and Wealth in Early Western Christianity*. Cambridge: Harvard University Press.

Bruand, Olivier. 2010. "La gestion du patrimoine des élites en Autunois. Le prieuré de Perrecy et ses obligés (fin IXe-Xe siècle)." In J.-P. Devroey, L. Feller and R. Le Jan (eds.), *Les élites et la richesse au haut Moyen Âge (Actes du colloque tenu à Bruxelles les 13–15 mars 2008)*. Turnhout: Brepols.

Brubaker, Leslie. 2013. "Looking at the Byzantine Family." In Leslie Brubaker and Shaun Tougher (eds.), *Approaches to the Byzantine Family*. London: Routledge.

Brubaker, Leslie and Haldon, John. 2011. *Byzantium in the Iconoclast Era, 680–850: a History*. Cambridge: Cambridge University Press.

Bruce-Mitford, Rupert Leo Scott. 1968. *The Sutton Hoo Ship Burial: a Handbook*. London: Trustees of the British Museum.

Buc, Philippe. 2001. *The Dangers of Ritual: between Early Medieval Texts and Social Scientific Theory*. Princeton: Princeton University Press.

Bynum, Carolyn W. 2007. *Wonderful Blood: Theology and Practice in Late Medieval Northern Germany and Beyond*. Philadelphia: University of Pennsylvania Press.

Capitani, Ovidio. 1990. *Tradizione ed interpretazione: dialettiche ecclesiologiche del sec. XI*. Roma: Jouvence.

Carlà, Filippo. 2010. "The End of Roman Gold Coinage and the Disintegration of a Monetary Area." *Annali dell'Istituto italiano di numismatica*, 56: 45–114.

Carver, Martin O.H. 1998. *Sutton Hoo: Burial Ground of Kings*. London: British Museum Press.

Castelin, Karel. 1973. *Grossus Pragensis: Der Prager Groschen und seine Teilstücke, 1300–1547*. Braunschweig: Klinkhardt and Biermann.

Castellanos, Santiago M. 2012. "Creating New Constantines at the End of the Sixth Century." *Historical Research*, 85: 556–75.

Ceccarelli, Giovanni. 2001. "Risky Business. Theological and Canonical Thought on Insurance from the Thirteenth to the Seventeenth Centuries." *The Journal of Medieval and Early Modern Studies*, 31(3): 607–58.

Ceccarelli, Giovanni. 2003. *Il gioco e il peccato. Economia e rischio nel tardo Medioevo*. Bologna: Il Mulino.

Ceccarelli, Giovanni. 2007. "Notai, confessori e usurai: concezioni del credito a confronto (secc. XIII-XIV)." *Quaderni/Cahiers del Centro Studi sui Lombardi, sul credito e sulla banca*, 1: 113–53.

Challis, Christopher E. 1992. *A New History of the Royal Mint*. Cambridge: Cambridge University Press.

Chevalier, Bernard. 1973. "Les changeurs en France dans la première moitié du XIVe siècle." In *Économie et sociétés au moyen âge. Mélanges offerts à Edouard Perroy*. Paris: Publications de la Sorbonne.

Chilosi, David and Volckart, O. 2011. "Money, States and Empire: Financial Integration and Institutional Change in Central Europe, 1400–1520." *Journal of Economic History*, 71: 762–91.

Cipolla, C.M. 1963. "The Italian and Iberian Peninsulas." In M.M. Postan, E.E. Rich and E. Miller (eds.), *The Cambridge Economic History of Europe, vol. III. Economic Organization and Policies in the Middle Ages*. Cambridge: Cambridge University Press.

Clark, Gregory. 2005. "The Condition of the Working Class in England, 1209–2004." *Journal of Political Economy*, 113: 1307–40.

Cohn, Samuel Cline. 2004. *Popular Protest in Late-Medieval Europe*. Manchester: Manchester University Press.

Coleman, Janet. 1987. "The Two Jurisdictions: Theological and Legal Justifications of Church Property in the Thirteenth Century." *Studies in Church History*, 24: 75–110.

Colgan, Edward. 2003. *For Want of Good Money: the Story of Ireland's Coinage*. Bray: Wordwell.

Cook, Barrie J. 1999. "Foreign Coins in Medieval England." In Lucia Travaini (ed.), *Local Coins, Foreign Coins: Italy and Europe 11th–15th Centuries*. Milan: Società Numismatica Italiana.

Cook, Barrie J. 2006. "*En Monnaie Aiant Cours*: the Monetary System of the Angevin Empire." In Barrie Cook and Gareth Williams (eds.), *Coinage and History in the North Sea World c.500–1250. Essays in Honour of Marion Archibald*. Leiden: Brill.

Cornell, Vincent J. 2006. "In the Shadow of Deuteronomy: Approaches to Interest and Usury in Judaism and Christianity." In Abdulkader Thomas (ed.), *Interest in Islamic Economics: Understanding Riba*. London: Routledge.

*Corpus iuris civilis*. 1870–1895. Edited by Theodor Mommsen *et al*. Berlin: Weidmann.

Coulton, C.G. 1925. *The Medieval Village*. Cambridge: Cambridge University Press.

Coupland, Simon. 1990. "Money and Coinage under Louis the Pious." *Francia*, 17(1): 23–54.

Coupland, Simon. 2010. "Boom and Bust at Ninth-Century Dorestad." In Annemarieke Willemsen and Hanneke Kik (eds.), *Dorestad in an International Framework: New Research on Centres of Trade and Coinage in Carolingian Times*. Turnhout: Brepols.

Coupland, Simon. 2014. "The Use of Coin in the Carolingian Empire in the Ninth Century." In Naismith, Allen and Screen 2014.

Courtnay, W.J. 1972–3. "Token Coinage in the Administration of Poor Relief during the Later Middle Ages." *Journal of Interdisciplinary History*, 3: 175–95.

Crosby, Alfred W. 1997. *The Measure of Reality: Quantification of Western Society, 1250–1600*. Cambridge: Cambridge University Press.

Crusafont, Miquel, Balaguer, Anna M., and Grierson, Philip. 2013. *Medieval European Coinage 6: the Iberian Peninsula*. Cambridge: Cambridge University Press.

Curta, Florin and Gândilă, Andrei. 2012. "Hoards and Hoarding Patterns in the Early Byzantien Balkans." *Dumbarton Oaks Papers*, 65–6: 45–111.

Dales, Douglas. 2012. *Alcuin: His Life and Legacy*. Cambridge: James Clarke & Co.

Darley, Rebecca R. 2015. "Self, Other and the Use and Appropriation of Late Roman Coins in South India and Sri Lanka (4th–7th Centuries AD)." In Himanshu Prabha Ray (ed.), *Negotiating Cultural Identity: Landscapes in Early Medieval South Asian History*. London and New Delhi: Routledge.

Davies, Wendy. 2002. "Sale, Price and Valuation in Galicia and Castile-León in the Tenth Century." *Early Medieval Europe*, 11(2): 149–74.

Davies, Wendy. 2007. *Acts of Giving: Individual, Community and Church in Tenth-Century Christian Spain*. Oxford: Oxford University Press.

Davies, Wendy. 2010. "Notions of Wealth in the Charters of Ninth- and Tenth-Century Christian Iberia." In Régine Le Jan, Laurent Feller and Jean-Pierre Devroey (ed.), *Les élites et la richesse au haut Moyen Âge*. Turnhout: Brepols.

Davis, Charles T. 1960. "An Early Florentine Political Theorist: Fra Remigio de'Girolami." *Proceedings of the American Philosophical Society*, 104(6): 662–76.

Day, Rebecca R. 2012. "A Tale of 'Four' Hoards (or Unpicking Akki Alur)." *Journal of the Oriental Numismatic Society*, 211: 5–14.

Day, William R., Matzke, Michael and Saccocci, Andrea. 2016. *Medieval European Coinage, with a Catalogue of the Coins in the Fitzwilliam Museum, Cambridge, vol. 12, Italy (i) (Northern Italy)*. Cambridge: Cambridge University Press.

De Roover, Raymond. 1971. *La pensée économique des Scolastiques*. Montréal-Paris: Institut d'Etudes Médiévales.

*Decretales Gregorii IX*. [1879] 1959. *Corpus Iuris Canonici* ed. Aemilius Friedberg et al., vol. II. Graz: Akademische Druck- u. Verlagsanstalt.

*Decretum Gratiani*. [1879] 1959. *Corpus Iuris Canonici* ed. Aemilius Friedberg et al., vol. I. Graz: Akademische Druck- u. Verlagsanstalt.

Della Valle, Pietro. 1843. *Viaggi di Pietro Della Valle il pellegrino descritti da lui medesimo in 54 lettere familiari all'erudito suo amico Mario Schipano*. 2 vols. Turin: G. Gancia.

Dennis, Andrew, Foote, Peter and Perkins, Richard (trans.). 1980–2006. *Laws of Early Iceland: Grágás, the Codex Regius of Grágás, with Material from Other Manuscripts*. 2 vols. Winnipeg: University of Manitoba Press.

Dennis, George. T. 1984. *Maurice's Strategikon: Handbook of Byzantine Military Strategy*. Philadelphia: University of Pennsylvania Press.

Desan, Christine. 2014. *Making Money: Coin, Currency, and the Coming of Capitalism*. Oxford: Oxford University Press.

Despy, Georges. 1968. "Villes et campagnes aux IXe et Xe siècles: l'exemple des pays mosans." *Revue du Nord*, 50: 145–68.

Devroey, Jean-Pierre. 1993a. "*Ad utilitatem monasterii*. Mobiles et préoccupations de gestion dans l'économie monastique du monde franc." In Alain Dierkens, Daniel Misonne, and Jean-Marie Sansterre (eds.), *Le monachisme à Byzance et en Occident du VIIIe au Xe siècle. Aspects internes et relations avec la société* (*Revue Bénédictine* 103(1–2)). Namur: Abbaye de Maredsous.

Devroey, Jean-Pierre. 1993b. "Courants et réseaux d'échange dans l'économie franque entre Loire et Rhin." *Settimane di studio del centro italiano di studi sull'alto medioevo*, 40: 327–93.

Devroey, Jean-Pierre. 2003. *Economie rurale et société dans l'Europe franque (VIe-IXe siècles)*. Paris: Belin.

Dewing, H.B. (ed. and trans.). 1914–40. *Procopius*. 7 vols. Cambridge: Harvard University Press.

Dini, Bruno. 1999. *I mercanti-banchieri e la Sede apostolica (XIII—prima metà del XIV secolo)*, in *Gli spazi economici della Chiesa nell'Occidente mediterraneo*. Pistoia: Centro italiano di studi di storia e d'arte.

Dinkova-Bruun, Greti. 2015. "Nummus falsus: the Perception of Counterfeit Money in the Eleventh and Early Twelfth Century." In Giles E.M. Gasper and

S.H. Gullbekk (eds.), *Money and the Church in Medieval Europe, 1000–1200: Practice, Morality and Thought*. Farnham: Ashgate.

Douglas, John M. 1992. *The Armenians*. New York: J.J. Winthrop Corporation.

Duby, Georges. 1961. "La seigneurie et l'économie paysanne. Alpes du sud, 1338." *Etudes Rurales*, 2: 5–36 [reprinted in Duby 1973b: 167–201].

Duby, Georges. 1962. *L'économie rurale et la vie des campagnes dans l'Occident medieval*. Paris: Aubier Montaigne.

Duby, Georges. 1973a. *Guerriers et paysans. VIIIe-XIIe siècle. Premier essor de l'économie européenne*. Paris: Gallimard.

Duby, Georges. 1973b. *Hommes et structures du Moyen Âge*. Paris: Mouton.

Dumas, Françoise. 1991. "La monnaie au Xe siècle." *Settimane di studio del Centro italiano di studi sull'alto medioevo*, 38: 565–609.

Dümmler, Ernst (ed.). 1925. "Epistolae variorum inde a saeculo nono medio usque ad mortem Karoli II. (Calvi) imperatoris collectae." In *Monumenta Germaniae Historica: Epistolarum tomus VI: Epistolae karolini aevi tomus IV*. Berlin: Weidmann.

Dyer, Christopher. 1997. "Peasants and Coins: the Uses of Money in the Middle Ages." *British Numismatic Journal*, 67: 31–47.

Einaudi, Luigi. 1936. "Teoria della moneta immaginaria nel tempo di Carlomagno alla rivoluzione francese." *Rivista di storia economica*, 1: 1–36.

Ellard, Gerald. 1943. "Bread in the Form of a Penny." *Theological Studies*, 4: 319–46.

Emmerig, Hubert. 2006. "Der Münzbetrieb in Mittelalter und früher Neuzeit: Personal, Ausrüstung, Tätigkeiten." *Vorträge zur Geldgeschichte*, 3: 5–23.

Engel, Arthur and Serrure, Raymond. 1891–1905. *Traité de numismatique du moyen âge*. 2 vols. Paris: Leroux.

Ennen, Edith. 1972/87. *Die europäische Stadt des Mittelalters*. Göttingen: Vandenhoeck & Ruprecht.

Epstein, Stephen R. 1994. "Regional Fairs, Institutional Innovation, and Economic Growth in Late Medieval Europe." *Economic History Review*, 47: 459–82.

Ermisch, Hubert. 1887. *Das sächsische Bergrecht des Mittelalters*. Leipzig: Gieseke & Devrient.

Evans, Allan. 1936. *Francesco Balducci Pegolotti: La Pratica della Mercatura*. Cambridge: Medieval Academy of America.

Evans, David H. and Jarrett, Michael G. 1987. "The Deserted Village of West Whelpington, Northumberland: Third Report Part One." *Archaeologia Aeliana*, 5th series, 15: 254–5.

Farber, Lianna. 2006. *An Anatomy of Trade in Medieval Writing: Value, Consent, and Community*. Ithaca: Cornell University Press.

Fedele, P. 1934. "Il giubileo del 1300." *Gli Anni Santi*. Turin: SEI.

Feger, O. (ed.). 1956. *Die Chronik des Klosters Petershausen*. Sigmaringen: Thorbecke.

Feller, Laurent. 1998a. *Les Abruzzes médiévales: territoire, économie et société en Italie centrale du IXe au XIIe siècle*. Rome: École française de Rome.

Feller, Laurent. 1998b. "Les conditions de la circulation monétaire dans les régions périphériques du royaume d'Italie (Sabine et Abruzzes, IXe-XIIe s.)." In *L'argent au Moyen Age: idéologie, finances, fiscalité, monnaie* (Actes du XXVIIe congrès de la Société des Médiévistes de l'Enseignement Supérieur, Clermont-Ferrand, 30 mai–1er juin, 1997). Paris: Publications de la Sorbonne.

Feller, Laurent. 2009. "Les conversions de redevances. Pour une problématique des revenus seigneuriaux." In Laurent Feller (ed.), *Calculs et rationalités dans la seigneurie médiévale: les conversions de redevances entre XIe et XVe siècles*. Paris: Publications de la Sorbonne.

Feller, Laurent. 2011. *Sur la formation des prix dans l'économie du haut Moyen Âge*, in *Annales. Histoire, Sciences Sociales*, 66, 3, p. 627–61.

Feller, Laurent. 2013. "Transformation des objets et valeur des choses. L'exemple de la Vita Meinwerici." In L. Feller and A. Rodriguez (eds.), *Objets sous contrainte. Circulation des richesses et valeur des choses au Moyen Âge*. Paris: Publications de la Sorbonne.

Feller, Laurent. 2014. "Measuring the Value of Things in the Middle Ages." *Economic Sociology: the European Electronic Newsletter*, 15(3): 30–40.

Feller, Laurent. 2016. "Mesurer la valeur des choses au haut Moyen Âge: les transactions dans la vie de Géraud d'Aurillac." In Alain Dierkens, Nicolas Schroeder and Alexis Wilkin (eds.), *Mélanges Devroey*. Paris: Publications de la Sorbonne (forthcoming).

Feller, Laurent. 2018a. "Autour d'une nouvelle de Boccace : l'économie immorale." In Marie Dejoux and Diane Chamboduc de Saint-Pulgent (eds.), *La fabrique des sociétés médiévales méditerranéennes. Le Moyen Âge de François Menant*. Paris: Éditions Rue d'Ulm.

Feller, Laurent. 2018b. "Travail, salaire et pauvreté au Moyen Âge." In Ross Balzaretti, Julia Barrow and Patricia Skinner (eds.), *Italy and Early Medieval Europe: Papers for Chris Wickham*.

Feller, Laurent, Gramain, Agnès and Weber, Florence. 2005. *La fortune de Karol: marché de la terre et liens personnels dans les Abruzzes au haut Moyen Âge*. Rome: École française de Rome.

Feveile, Claus. 2008. "Series X and Coin Circulation in Ribe." In Tony Abramson (ed.), *Studies in Early Medieval Coinage 1: Two Decades of Discovery*. Woodbridge: Boydell Press.

Finlay, Alison and Faulkes, Anthony (trans.). 2011. *Snorri Sturluson: Heimskringla. Volume I: the Beginnings to Óláfr Tryggvason*. London: Viking Society for Northern Research.

Finucane, Ronald C. 1977. *Miracles and Pilgrims: Popular Beliefs in Medieval England*. London: Dent.

Flandreau, Mark. 2002. "'Water Seeks Level': Modelling Bimetallic Exchange Rates and the Bimetallic Band." *Journal of Money, Credit and Banking*, 34: 491–519.

Flori, Jean. 2006. *Richard the Lionheart: King and Knight*. Edinburgh: Edinburgh University Press.

Fossier, Robert. 1981. "Les tendances de l'économie: stagnation ou croissance?" *Settimane di studio del centro italiano di studi sull'alto medioevo*, 27: 261–74 [reprinted in Fossier 1992: 341–50].

Fossier, Robert. 1992. *Hommes et villages d'Occident au Moyen Âge*. Paris: Publications de la Sorbonne.

Füeg, Franz. 2007. *Corpus of the Nomismata from Anastasius II to John I in Constantinople, 713–979*, vol. 1. London and Lancaster: Classical Numismatic Group.

Furió, Antonì and Garcia Marsilla, Juan Vicente. 2014. "Espèces et créances en circulation: monnaie métallique et crédit comme monnaie dans le royaume de Valence vers 1300." In Monique Bourin, François Menant et Lluis To Figueras (eds.), *Dynamiques du monde rural dans la conjoncture de 1300*. Rome: École française de Rome.

Gaettens, Richard. [1957] 1982. *Geschichte der Inflationen vom Altertum bis zur Gegenwart*. Munich: Battenberg.

Galster, Georg. 1972. *Unionstidens udmøntninger. Danmark og Norge 1397–1540. Sverige 1363–1521*. Copenhagen: Dansk numismatisk forening.

Gamberini, Andrea *et al*. 2011. *The Languages of Political Society*. Roma: Viella.

Ganz, David. 2010. "Giving to God in the Mass." In Wendy Davies and Paul Foracre (eds.), *The Languages of Gift in the Early Middle Ages*. Cambridge: Cambridge University Press.

Garcia Marsilla, J.V. 2013. "Avec les vêtements des autres. Le marché du textile d'occasion dans la Valence médiévale." In Laurent Feller and Ana Rodriguez (eds.), *Objets sous contrainte. Circulation des richesses et valeur des choses au Moyen Âge*. Paris: Publications de la Sorbonne.

Garipzanov, Ildar. 2016. "Regensburg, Wandalgarius and the *novi denarii*: Charlemagne's Monetary Reform Revisited." *Early Medieval Europe*, 24: 58–73.

Gasper, Giles E.M. 2015. "Contemplating Wealth in Monastic Writing *c*. 1060–*c*. 1160." In Giles E.M. Gasper and S.H. Gullbekk (eds.), *Money and the Church in Medieval Europe, 1000–1200: Practice, Morality and Thought*. Farnham: Ashgate.

Gasper, Giles E.M. and Gullbekk, Svein H. 2012. "Money and its Use in the Thought and Experience of Anselm, Archbishop of Canterbury (1093–1109)." *Journal of Medieval History*, 38: 155–82.

Gautier-Dalché, Jean. 1969. "L'histoire monétaire de l'Espagne septentrionale du IXe siècle au XIIe siècle. Quelques réflexions sur divers problèmes." *Anuario de Estudios Medievales*, 6: 43–95. Repr. 1982 in *Economie et Société dans les pays de la Couronne de Castille*. London: Variorum.

Geary, Patrick J. 1990. *Furta Sacra: Thefts of Relics in the Central Middle Ages*. Princeton: Princeton University Press.

Geisst, Charles R. 2013. *Beggar Thy Neighbor: A History of Usury and Debt*. Philadelphia: University of Pennsylvania Press.

Georganteli, Eurydice. 2012. "Transposed Images: Currencies and Legitimacy in the Late Medieval Eastern Mediterranean." In Jonathan Harris, Catherine J. Holmes and Eugenia Russell (ed.), *Byzantines, Latins, and Turks in the Eastern Mediterranean World after 1150*. Oxford: Oxford University Press.

Geva, Benjamin. 2011. *The Payment Order of Antiquity and the Middle Ages: a Legal History*. Oxford: Hart Publications.

Giard, John Baptiste. 1967. "Le Florin d'or au Baptiste et ses imitations en France au XIVe siècle." *Bibliotheque de l'Ecole des Chartes*, 125: 94–141.

Gieysztor, Aleksander. 1959. *La porte de bronze à Gniezno: document de l'histoire de la Pologne au XIIe siècle*. Rome: Angelo Signorelli.

Gilchrist, John. 1972. "Eleventh and Early Twelfth-Century Collections and the Economic Policy of Gregory VII." *Studi Gregoriani*, 9: 377–417.

Gioanni, Stéphane. 2015. "Réceptions et représentations du De Gloria de Cicéron de l'Antiquité au premier humanism." In Jean-Philippe Genet (ed.), *La légitimité implicite (actes des conférences organisées à Rome en 2010 et 2011)*. Rome: École française de Rome.

Girard, Albert. 1940. "Un phénomène économique: la guerre monétaire, XIVe-XVe siècles." *Annales d'histoire sociale*, 2: 207–18.

Göbl, Robert. 1971. *Sasanian Numismatics*. Braunschweig: Klinkhardt and Biermann.

Goldberg, Jessica. 2012. *Trade and Institutions in the Medieval Mediterranean: the Geniza Merchants and their Business World*. Cambridge: Cambridge University Press.

Goudsmit, Simon. 2004. *The Limits of Money: Three Perceptions of Our Most Comprehensive Value System*. Delft: Eburon.
Greenblatt, Stephen. 2011. *The Swerve: How the Renaissance Began*. London: The Bodley Head.
Grierson, Philip. 1957. "The Coin List of Pegolotti." In *Studia in onore di Armando Sapori*. Milan: Istituto Editoriale Cisalpino. (reprinted in Grierson 1979: ch. XI).
Grierson, Philip. 1959. "Commerce in the Dark Ages: a Critique of the Evidence." *Transactions of the Royal Historical Society*, 5th series, 9: 123–40.
Grierson, Philip. 1970. "The Purpose of the Sutton Hoo Coins." *Antiquity*, 44: 14–18.
Grierson, Philip. 1975. *Numismatics*. Oxford: Oxford University Press.
Grierson, Philip. 1976. *Monnaies du moyen âge*. Fribourg: Office du livre.
Grierson, Philip. 1979. *Later Medieval Numismatics (11th–16th Centuries)*. London: Variorum.
Grierson, Philip. 1982. *Byzantine Coins*. Berkeley and Los Angeles: University of California Press.
Grierson, Philip. 1991. *The Coins of Medieval Europe*. London: Seaby.
Grierson, Philip. 1999. *Byzantine Coinage*. Washington DC: Dumbarton Oaks.
Grierson, Philip and Blackburn, Mark. 1986. *Medieval European Coinage, with a Catalogue of the Coins in the Fitzwilliam Museum, Cambridge. 1: the Early Middle Ages (5th–10th Centuries)*. Cambridge: Cambridge University Press.
Grierson, Philip and Travaini, Lucia. 1998. *Medieval European Coinage, with a Catalogue of the Coins in the Fitzwilliam Museum, Cambridge, vol. 14, Italy (iii) (South Italy, Sicily, Sardinia)*. Cambridge: Cambridge University Press.
Grinder-Hansen, Keld. 2000. *Kongemagtens krise. Det danske møntvæsen 1241–1340*. Copenhagen: Museum Tusculanums Forlag.
Guest, Peter. 2012. "The Production, Supply and Use of Late Roman and Early Byzantine Copper Coinage in the Eastern Empire." *Numismatic Chronicle*, 172: 105–31.
Gullbekk, Svein H. 1991. "Some Aspects of Coin Import to Norway and Coin Circulation in the Late Viking-Age." *Nordisk Numismatisk Årsskrift* 1991: 63–88.
Gullbekk, Svein H. 2003. *Pengevesenets fremvekst og fall i Norge i middelalderen*. Dr. thesis. Oslo: Unipub.
Gullbekk, Svein H. 2009. *Pengevesenets fremvekst og fall i Norge i middelalderen*. Copenhagen: Museum Tusculanum Press.
Gullbekk, Svein H. 2011. "Monetisation in Medieval Scandinavia." In Nicholas Holmes (ed.), *Proceedings of the XIVth International Numismatic Congress, Part 2*. Glasgow: International Numismatic Council.
Gullbekk, Svein H. 2014. "Vestfold: a Monetary Perspective on the Viking Age." In Naismith, Allen and Screen.
Gullbekk, S.H., Kilger, C.K., Roland, H. and Kristoffersen, S. (eds.). (Forthcoming) *The Use of Money in Religious and Devotional Contexts: Coin Finds in Churches in Scandinavia, Iceland and the Alpine Region*.
Hägermann, Dieter. 1999/2003. "Regalien, -politik, -recht." In *Lexikon des Mittelalters, Vol. VII: Planudes-Stadt (Rus')*. Munich: dtv.
Hall, Mark A. 2016. "'Pennies from Heaven': Money in Ritual in Medieval Europe." In Colin Haselgrove and Stefan Krmnicek (eds.), *The Archaeology of Money: Proceedings of the Workshop 'Archaeology of Money', University of Tübingen, October 2013*. Leicester: Leicester Archaeology Monographs.
Hamp, K. 1889. "Einharti epistolae." In Ernst Dümmler (ed.), *Monumenta Germaniae Historica: Epistolarum tomus V; Epistolae Karolini Aevi tomus III*. Berlin: Weidmann.

Hardt, Matthias. 2016. "The Importance of the Slave Trade for the Slavic Princes of the Early and High Middle Ages." In Geneviève Bührer-Thierry, Régine Le Jan and Vito Loré (eds.), *Acquérir, prélever, contrôler. Les ressources en compétition (400–1100)*. Turnhout: Brepols (forthcoming).

Haselgrove, Colin and Webley, Leo. 2016. "Lost Purses and Loose Change? Coin Deposition on Settlements in Iron Age Europe." In Colin Haselgrove and Stefan Krmnicek (eds.), *The Archaeology of Money: Proceedings of the Workshop 'Archaeology of Money', University of Tübingen, October 2013*. Leicester: Leicester Archaeology Monographs.

Hauberg, Peter. 1884. "Danmarks Mytnvæsen og Mynter i Tidsrummet 1241–1377." *Aarbøger for Nordisk Oldkyndighed og Historie* 1884: 217–374.

Hauberg, Peter. 1900. *Myntforhold og Udmyntninger i Danmark indtil 1146*. Copenhagen: Bianco Lunos Bogtrykkeri.

Heidemann, Stefan. 1998. "The Merger of Two Currency Zones in Early Islam: the Byzantine and Sasanian Impact on the Circulation in Former Byzantine Syria and Northern Mesopotamia." *Iran*, 36: 95–112.

Hendy, Michael. 1985. *Studies in the Byzantine Monetary Economy, c. 300–1450*. Cambridge: Cambridge University Press.

Henry of Segusio. 1574. *Summa aurea*. Venezia: Jacobus Vitalis.

Herz, M. 1958. *Sacrum Commercium. Eine begriffgeschichtliche Studie zur Theologie der Römischen Liturgiesprache*. Munich: K. Zink.

Hill, Brian E. 2013. "Charles the Bald's Edict of Pîtres: a Translation and Commentary." MA thesis, University of Minnesota: Minneapolis.

Hill, P. (ed.). 1997. *Whithorn and St. Ninian: the Excavations of a Monastic Town, 1984–91*. Stroud: Sutton.

Hillebrand, Werner. 1967. "Von den Anfängen des Erzbergbaus am Rammelsberg bei Goslar." *Niedersächsisches Jahrbuch für Landesgeschichte*, 39: 103–14.

Hillenbrand, Carole. 1990. *A Muslim Principality in Crusader Times: the Early Artuqid State*. Istanbul: Nederlands Historisch-Archaeologisch Instituut.

Hilsdale, Cecily J. 2005. "Constructing a Byzantine 'Augusta': a Greek Book for a French Bride." *The Art Bulletin*, 87: 458–83.

Hilton, Rodney H. 1992. *English and French Towns in Feudal Society*. Cambridge: Cambridge University Press.

Hokenson, Jan Walsh and Munson, Marcella. 2014. *The Bilingual Text: History and Theory of Literary Self-Translation*. London: Routledge.

Hollander, Robert and Hollander, Jean (trans.). 2000. *Dante Alighieri: Inferno*. New York: Doubleday.

Holmes, Catherine and Standen, Naomi. 2015. "Defining the Global Middle Ages." *Medieval Worlds*, 1: 106–17.

Holmes, Nicholas M. McQ. 2004. "The Evidence of Finds for the Circulation and Use of Coins in Medieval Scotland." *Proceedings of the Society of Antiquaries of Scotland* 134: 241–80.

Honorius of Autun. *Gemma animae*, in Migue 1844–64, vol. 172: 541–738.

Horden, Peregrine and Purcell, Nicholas. 2000. *The Corrupting Sea: a Study of Mediterranean History*. Oxford: Blackwell.

Hoskin, Philippa. 2014. "Robert Grosseteste and the simple benefice: a novel solution to the complexities of lay presentation." *Journal of Medieval History*, 40 (1): 24–43.

Hunt, Edwin, S. and Murray, James M. 1999. *A History of Business in Medieval Europe, 1200–1550*. Cambridge: Cambridge University Press.

Hunter, Fraser and Painter, Kenneth (eds.). 2013. *Late Roman Silver: the Traprain Treasure in Context*. Edinburgh: Society of Antiquaries of Scotland.

Ilisch, Lutz. 1990. "Whole and Fragmented Dirhams in Near Eastern Hoards." In Kenneth Jonsson and Brita Malmer (ed.), *Sigtuna Papers: Proceedings of the Sigtuna Symposium on Viking-Age Coinage 1–4 June 1989*. Stockholm: Kungl. Vitterhets Historie och Antikvitets Akademien.

Ilisch, Peter. 1988. "Münzmeister in Deutschland 1400–1500." In N.J. Mayhew and P. Spufford (eds.), *Later Medieval Mints: Organisation, Administration and Techniques. The Eighth Oxford Symposium on Coinage and Monetary History*. Oxford: Archaeopress.

Isidore of Seville. 1911. *Isidori Hispalensis episcopi Etymologiarum sive Originum libri XX*. Wallace Martin Lindsay (ed.). 2 vols. Oxford: Oxford University Press.

James, Edward. 1988. "The Northern World in the Dark Ages, 400–900." In George A. Holmes (ed.). *The Oxford Illustrated History of Medieval Europe*. London: Guild Publishing.

Jarnut, Jörg and Strothmann, Jürgen. (eds.). 2013. *Die Merowingischen Monetarmünzen als Quelle zum Verständnis des 7. Jahrhunderts in Gallien*. Paderborn: Wilhelm Fink.

Jarrett, Jonathan. 2014. "*Bovo Soldare*: a Sacred Cow of Spanish Economic History Re-Evaluated." In Rory Naismith, Martin Allen and Elina Screen (eds.), *Early Medieval Monetary History: Studies in Memory of Mark Blackburn*. Farnham: Ashgate.

Jasper, Kathryn L. 2012. "The Economics of Reform in the Middle Ages." *History Compass*, 10: 440–54.

Jensen, Jørgen Steen (ed.). 1989. *De skriftlige kilder til Danmarks middelalderlige møntvæsen*. Copenhagen: Den kgl. Mønt- og Medaillesamling, Nationalmuseet.

Jesse, Wilhelm (ed.). 1924. *Quellenbuch zur Münz- und Geldgeschichte des Mittelalters*. Halle: Münzhandlung A. Riechmann and Co.

Jesse, Wilhelm. 1928. *Der Wendische Münzverein*. Lübeck: Hansischer Geschichtsverein.

Jesse, Wilhelm. 1930. "Die deutschen Münzer-Hausgenossen." *Numismatische Zeitschrift*, 63: 47–92.

Johns, Jeremy. 2003. "Archaeology and the History of Early Islam: the first Seventy Years." *Journal of the Economic and Social History of the Orient*, 46: 411–96.

Johnson, Charles (ed. and trans.). 1956. *The De moneta of Nicholas Oresme, and English Mint Documents*. London: Nelson.

Jonsson, Eeva. Forthcoming. "Jomala Church, Åland Islands—Coin Offerings and the Cult of the Virgin Mary." In Gullbekk, Kilger, Roland and Kristoffersen.

Jordan, William Chester 1996. *The Great Famine: Northern Europe in the Early Fourteenth Century*. Princeton: Princeton University Press.

Jordan, William Chester. 2009. *A Tale of Two Monasteries: Westminster and Saint-Denis in the Thirteenth Century*. Princeton: Princeton University Press.

Jungner, Hugo and Svardström, Elisabeth. 1940–70. *Västergötlands runinskrifter*. 5 vols. Stockholm: Almqvist and Wiksell.

Kaegi, Walter Emil. 2003. *Heraclius: Emperor of Byzantium*. Cambridge: Cambridge University Press.

Kano, Osamu. 2013. "«Configuration» d'une espèce diplomatique: le *praeceptum denariale* dans le haut moyen âge." In *Configuration du texte en histoire*. Nagoya: Nagoya University.

Kaye, Joel. 1998. *Economy and Nature in the Fourteenth Century: Money, Market Exchange and Emergence of Scientific Thought*. Cambridge: Cambridge University Press.
Kaye, Joel. 2014. *A History of Balance, 1250–1375: the Emergence of a New Model of Equilibrium and Its Impact on Thought*. Cambridge: Cambridge University Press.
Kelleher, Richard. 2012. "The Re-Use of Coins in Medieval England and Wales c. 1050–1550: an Introductory Survey." *Yorkshire Numismatist*, 4: 183–200.
Kelleher, Richard. 2015. *A History of Coinage in Medieval England*. Witham: Greenlight.
Kelleher, Richard. In press. "Old Money, New Methods: Coins and Later Medieval Archaeology." In Christopher Gerrard and Alejandra Gutierrez (eds.), *Oxford Handbook of Later Medieval Archaeology in Britain*. Oxford: Oxford University Press.
Kelleher, R. forthcoming. British Numismatic Society Special Publication 13: London.
Kelleher, Richard, Leins, Ian and Cook, Barrie J. 2008. "Roman, Medieval and Later coins from the Vintry, City of London." *Numismatic Chronicle*, 168: 167–233.
Kelleher, Richard and Williams, Gareth. 2011. "The Tutbury Hoard." In Malcolm Hislop, Mark Kincey and Gareth Williams (eds.), *Tutbury: 'A Castle Firmly Built'. Archaeological and historical investigations at Tutbury Castle, Staffordshire*. British Archaeological Reports: British Series 546. Oxford: Archaeopress.
Keller, Rodolphe. 2013. "Les profits de la guerre. Prédation et pouvoir dans le monde franc (VIe-Xe siècle)." Unpubl. Ph.D. dissertation: Université Paris Est-Marne-la-Vallée.
Kelly, Fergus. 1997. *Early Irish Farming: a Study Based Mainly on the Law-Texts of the 7th and 8th Centuries AD*. Dublin: School of Celtic Studies.
Kelly, Susan E. (ed.). 2009. *Charters of Peterborough Abbey*. Anglo-Saxon Charters 14. Oxford: Oxford University Press.
Kemmers, Fleur and Myrberg, Nanouschka. 2011. "Rethinking Numismatics. The Archaeology of Coins." *Archaeological Dialogues*. 18(1): 87–108.
Kempshall, Matthew S. 1999. *The Common Good in Late Medieval Political Thought*. Oxford: Oxford University Press.
Kennedy, Hugh. 2004. *The Prophet and the Age of the Caliphate*. Revised ed. London: Routledge.
Kent, John. 2005. *Coinage and Currency in London from the London and Middlesex Records and Other Sources. From Roman times to the Victorians*. London: Baldwin.
Kessler, Herbert. 2004. *Seeing Medieval Art*. Plymouth: Broadview Press.
Keydell, R. (ed.). 1967. *Agathias Myrinaei: Historiarum libri quinque*. Berlin: De Gruyter.
Keynes, Simon. 1985. "King Athelstan's Books." In Michael Lapidge and Helmut Gneuss (eds.), *Learning and Literature in Anglo-Saxon England: Studies Presented to Peter Clemoes on the Occasion of his Sixty-Fifth Birthday*. Cambridge: Cambridge University Press.
Kilger, Christoph. 2007. "Kaupang from Afar: Aspects of the Interpretation of Dirham Finds in Northern and Eastern Europe between the Late 8th and Early 10th Centuries." In Dagfinn Skre (ed.), *Means of Exchange: Dealing with Silver in the Viking Age*. Kaupang Excavation Project Publication Series 2. Aarhus: Aarhus University Press.
Kilger, Christoph. Forthcoming. "Moving Money, Ritual Money—Studying Use of Coins in Bunge Church on Medieval Gotland, 12th–15th Centuries." In Gullbekk, Kilger, Roland and Kristoffersen.

Kimball, Elisabeth G. (ed.). 1962. *Records of Some Sessions of the Peace in Lincolnshire: 1381–1396. 2. The Parts of Lindsey*. Lincoln: Lincoln Records Society.

King, Peter. 1985. *The Finances of the Cistercian Order in the Fourteenth Century* (Cistercian Studies Series 85). Kalamazoo: Cistercian Publications.

Kiser, Edgar. 1994. "Markets and Hierarchies in Early Modern Tax Systems: a Principal-Agent Analysis." *Politics and Society*, 22: 284–315.

Klackenberg, Henrik. 1992. *Moneta Nostra. Monetariseringen i Medeltidens Sverige*. Stockholm: Almqvist and Wiksel International.

Kluge, Bernd. 1991. *Deutsche Münzgeschichte von der späten Karolingerzeit bis zum Ende der Salier*. Sigmaringen: Thorbecke.

Kluge, Bernd. 2007. *Numismatik des Mittelalters*. Vienna: Verlag der Österreichischen der Wissenschaften.

Kool, Robert. 2007. "Coin Circulation in the Villeneuves of the Latin Kingdom of Jerusalem: the Cases of Parva Mahumeria and Bethgibelin." In Peter Edbury and Sophia Kalopissi-Verti (eds.), *Archaeology and the Crusades*. Athens: Pierides Foundation.

Kool, Robert, et al. 2011. "A Late Tenth-Century Fatimid Coin Purse from Bet She'an." *'Atiqot*, 67: 31–41.

Koppmann, Karl (ed.). 1878. *Kämmereirechnungen der Stadt Hamburg, Vol. 3: 1471–1500*. Hamburg: Hermann Grüning.

Kotsis, Kriszta. 2012. "Defining Female Authority in Eighth-Century Byzantium: the Numismatic Images of the Empress Irene (797–802)." *Journal of Late Antiquity*, 5: 185–215.

Kroll, John H. 2012. "The Monetary Background of Early Coinage." In William E. Metcalf (ed.), *The Oxford Handbook of Greek and Roman Coinage*. Oxford: Oxford University Press.

Krusch, Bruno (ed.). 1896. *Monumenta Germaniae Historica: Scriptorum rerum Merovingicarum tomus III: Passiones vitaeque sanctorum aevi Merovingici et antiquorum aliquot I*. Hanover: Hahn.

Kruse, Susan E. 1988. "Ingots and Weight Units in Viking Age Silver Hoards." *World Archaeology*, 20(2): 285–301.

Kumler, Aden. 2011. "The Multiplication of the Species. Eucharistic Morphology in the Middle Ages." *RES: Anthropology and Aesthetics*, 59/60: 179–91.

Lafaurie, Jean. 1980. "La surveillance des ateliers monétaires au IXe siècle." *Francia*, 9: 486–96.

Laing, Samuel (trans.). 1964. *Snorri Sturluson: Heimskringla. Pt 1: the Olaf Sagas*. Rev. with introduction and notes by Jacqueline Simpson. 2 vols. London: Dent.

Lambert, M.D. 1961. *Franciscan Poverty. The Doctrine of Absolute Poverty of Christ and the Apostles in the Franciscan Order, 1210–1323*. London: SPCK.

Lange, Christian C.A. et al. 1847–2011. *Diplomatarium Norvegicum*. 23 vols. Christiania/Oslo: P.T. Malling.

Langholm, Odd. 1979. *Price and Value in the Aristotelian Tradition. A Study in Scholastic Economic Sources*. Oslo: Universitetsforlaget.

Langholm, Odd. 1983. *Wealth and Money in the Aristotelian Tradition: a Study in Scholastic Economic Sources*. Bergen: Universitetsforlaget.

Langholm, Odd. 1992. *Economics in Medieval Schools: Wealth, Exchange, Value, Money and Usury according to the Paris Theological Tradition, 1200–1350*. Leiden: Brill.

Langholm, Odd. 2015. "A Herald of Schoolasticism: Alain of Lille on Economic Virtue." In Giles E. M. Gasper and S. H. Gullbekk (eds.), *Money and the Church in Medieval Europe, 1000–1200. Practice, Morality and Thought*. Farnham: Ashgate.

Lauwers, Michel. 2009. "Déposer, cacher, fonder. À propos de quelques formes de dépôt ritual dans l'Occident médiéval." In Sandrine Bonnardin, Caroline Hamon, Michel Lauwers and Bénédicte Quilliec (eds.), *Du matériel au spirituel: réalités archéologiques et historiques des «dépôts» de le Préhistoire à nos jours*. Antibes: Éditions APDCA.

Lauwers, Michel. 2012. *La dîme, l'église et la société féodale*. Turnhout: Brepols.

Lawrence, C.H. 1994. *The Friars. The Impact of the Early Mendicant Movement on the Western Society*. London: Longman.

Le Goff, Jacques. 2005. *The Birth of Europe*. Oxford: Blackwell.

Le Goff, Jacques. 2012. *Money and the Middle Ages: an Essay in Historical Anthropology*. Cambridge: Polity.

Leader-Newby, Ruth. 2004. *Silver and Society in Late Antiquity: Functions and Meaning of Silver Plate in the Fourth to Seventh Centuries*. Aldershot: Ashgate.

Lecuppre-Desjardin, Élodie, Van Bruaene, Anne-Laure (eds.). 2010. *De bono communi. The Discourse and Practice of the Common Good in the European City (13th–16th c.)*. Turnhout: Brepols.

Lenoble, Clément. 2013. *L'exercice de la pauvreté. Économie et religion chez les franciscains d'Avignon (XIIIe-XVe siècle)*. Rennes: Presses Universitares de Rennes.

Leonard Jr., Robert. D. 2008. "Effects of the Fourth Crusade on European Gold Coinage." In Thomas F. Madden (ed.). *The Fourth Crusade: Event, Aftermath, and Perceptions*. Aldershot: Ashgate from the Society for the Study of the Crusades and the Latin East.

Levillain, Léon (ed.). 1927–35. *Loup de Ferrières. Correspondance*. 2 vols. Paris: Les Belles Lettres.

Leyser, Karl. 1994. "The Carolingian and Ottonian Centuries." In Timothy Reuter (ed.), *Communication and Power in Medieval Europe*. London: Hambledon.

Liebermann, F. (ed.). 1903–16. *Die Gesetze der Angelsachsen*. 3 vols. Halle: Niemeyer.

Liestøl, A. 1979. "Runeringen i Forsa: Kva er han, og når vart han smidd?" *Saga och Sed: Gustav Adolfs Akademiens Årsbok*: 12–27.

Limentani, Alberto (ed.). 1972. *Les estoires de Venise: Cronaca veneziana in lingua francese dalle origini al 1275*. Florence: Okschki.

Lindsay, W.M. (ed.). 1911. *Isidori Hispalensis Episcopi Etymologiarum sive Originum libri xx*. 2 vols. Oxford: Clarendon Press.

Little, Lester K. 1978. *Religious Poverty and the Profit Economy in Medieval Europe*. London: Paul Elek.

Lopez, Robert S. 1956. Back to Gold, 1252. *Economic History Review*, 9: 219–40.

Lopez, Robert S. 1971. *The Commercial Revolution of the Middle Ages*. Englewood Cliffs: Prentice-Hall.

Lopez, Robert S. and Miskimin, Harry A. 1962. "The Economic Depression of the Renaissance." *Economic History Review*, 14: 408–26.

Loveluck, Chris. 2013. *Northwest Europe in Early Middle Ages. A Comparative Archaeology*. Cambridge: Cambridge University Press.

Loveluck, Chris. 2016. "The Dynamics of Portable Wealth, Social Status and Competition in the Ports, Coastal Zones and River Corridors of Northwest Europe, c. AD 650–1100." In Geneviève Bührer-Thierry, Régine Le Jan and Vito Loré (eds.), *Acquérir, prélever, contrôler. Les ressources en compétition (400–1100)*. Turnhout: Brepols.

Lunden, Kåre. 1978. *Korn og kaup, studiar over prisar og jordbruk på Vestlandet i mellomalderen*. Oslo, Bergen and Tromsø: Universitetsforlaget.

Lunt, William. 1934. *Papal Revenues in the Middle Ages*. 2 vols. New York: Columbia University Press.

Maddicott, John R. 1989. "Trade, Industry and the Wealth of King Alfred." *Past and Present*, 123: 3–51.

Magnou Nortier, Elizabeth (ed.). 1993–7. *Aux sources de la gestion publique*. Lille: Presses Universitaires de Lille.

Malamoud, Charles (ed.). 1983. *Debts and Debtors*. New Delhi: Indian Council of Social Science Research and Maison des Sciences de l'Homme.

Malamoud, Charles (ed.). 1988. *Lien de vie, nœud mortel: les représentations de la dette en Chine, au Japon et dans le monde indien*. Paris: Éditions de l'EHESS.

Malkmus, William. 2007. "Ancient and Medieval Coin Dies: Catalogue and Notes." In Lucia Travaini and Alessia Bolis (eds). *Conii e scene di coniazione*. Rome: Quasar.

Malloy, Alex G., et al. 1994. *Coins of the Crusader States, 1098–1291: Including the Kingdom of Jerusalem and Its Vassal States of Syria and Palestine, the Lusignan Kingdom of Cyprus (1192–1489), and the Latin Empire of Constantinople and its Vassal States of Greece and the Archipelago*. Cheltenham: Attic Books.

Malmer, Brita. 1985. "Some Thoughts on the Secondary Treatment of Viking-Age Coins Found on Gotland and in Poland." In Stefan K. Kuczyński and Stanisław Suchodolski (eds.), *Numus et Historia. Polskie Towarzystwo Archeologiczne i Numizmatyczne Komisja Numizmatyczna*. Warsaw: Polskie Towarzystwo Archeologiczne i Numizmatyczne.

Manchester, William. 1992. *A World Lit only by Fire: the Medieval Mind and the Renaissance*. London: Macmillan.

Manzano, Eduardo. 2013. "Circulation des biens et des richesses entre al-Andalus et l'Occident européen durant les 'siècles obscurs'." In Laurent Feller and Ana Rodriguez (eds.), *Les objets sous contrainte. Circulation des objets et valeur des choses au Moyen Âge*. Paris: Publications de la Sorbonne.

Marcone, Arnaldo. 2008. "A Long Late Antiquity? Considerations on a Controversial Periodization." *Journal of Late Antiquity*, 1(1): 4–19.

Marcos Casquero, Manuel-Antonio. 2005. "*Pecunia*. Historia de un vocablo." *Pecvnia*, 1: 1–12.

Maurer, Bill. 2016. "Cashlessness, Ancient and Modern." In Colin Haselgrove and Stefan Krmnicek (ed.), *The Archaeology of Money: Proceedings of the Workshop 'Archaeology of Money', University of Tübingen, October 2013*. Leicester: Leicester Archaeology Monographs.

Mayhew, Nicholas J. 1983. *Sterling Imitations of Edwardian Type*. London: Royal Numismatic Society.

Mayhew, Nicholas J. 1992. "From Regional to Central Minting, 1158–1464." In Christopher E. Challis (ed.), *A New History of the Royal Mint*. Cambridge: Cambridge University Press.

Mayhew, Nicholas J. 1995. "Modelling Medieval Monetisation." In Richard H. Britnell and Bruce M.S. Campbell (eds.), *A Commercialising Economy: England 1086 to c. 1300*. Manchester: Manchester University Press.

Mayhew, Nicholas J. 2002. "Money in the Late Medieval Countryside: Britain." In Paolo Delogu and Sara Sorda (ed.), *La Moneta in Ambiente Rurale Nell'Italia Tardomedioevale*. Rome: Istituto italiano di numismatica.

Mayhew, Nicholas J. 2013a. "Prices in England, 1170–1750". *Past and Present*, 219: 3–39.
Mayhew, Nicholas J. 2013b. "La richesse de l'Angleterre médiévale dans ses rapports à la masse monétaire." In Laurent Feller and Ana Rodriguez (eds.), *Objets sous contrainte. Circulation des richesses et valeur des choses au Moyen Âge*. Paris: Publications de la Sorbonne.
Mayhew, Nicholas J. and Gemmill, Elizabeth. 1995. *Changing Values in Medieval Scotland: A Study of Prices, Money, and Weights and Measures*. Cambridge: Cambridge University Press.
McCormick, Michael. 2001. *Origins of the European Economy: Communications and Commerce, AD 300–900*. Cambridge: Cambridge University Press.
McCormick, Michael. 2002. "New Light on the 'Dark Ages': How the Slave Trade Fuelled the Carolingian Economy." *Past and Present*, 177: 17–54.
McKinnon, Andrew M. 2013. "Ideology and the market metaphor in rational choice theory of religion: a rhetorical critique of 'religious economies'." *Critical Sociology*, 39/4: 529–43.
McLaughlin, Terence P. 1939–40. "The Teaching of the Canonists on Usury (XII, XIII and XIV Centuries." *Mediaeval Studies*, 1: 81–147; 2: 1–22.
McNamara, Jo Ann. 2001. "Life of Saint Eligius by Dado, Bishop of Rouen." In T. Head (ed.). *Medieval Hagiography: a Sourcebook*. London: Routledge, 137–67.
Merlo, G. G. 2009. "Francesco d'Assisi e il denaro." In L. Travaini (ed.), *Valori e disvalori simbolici delle monete. I 30 denari di Giuda*. Rome: Quasar.
Metcalf, David Michael. 1992. "The Rome (Forum) Hoard of 1883." *British Numismatic Journal*, 62: 62–96.
Metcalf, David Michael. 1995. *Coinage of the Crusades and the Latin East in the Ashmolean Museum Oxford*. 2nd ed. Royal Numismatic Society: Special Publication 28. London: Royal Numismatic Society.
Metcalf, David Michael. 2006. "Monetary Circulation in Merovingian Gaul, 561–674. A propos Cahiers Ernest Babelon, 8." *Revue numismatique*, 162: 337–94.
Migne, J.P. (ed.). 1844–64. *Patrologiae cursus completus. Series (latina) prima*. 221 vols. Paris: Excudebat Migne.
Miller, William Ian. 2004. *Eye for an Eye*. Cambridge: Cambridge University Press.
Moeser, Karl and Dworschak, Fritz. 1936. *Die große Münzreform unter Erzherzog Sigmund von Tirol (Die ersten großen Silber- und deutschen Bildnismünzen aus der Münzstätte Hall im Inntal)*. Vienna: Verlag Dr. Eduard Stepan.
Mommsen, Theodor and Meyer, Paul. M. (eds.). 1905. *Theodosiani libri XVI cum Constitutionibus Sirmondianis, et leges novella ad Theodosianum pertinentes*. 2 vols. Berlin: Weidmann.
Morrison, Karl F. 1961. "The Gold Medallions of Louis the Pious and Lothaire I and the Synod of Paris (825)." *Speculum*, 36: 592–600.
Morrisson, Cécile. 1992. "Monnaie et finances dans l'empire byzantin, Xe–XIVe siècle." In *Hommes et richesse dans l'Empire byzantin, II: VIIIe–Xve siècle*. Paris: Lethielleux.
Morrisson, Cécile. 2002. "Byzantine Money: its Production and Circulation." In Angeliki E. Laiou (ed.), *The Economic History of Byzantium: from the Seventh through the Fifteenth Century*. 3 vols. Washington DC: Dumbarton Oaks Research Library and Collection.
Mouton, D. 2008. *Mottes castrales en Provence. Les origines de la fortification privée au Moyen Âge*. Paris: Éditions de la Maison des sciences de l'homme.

Munro, John H. 1972. *Wool, Cloth, and Gold: the Struggle for Bullion in Anglo-Burgundian Trade, 1340–1478*. Brussels and Toronto: University of Toronto Press.

Munro, John H. 2003. "The Monetary Origins of the 'Price Revolution': South German Silver Mining, Merchant-Banking, and Venetian Commerce, 1470–1540." In D.O. Flynn, A. Giráldez and R. von Glahn (eds.), *Global Connections and Monetary History, 1470–1800*. Aldershot, Brookfield: Ashgate Publishing.

Munro, John H. 2009. *Warfare, Liquidity Crises, and Coinage Debasements in Burgundian Flanders, 1384–1482: Monetary or Fiscal Remedies?* Toronto: University of Toronto, Department of Economics.

Murray, Albert Victor. 1967. *Abélard and St. Bernard: A Study in Twelfth Century "Modernism"*. Manchester: Manchester University Press.

Murray, Alexander. 1992. *Reason and Society in the Middle Ages*. Oxford: Oxford University Press.

Murray, Alexander. 2004. "Should the Middle Ages be Abolished?" *Essays in Medieval Studies*, 21: 1–22.

Murray, J.E.L. 1977. "The Black Money of James III." In D.M. Metcalf (ed.) *Coinage in Medieval Scotland*. Oxford: Archaeopress.

Muzzarelli, Maria-Giuseppina and Campanini, Antonella (eds.). 2003. *Disciplinare il lusso. La legislazione suntuaria in Italia e in Europa tra Medioevo ed Età modern*. Rome: Carocci.

Myrberg, Nanouschka. 2007. "The Social Identity of Coin Hoards: an Example of Theory and Practice in the Space between Numismatics and Archaeology." In Hans-Markus von Kaenel and Fleur Kemmers (eds.), *Coins in Context I: New Perspectives for the Interpretation of Coin Finds*. Mainz: Verlag Philipp von Zabern.

Myrberg, Nanouschka. 2009. "The Hoarded Dead. Late Iron Age Silver Hoards as Graves." In Ing-Marie Back-Danielsson, Ingrid Gustin, Annika Larsson, Nanouschka Myrberg and Susanne Thedéen (eds.), *On the Threshold: Burial Archaeology in the Twenty-First Century*. Postdoctoral Archaeological Group 1/Stockholm Studies in Archaeology 47. Stockholm: Insitutionen för arkeologi och antikens kultur, Stockholms universitet.

Naismith, Rory. 2011. *Money and Power in Anglo-Saxon England: the Southern English Kingdoms, 757–865*. Cambridge: Cambridge University Press.

Naismith, Rory. 2012. "Kings, Crisis and Coinage Reforms in the Mid-Eighth Century." *Early Medieval Europe*, 20(3): 291–332.

Naismith, Rory. 2014a. "Gold Coinage and Its Use in the Post-Roman West." *Speculum* 89(2): 273–306.

Naismith, Rory. 2014b. "The Social Significance of Monetization in the Early Middle Ages." *Past and Present*, 223: 3–39.

Naismith, Rory. 2015. "*Turpe lucrum*? Wealth, Money and Coinage in the Millennial Church." In Giles M. Gasper and Svein H. Gullbekk (eds.), *Money and Church in Medieval Europe, 1000–1200: Practice, Morality and Thought*. Farnham: Ashgate.

Naismith, Rory. 2016a. "The Economy of *Beowulf*." In Leonard Neidorf, Rafael J. Pascual and Tom Shippey (eds.), *Old English Philology: Studies in Honour of R.D. Fulk*. Cambridge: D.S. Brewer.

Naismith, Rory. 2016b. "The Forum Hoard and Beyond: Money, Gift, and Religion in the Early Middle Ages." *Viator*, 47(2): 35–56.

Naismith, Rory. 2017. *Medieval European Coinage, with a Catalogue of the Coins in the Fitzwilliam Museum, Cambridge, vol. 8, Britain and Ireland c. 400–1066*. Cambridge: Cambridge University Press.

Naismith, Rory, Allen, Martin and Screen, Elina (eds.). 2014. *Early Medieval Monetary History: Studies in Memory of Mark Blackburn*. Farnham: Ashgate.

Naismith, Rory and Tinti, Francesca. 2016. *The Forum Hoard of Anglo-Saxon Coins/Il ripostiglio dell'Atrium Vestae nel Foro Romano*. Bollettino di numismatica 55–6. Rome: Istituto poligrafico e Zecca dello Stato.

Naismith, Rory. n. d. *Medieval European Coinage, with a Catalogue of Coins in the Fitzwilliam Museum, Cambridge. 8: Britain and Ireland c. 400–1066*. Cambridge: Cambridge University Press. Forthcoming.

Nederman, Cary J. 2000. "Community and the Rise of Commercial Society: Political Economy and Political Theory in Nicholas Oresme's *De moneta*." *History of Political Thought*, 21(1): 1–15.

Nelson, Benjamin. 1969. *The Idea of Usury: From Tribal Brotherhood to Universal Otherhood*. Chicago and London: University of Chicago Press (second edition).

Nelson, Janet L. 1987. "Making Ends Meet: Wealth and Poverty in the Carolingian Church." *Studies in Church History*, 24: 25–35.

Nelson, Janet L. 2010. "*Munera*." In J.-P. Devroey, L. Feller and R. Le Jan (eds.), *Les élites et la richesse au Moyen Âge*. Turnhout: Brepols.

Newhauser, Richard G. 2014. "Introduction: the Sensual Middle Ages." In Richard G. Newhauser (ed.) 2014. *A Cultural History of the Senses in the Middle Ages*. London: Bloomsbury.

Nicholas of Cusa. 1998. *De ludo globi*, ed. I.G. Senger, in *Opera omnia*, vol IX. Hamburg: Felix Meiner.

Nightingale, Pamela. 2004. "Money and Credit in the Economy of Late Medieval England." In D. Wood (ed.), *Medieval Money Matters*. Oxford: Oxbow.

Noell, Brian. 2008. "Cistercian Monks in the Market. Legal Studies, Economic Statutes and Institutional Evolution in the Twelfth Century." *Citeaux*. 59: 169–92.

Noonan, John Thomas. 1957. *The Scholastic Analysis of Usury*. Cambridge: Harvard University Press.

North, Douglas C. and Thomas, Robert P. 1971. "The Rise and Fall of the Manorial System: A Theoretical Model." *Journal of Economic History*, 31: 777–803.

North, Michael. 1990. *Geldumlauf und Wirtschaftskonjunktur im südlichen Ostseeraum an der Wende zur Neuzeit (1440–1570): Untersuchungen zur Wirtschaftsgeschichte am Beispiel des Großen Lübecker Münzschatzes, der norddeutschen Münzfunde und der schriftlichen Überlieferung*. Sigmaringen: Thorbecke.

O'Meara, John (trans.). 1982. *Gerald of Wales: The History and Topography of Ireland*. London: Penguin.

Palmer, Andrew. 1993. *The Seventh Century in the West-Syrian Chronicles*. Liverpool: Liverpool University Press.

Palmer, James T. 2014. *The Apocalypse in the Early Middle Ages*. Cambridge: Cambridge University Press.

Parisse, Michel (ed.). 1998. *La correspondance d'un évêque carolingien, Frothaire de Toul (ca 813–847)*. Paris: Publications de la Sorbonne.

Penn, Simon, A.C. and Dyer, Christopher. 1990. "Wages and Earnings in Late Medieval England: Evidence from the Enforcement of the Labour Laws." *Economic History Review*, 43: 356–76.

Perea Caveda, Alicia. 2001. *El Tesoro Visigodo de Guarrazar*. Madrid: Consejo Superior de Investigaciones Científicas.

Pestell, Tim and Ulmschneider, Katharina (eds.). 2003. *Markets in Early Medieval Europe. Trading and 'Productive' Sites, 650–850*. Macclesfield: Windgather Press.

Piergiovanni, Vito. 1993. *The Growth of the Bank as Institution and the Development of Money-Business Law*. Berlin: De Gruyter.

Pinto, Giuliano. 2013. "Les rémunérations des salariés du bâtiment (Italie, XIIIe-XVe siècle): les critères d'évaluation." In Patrice Beck, Philippe Bernardi and Laurent Feller (eds.), *Rémunérer le travail au Moyen Âge*. Paris: Picard.

Pirenne, Henri. 1936 [2005]. *Mahomet et Charlemagne*. Paris: PUF.

Pirenne, Henri. 1951. *Histoire économique de l'Occident medieval*. Bruges: Desclee.

Pliego Vázquez, Ruth. 2009. *La moneda visigoda*. 2 vols. Seville: Secretariado de Publicaciones, Universidad de Sevilla.

Plummer, Charles (ed.). 1892. *Two of the Saxon Chronicles Parallel with Supplementary Extracts from the Others*. 2 vols. Oxford: Clarendon Press.

Polanyi, Karl. 1968. *Primitive, Archaic and Modern Economies. Essays of Karl Polanyi*. Ed. by George Dalton. Boston: Beacon Press.

Polo, Marco. 2005. *Travels in the Land of Kubilai Khan*. London: Penguin.

Poly, Jean-Pierre and Bournazel, Eric. 1991. *La mutation féodale, Xe-XIIe siècle*. Paris: Presses Universitaires de France.

Poque, Suzanne. 1960. "Christus Mercator. Notes augustiniennes." *Recherches de Science Religieuse*, 48: 564–77.

Poque, Suzanne. 1984. *Le langage symbolique dans la prédication d'Augustin d'Hippone*. Paris: Etudes Augustiniennes.

Prestwich, Michael. 1988. *Edward I*. London: Methuen.

Prigent, Vivien. 2014. "Le mythe du mancus et les origins de l'économie européenne." *Revue numismatique*, 180: 701–28.

Prodi, Paolo (ed.). 2008. *La fiducia secondo i linguaggi del potere*. Bologna: il Mulino.

Prodi, Paolo. 2009. *Settimo non rubare. Furto e mercato nella storia dell'Occidente*. Bologna: il Mulino.

Quaglioni, Diego and Todeschini, Giacomo et al. (eds.). 2005. *Credito e usura fra teologia, diritto e amministrazione: Linguaggi a confronto (sec. XII-XVI)*. Rome: École française de Rome.

Rahner, H. 1956. "Werdet kundige Geldwechsler. Zur Geschichte der Lehre des hl. Ignatius von der Unterscheidung der Geister." *Gregorianum*, 37: 444–83.

Ramsey, Boniface (trans.). 1997. *John Cassian: the Conferences; Ancient Christian Writers 57*. Mahwah: Paulist Press.

Redford, Scott. 1998. *The Archaeology of the Frontier in the Medieval Near East: Excavations at Gritille, Turkey*. Boston: Archaeological Institute of America.

Redish, Angela. 2000. *Bimetallism: An Economic and Historical Analysis*. Cambridge and New York: Cambridge University Press.

Reece, Richard. 1987. *Coinage in Roman Britain*. London: Seaby.

Reisch, Gregor. 1503. *Margarita philosophica*. Freiburg im Breisgau: Johannes Schotten.

Resch, Alfred. 1906. *Agrapha. Aussercanonische Evangelienfragmente*, Leipzig: J.C. Hinrichs (second edition).

Reuter, Timothy. 2000. "'You Can't Take it with You': Testaments, Hoards and Moveable Wealth in Europe, 600–1100." In Elizabeth M. Tyler (ed.), *Treasure in the Medieval West*. York: York Medieval Press.

Reynolds, Andrew. 2009. *Anglo-Saxon Deviant Burial Customs*. Oxford: Oxford University Press.

Reynolds, Susan. 2012. "Trust in Medieval Society and Politics." In her *The Middle Ages Without Feudalism. Essays in Criticism and Comparison on the Medieval West*. Farnham: Ashgate.

Richter, Michael. 1998. "William ap Rhys, William de Braose, and the Lordship of Gower, 1289 and 1307." *Studia Celtica*, 32: 189–209.

Risvaag, Jon Anders. Forthcoming. "Coin Finds of Høre Stave Church, Oppland Norway: Reflections of Regulation and Conflict in the Middle Ages." In Gullbekk, Kilger, Roland and Kristoffersen.

Robson, M. (ed.). 2011. *The Cambridge Companion to Saint Francis of Assisi*. Cambridge: Cambridge University Press.

Rodolico, Niccolò. 1889 [ed. 1968]. *Il popolo minuto. Note di storia fiorentina (1343–1378)*. Florence: Olschki.

Rogers, James. E. Thorold. 1866. *A History of Agriculture and Prices in England: from the Year after the Oxford Parliament (1259) to the Commencement of the Continental War (1793)*. Oxford: Clarendon Press.

Rosenwein, Barbara H. 1989. *To Be the Neighbor of Saint Peter. The Social Meaning of Cluny's Property, 909–1049*. Ithaca-London: Cornell University Press.

Rosenwein, Barbara H. and Little, Lester K. 1974. Social Meaning in the Monastic and Mendicant Spiritualities, *Past and Present* 63: 4–32.

Ross, Marvin Chauncey. 1965. 2nd ed. with addendum by Susan A. Boyd and Stephen R. Zwirn. 2005. *Catalogue of the Byzantine and Early Mediaeval Antiquities in the Dumbarton Oaks Collection, Vol. 2, Jewelry, Enamels, and Art of the Migration Period*. Washington DC: Dumbarton Oaks Research Library and Collection.

Rössner, Philipp R. 2012. *Deflation—Devaluation—Rebellion: Geld im Zeitalter der Reformation*. Stuttgart: Steiner.

Rovelli, Alessia. 1992. "La funzione della moneta tra l'VIII e X secolo. Un analisi della documentazione archelogica." In Riccardo Francovich and Ghislaine Noyé (eds.), *La storia dell'alto Medioevo italiano alla luce dell'archeologia*. Florence: a l'Insegna del Giglio.

Rovelli, Alessia. 2009. "Coins and Trade in Early Medieval Italy." *Early Medieval Europe*, 17(1): 45–76.

Rovelli, Alessia. 2012. "Coin Hoards." In her *Coinage and Coin Use in Medieval Italy*. Farnham: Ashgate Variorum. English translation of Rovelli, Alessia. 2004. "I tesori monetali." In Sauro Gelichi and Cristina La Rocca (eds.), *Tesori. Forme di accumulazione della ricchezza nell'alto medioevo (secoli V–XI)*. Rome: Viela.

Rubin, Miri. 1991. *Corpus Christi: The Eucharist in Late Medieval Culture*. Cambridge: Cambridge University Press.

Saccocci, Andrea. 1999. "Billon and Bullion: Local and Foreign Coins in Northern Italy (11th–15th Centuries)." In Travaini 1999.

de Salis, Ludwig Rudolf (ed.). 1892. *Leges nationum Germanicarum II.1: Leges Burgundionum*. Monumenta Germaniae Historica. Hanover: Hahn.

Salvesen, Astrid (ed.). 1969. *Historien om Danenes ferd til Jerusalem*. Oslo: Thorleif Dahls kulturbibliotek.

Salvesen, Astrid (ed.). 1971. *Gammelnorsk Homiliebok*. Oslo-Bergen-Tromsø: Universitetsforlaget.

Santarelli, Umberto. 1984. *La categoria dei contratti irregolari. Lezioni di storia del diritto*. Torino: Giappichelli.

Sargent, Thomas J. and Velde, François R. 2002. *The Big Problem of Small Change*. Princeton: Princeton University Press.

Sarris, Peter. 2006. *Economy and Society in the Age of Justinian*. Cambridge: Cambridge University Press.

Schefold, Bertram. 2016. *Great Economic Thinkers from Antiquity to the Historical School: Translations from the Series Klassiker Der Nationalökonomie*. London and New York: Routledge.

Schindel, Nikolaus. 2005. "Sasanian Mint Abbreviations: the Evidence of Style." *Numismatic Chronicle*, 165: 287–99.

Schirmer, Uwe. 2006. *Kursächsische Staatsfinanzen (1456–1656): Strukturen—Verfassung—Funktionseliten*. Stuttgart: Franz Steiner Verlag.

Schive, Claudius Iacob. 1867. "Skandinaviske Mynter, fundne ved Vevey i Schweitz. Beskrevne af A. Morel Fatio. Med Anmærkninger af Schive." *Forhandlinger* 1866: 257–81.

Schmoeckel, Mathias. 2014. "Das kanonische Zinsverbot und die Konfessionalisierung." In Wim Decock et al. (eds.), *Law and Religion: The Legal Teaching of the Protestant and Catholic Reformations*. Göttingen: Vandenhoeck and Ruprecht.

Schmutz, D. and Koenig, F.E. 2003. *Gespendet, verloren, wiedergefunden. Die Fundmünzen aus der reformierten Kirche Steffisburg als Quelle zum spätmittelalterlichen Geldumlauf*. Bern: Haupt Verlag.

Schnapper, Bernard. 1969. "La repression de l'usure et l'evolution économique." *Tijdschrift voor Rechtsgeschiedenis*, 37(1): 47–75.

Schreckenberg, Hans. 1982. *Die christliche Adversus Judaeos-Texte und ihr literarisches und historisches Umfeld (I-XI Jh.)*. Frankfurt-Bern: Peter Lang.

Schröder, Edward. 1918. "Studien zu den deutschen Münznamen." *Zeitschrift für vergleichende Sprachforschung auf dem Gebiete der Indogermanischen Sprachen*, 48: 241–75.

Schultz, Alwin (1888). *Der Weisskunig: Nach den Dictaten und eigenhändigen Aufzeichnungen Kaiser Maximilians I. zusammengestellt von Marx Treitzsauerwein von Ehrentreitz*. Vienna: Adolf Holzhausen.

Schüttenhelm, Joachim. 1987. *Der Geldumlauf im südwestdeutschen Raum vom Riedunger Münzvertrag 1423 bis zur ersten Kipperzeit 1618*. Stuttgart: Kohlhammer.

Schwabenicky, Wolfgang. 1994. "Archäologische und historische Forschungen zum hochmittelalterlichen Montanwesen im sächsischen Erzgebirge." *Mitteilungen der AG für Archäologie des Mittelalters und der Neuzeit*, 4: 25–7.

Schwiedland, Eugen Peter. 1899. *Die Hausierfrage in Österreich*. Leipzig: Duncker & Humblot.

Scull, Chris. 1990. "Scales and Weights in Early Anglo-Saxon England." *Archaeological Journal*, 147: 183–215.

Scull, Christopher, Minter, Faye and Plouviez, Jude. 2016. "Social and Economic Complexity in Early Medieval England: a Central Place Complex of the East Anglian Kingdom at Rendlesham, Suffolk." *Antiquity*, 354: 1594–612.

Screen, Elina. 2013. Sylloge of Coins of the British Isles 65. Norwegian Collections. Part 1: Anglo Saxon Coins to 1016. Oxford: Oxford University Press.

Sellwood, David. 1980. "The Production of Flans for Byzantine Trachy Issues." In David Michael Metcalf and Andrew Oddy (eds.), *Metallurgy in Numismatics*. London: Royal Numismatic Society.

Semmler, Josef (ed.). 1963. *Corpus consuetudinum monasticarum 1: Statuta seu Brevia Adalhardi abbatis Corbeiensis*. Siegburg: Franz Schmitt.

Serafini, Camillo. 1951. "Appendice numismatica." In Bruno M. Apollonj Ghetti (ed.), *Esplorazioni sotto la Confessione di San Pietro in Vaticano eseguite negli anni 1940–1949*. 2 vols. Vatican City: Tipografia poliglotta vaticana.

Shell, Marc. 1982. *Money, Language and Thought: Literary and Philosophical Economies from the Medieval to the Modern Era*. Berkeley: University of California Press.

Sibon, Juliette. 2013. "Du gage-objet au gage-chose. Une étude de cas au sommet de la société urbaine marseillaise à l'extrême fin du XIVe siècle." In Laurent Feller and Ana Rodriguez (eds.), *Objets sous contrainte: Circulation des richesses et valeur des choses au Moyen Âge*. Paris: Publications de la Sorbonne.

Siems, Harald. 1992. *Handel und Wucher im Spiegel frühmittelalterlicher Rechtsquellen*. Hanover: Hahnsche Buchhandlung.

Skaare, Kolbjørn. 1976. *Coins and Coinage in Viking Age Norway*. Lund: Universitetsforlaget.

Skaare, Kolbjørn. 1995. *Norges Mynthistorie. Mynter og utmynting i 1000 år. Pengesedler i 300 år. Numismatikk i Norge*. 2 vols. Oslo: Universitetsforlaget.

Skre, Dagfinn. 2007. "Dealing with Silver: Economic Agency in South-Western Scandinavia AD 600–1000." In Dagfinn Skre (ed.), *Means of Exchange: Dealing with Silver in the Viking Age*. Kaupang Excavation Project Publication Series 2. Aarhus: Aarhus University Press.

Sloane, Barney. 2011. *The Black Death in London*. Stroud: History Press.

Smail, Daniel Lord. 2013. "Les biens comme otages. Quelques aspects du processus de recouvrement des dettes à Lucques et à Marseille à la fin du Moyen Âge." In Laurent Feller and Ana Rodriguez (eds.), *Objets sous contrainte: Circulation des richesses et valeur des choses au Moyen Âge*. Paris: Publications de la Sorbonne.

Smith, Julia M.H. 2003. "Einhard: the Sinner and the Saints." *Transactions of the Royal Historical Society*, 13: 55–77.

Smith, Romney David. 2015. "Calamity and Transition: Re-Imagining Italian Trade in the Eleventh-Century Mediterranean." *Past and Present*, 228: 15–56.

Sortland, Svanhild. 2006. "An Analysis of the Coin Finds from the Church at Mære." *Nordisk Numismatisk Årsskrift*, 2000–2002: 304–18.

Southern, Richard W. 1990 [1970]. *Western Society and the Church in the Middle Ages*. London: Penguin.

Spufford, Peter. 1984. "Le rôle de la monnaie dans la révolution commerciale du XIIIe siècle." In John Day (ed.), *Etudes d'histoire monétaire*. Lille: Presses Universitaires de Lille.

Spufford, Peter. 1986. *Handbook of Medieval Exchange*. London: Offices of the Royal Historical Society.

Spufford, Peter. 1988a. "Mint Organisation in Late Medieval Europe." In N.J. Mayhew and P. Spufford (eds.), *Later Medieval Mints: Organisation, Administration and Techniques. The Eighth Oxford Symposium on Coinage and Monetary History*. Oxford: Archaeopress.

Spufford, Peter. 1988b. *Money and its Use in Medieval Europe*. Cambridge: Cambridge University Press.

Spufford, Peter. 1999. "Local Coins, Foreign Coins in Late Medieval Europe: an Overview." In Lucia Travaini (ed.), *Local Coins, Foreign Coins: Italy and Europe 11th–15th Centuries*. Milan: Società Numismatica Italiana.

Spufford, Peter. 2000. "Monetary Practice and Monetary Theory in Europe (12th–15th. Centuries)." In *Moneda y monedas en la Europa medieval, siglos XII–XV. Actas de la XXVI Semana de Estudios Medievales de Estella, 19 al 23 de julio de 1999*. Pamplona: Gobierno de Navarra.

Spufford, Peter. 2002. *Power and Profit: the Merchant in Medieval Europe*. London: Thames and Hudson.

Spufford, Peter. 2008. *How Rarely Did Medieval Merchants Use Coin?* Geldmuseum: Utrecht.

Spufford, Peter. 2015. "Debasement of the Coinage and its Effects on Exchange Rates and the Economy in England in the 1540s, and in the Burgundian-Habsburg Netherlands in the 1480s." In John H. Munro (ed.), *Money in the Pre-Industrial World: Bullion, Debasements and Coin Substitute*. London: Routledge.

Squatriti, Paolo (trans.). 2007. *The Complete Works of Liudprand of Cremona*. Washington DC: Catholic University of America Press.

Stahl, Alan. 1999. "The Circulation of Medieval Venetian Coinages." In Lucia Travaini (ed.), *Local Coins, Foreign Coins: Italy and Europe 11th–15th Centuries*. Milan: Società Numismatica Italiana.

Stahl, Alan. 2000. *Zecca: The Mint of Venice in the Middle Ages*. Baltimore: Johns Hopkins University Press.

Stark, Werner. 1966–72. *A Sociology of Religion: A Study of Christendom*. 5 vols. London: Routledge and Kegan Paul.

Steen Jensen, Jøergen. 1999. "Local and Foreign Coins in Denmark (11th–16th Centuries)." In Travaini 1999.

Steinbach, Sebastian. 2007. *Das Geld der Nonnen und Mönche: Münzrecht, Münzprägung und Geldumlauf der ostfränkisch-deutschaen Klöster in ottonisch-salischer Zeit (ca. 911–1125)*. Berlin: Winter Industries.

Steuer, Heiko. 2004. "Münzprägung, Silberströme und Bergbau um das Jahr 1000 in Europa: wirtschaftlicher Aufbruch und technische Innovation." In Achim Humbel and Bernd Schneidmüller (eds.), *Aufbruch ins zweite Jahrtausend: Innovation und Kontinuität in der Mitte des Mittelalters*. Ostfildern: Thorbecke.

Storm, Gustav. 1897. *Afgifter fra den norske kirkeprovins til det apostoliske kammer og Kardinalkollegiet 1311–1523*. Christiania/Oslo: I kommission hos H. Aschehoug and Co.

Szabò-Bechstein, Brigitte. 1985. *Libertas ecclesiae. Ein Schlüsselbegriff des Investiturstreits und seine Vorgeschichte. 4.–11. Jh.* Roma: Studi Gregoriani.

Taranger, Absalon. (ed.). 1970. *Magnus Lagabøtes Landslov*. Oslo-Bergen-Tromsø: Universitetsforlaget.

Tellenbach, Gerd. 1993. *The Church in Western Europe from the Tenth to the Early Twelfth Century*, Cambridge: Cambridge University Press.

Testart, Alain (ed.). 2001. *Aux origines de la monnaie*. Paris: Errance.

Testart, Alain. 2001. "Moyen d'échange/moyen de paiement. Des monnaie en général et plus particulièrement des primitives" in Alain Testart (ed.), *Aux origines de la monnaie*. Paris: Errance.

Thieme, Hans. 1942. "Die Funktion der Regalien im Mittelalter." *Zeitschrift der Savigny-Stiftung fur Rechtsgeschichte: germanistische Abteilung*, 62: 57–88.

Thomas, Gabor and Ottaway, Patrick. 2008. "The Symbolic Lives of Late Anglo-Saxon Settlements: a Cellared Structure and Iron Hoard from Bishopstone, East Sussex." *Archaeological Journal*, 165: 334–98.

Tobin, James. 1992. "Money." In *The New Palgrave dictionary of Money and Finance*. London: Macmillan.

Todeschini, Giacomo. 1994. *Il prezzo della salvezza. Lessici medievali del pensiero economico*. Roma: Nuova Italia Scientifica.

Todeschini, Giacomo. 2000. "Linguaggi economici ed ecclesiologia fra XI e XII secolo: dai Libelli de lite al Decretum Gratiani." In G. Rossetti and G. Vitolo (eds.), *Studi in onore di Mario del Treppo*. 2 vols. Naples: Liguori.

Todeschini, Giacomo. 2002. *I mercanti e il tempio. La società cristiana e il circolo virtuoso della ricchezza fra medioevo ed età moderna*. Bologna: il Mulino.

Todeschini, Giacomo. 2009a. *Franciscan Wealth. From Voluntary Poverty to Market Society*. New York: Bonaventure University Press.

Todeschini, Giacomo. 2009b. "Eccezioni e usura nel Duecento. Osservazioni sulla cultura economica medievale come realtà non dottrinaria" *Quaderni Storici*, 131/44(2): 443–60.

Todeschini, Giacomo. 2010. "The Incivility of Judas: 'Manifest' Usury as a Metaphor for the 'Infamy of Fact' (*infamia facti*)." In Juliann Vitullo and Diane Wolfthal (eds.), *Money, Morality and Culture in Late Medieval and Early Modern Europe*. Farnham: Ashgate.

Todeschini, Giacomo. 2011. *Come Giuda. La gente comune e i giochi dell'economia fra medioevo ed età moderna*. Bologna: il Mulino.

Todeschini, Giacomo. 2012. "Usury in the Christian Middle Ages. A Reconsideration of the Historiographical Tradition (1949–2010)." in Francesco Ammannati (ed.), *Religion and religious institutions in the European economy. 1000–1800*. Prato-Florence: Florence University Press.

Todeschini, Giacomo. 2016. "Jewish Usurers, Blood Libel and the Second-Hand Economy. The Medieval Origins of a Stereotype (from the Thirteenth to the Fifteenth Century)." In Cordelia Hess and Jonathan Adams (eds.), *The Medieval Roots of Antisemitism*. Farnham: Ashgate.

Toneatto, Valentina. 2012. *Les banquiers du Seigneur. Évêques et moines face à la richesse (IVe-début IXe siècle)*. Rennes: Presses Universitaires de Rennes.

Toubert, Pierre. 1983. "Il sistema curtense: la produzione e lo scambio interno in Italia nei secoli VIII, IX e X." In R. Romano and U. Tucci (eds.), *Economia naturale, economia monetaria: Storia d'Italia Einaudi, Annali 6*. Turin: Einaudi. [reprinted in Toubert 2004: 145–218].

Toubert, Pierre. 1990. "La part du grand domaine dans le décollage économique de l'Occident (VIIIe-Xe siècles)." In *La croissance agricole du haut Moyen-Age: chronologie, modalités, géographie (Actes des journées d'études de Flaran, 10, sept. 1988)*. Auch: Comité départemental du tourisme du Gers. [reprinted in Toubert 2004: 73–115].

Toubert, Pierre. 2004. *L'Europe dans sa première croissance. De Charlemagne à l'an Mil*. Paris: Fayard.

Travaini, Lucia. 1988. "Mint Organization in Italy between the Twelfth and the Fourteenth Centuries: a Survey." In N.J. Mayhew and P. Spufford (eds.), *Later Medieval Mints: Organisation, Administration and Techniques*. Oxford: Archaeopress.

Travaini, Lucia (ed.). 1999. *Moneta locale, moneta straniera: Italia ed Europa, XI–XV secolo/Local Coins, Foreign Coins: Italy and Europe, 11th–15th Centuries. The Second Cambridge Numismatic Symposium*. Milan: Società numismatica italiana.

Travaini, Lucia. 2001. "The Normans between Byzantium and the Islamic World." *Dumbarton Oaks Papers*, 55: 179–96.

Travaini, Lucia. 2004. "Saints and Sinners: Coins in Medieval Italian Graves." *Numismatic Chronicle*, 164: 159–81.

Travaini, Lucia. 2009. "Monete e sangue." In Francesca Ceci (ed.), *Valori e disvalori simbolici delle monete: I trenta denari di Giuda*. Rome: Quasar.

Travaini, Lucia. 2011. "Le zecche italiane." In Lucia Travaini (ed.), *Le zecche italiane fino all'Unità*. 2 vols. Rome: Libreria dello Stato.

Travaini, Lucia. 2013. "Coins as Bread. Bread as Coins." *Numismatic Chronicle* 172: 187–200.

Travaini, Lucia. 2015. "Saints, Sinners and . . . a Cow: Offerings, Alms and Tokens of Memory." In Giles E.M. Gasper and Svein H. Gullbekk (eds.), *Money and the Church in Medieval Europe, 1000–1200: Practice, Morality and Thought*. Farnham: Ashgate.

Treadwell, Luke. 2009. "'Abd al-Malik's Coinage Reforms: the Role of the Damascus Mint." *Revue numismatique*, 165: 357–81.

Turtledove, Harry. 1982. *The Chronicle of Theophanes, Anni Mundi 6095–6305 (AD 602–813)*. Philadelphia: University of Pennsylvania Press.

Tveito, Olav. 2015. "Mynter i messen—Kirkefunnene som bidrag til kunnskap om offerpraksis og kirkeskikker (11.–17. årh.)." *Historisk Tidsskrift*, 2015(3): 383–417.

Van Vilsteren, Vincent T. 2000. "Hidden and Not Intended to be Recovered: an Alternative Approach to Hoards of Medieval Coins." *Jaarboek voor Munt-en Penningkunde*, 87: 51–63.

Van Vilsteren, V. "Hidden and Not Intended to be Recovered: an Alternative Approach to Hoards of Medieval Coins." *Jaarboek voor Munt-en Penningkunde*, 87: 51–00.

Van Werveke, Henri. 1932. "Monnaie, lingots ou marchandises? Les instruments d'échange aux XIe et XIIe siècles." *Annales d'histoire économique et sociale*, 4(17): 452–68.

Vaughan, Richard (ed.). 1993. *The Illustrated Chronicles of Matthew Paris*. Stroud: Alan Sutton.

Verhulst, Adriaan. 2002. *The Carolingian Economy*. Cambridge: Cambridge University Press.

Verna, Catherine. 2010. "Qualité des fers, prix des marchés, valeurs des hommes et des alliances (haut Vallespir, XVe siècle)." In Claude Denjean (ed.), *Sources sérielles et prix au Moyen Âge. Travaux offerts à Maurice Berthe*. Toulouse: Méridiennes.

Victor, S. 2013. "Les formes de salaires sur les chantiers de construction: l'exemple de Gérone au bas Moyen Âge." In Patrice Beck, Philippe Bernardi Laurent and Feller (eds.), *Rémunérer le travail au Moyen Âge*. Paris: Picard.

Vilar, Pierre. 1984. *A History of Gold and Money 1450–1920*. London: Verso.

Vogel, Kurt. 1954. *Die Practica des Algorismus Ratisbonensis: Ein Rechenbuch des Benediktinerklosters St. Emmeram aus der Mitte des 15. Jahrhunderts nach den Handschriften der Münchner Staatsbibliothek und der Stiftsbibliothek St. Florian*. Munich: Beck.

Volckart, Oliver. 1996. *Die Münzpolitik im Deutschordensland und Herzogtum Preußen von 1370 bis 1550*. Wiesbaden: Harrassowitz.

Volckart, Oliver. 2009. "Regeln, Willkur und der gute Rut: Geldpolitik und Finanzmarkteffizienz in Deutschland, 14. bis 16. Jahrhundert." *Jahrbuch für Wirtschaftsgeschichte*, 2: 101–29.

Volckart, Oliver. 2016. "Währungsvielfalt, Wechselkurse und Geldmarktintegration im Hanseraum, ca. 1350–1550." *Hansische Studien* 25: 11–29.

von der Hagen, Friedrich Heinrich. 1850. *Gesammtabenteuer, Vol. 1*. Stuttgart, Tübingen: J.G. Cotta.

von Stromer, Wolfgang. 1973–75. "Die ausländischen Kammergrafen der Stephanskrone—unter den Königen aus den Häusern Anjou, Luxemburg und Habsburg—Exponenten des Großkapitals." *Hamburger Beiträge zur Numismatik*, 27/29: 85–106.

von Wolfstrigl-Wolfskron, Max R. 1903. *Die Tiroler Erzbergbaue 1301–1665*. Innsbruck: Wagner'sche Universitäts-Buchhandlung.

Waitz, Georg (ed.). 1887. "Translatio et miracula sancti Petri et Marcellini." In *Monumenta Germaniae Historica: Scriptorum tomus 15.1*. Stuttgart: Hahn.

Walburg, Reinhold. 2008. *Coins and Tokens from Ancient Ceylon: Ancient Ruhuna—Sri Lankan-German Archaeological Project in the southern Province*, vol. 2. Wiesbaden: Reichert Verlag.

Walker Bynum, C. 1991. *Fragmentation and Redemption. Essays on Gender and the Human Body in Medieval Religion*. New York: Zone Books.

Webb, Diana. 2001. *Pilgrims and Pilgrimage in the Medieval West*. London: I.B. Tauris.

Weber, Max. 1958. "Religious Rejections of the World and Their Directions." In H.H. Gerth and C. Wright Mills (eds.), *From Max Weber: Essays in Sociology*. Oxford: Oxford University Press.

Weisenstein, Karl. 1995. *Das Kurtriersche Münz- und Geldwesen vom Beginn des 14. bis zum Ende des 16. Jahrhunderts: Auch ein Beitrag zur Geschichte des Rheinischen Münzvereins*. Koblenz: Numismatischer Verlag.

Welch Williams, Jane. 1993. *Bread, Wine and Money: The Windows of the Trades at Chartres Cathedral*. Chicago: University of Chicago Press.

Welter, J.T. (ed.). 1926. *Tabula exemplorum secundum ordinem Alphabeti*. Paris and Toulouse: Occitania, E.H. Guitard.

Werminghoff, Albert (ed.). 1906–8. *Concilia aevi Karolini*. 2 vols. Monumenta Germaniae Historica Concilia 2.1–2. Hanover and Leipzig: Hahn.

West, Charles. 2013. *Reframing the Feudal Revolution: Political and Social Transformation between Marne and Moselle, c. 800–c. 1100*. Cambridge: Cambridge University Press.

West, Shearer. 2004. *Portraiture*. Oxford: Oxford University Press.

Whelan, Estelle J. 2006. *The Public Figure: Political Iconography in Medieval Mesopotamia*. London: Melisende.

Whitelock, Dorothy (trans.). 1979. *English Historical Documents I: c. 500–1042*. 2nd ed. London: Eyre Methuen.

Wickham, Chris. 2005. *Framing the Early Middle Ages: Europe and the Mediterranean (400–800)*. Oxford: Oxford University Press.

Wickham, Chris. 2008. "Rethinking the Structure of the Early Medieval Economy." In Jennifer R. Davis and Michael McCormick (eds.), *The Long Morning of Medieval Europe: New Directions in Early Medieval Studies*. Aldershot: Ashgate.

Wickham, Chris. 2016. *Medieval Europe*. New Haven and London: Yale University Press.

Wilkin, Alexis, Naylor, John, Keene, Derek and Bijsterveld, Arnoud-Jan (eds.). 2015. *Town and Country in Medieval North Western Europe*. Turnhout: Brepols.

Williams, Gareth. 2006a. "The Circulation and Function of Coinage in Conversion-Period England, *c*. AD 580–675." In Barrie Cook and Gareth Williams (eds.), *Coinage and History in the North Sea World, c. AD 500–1250: Essays in Honour of Marion Archibald*. Leiden: Brill.

Williams, Gareth. 2006b. "Monetary Economy in Viking-Age Scotland in the Light of Single Finds." *Nordisk Numismatisk Årsskrift*, 2000–2002: 163–72.

Williams, Gareth. 2011a. "Coinage and Monetary Circulation in the Northern Danelaw in the 920s in the Light of the Vale of York Hoard." In Tony Abramson (ed.), *Studies in Early Medieval Coinage, vol. 2: New Perspectives*. Woodbridge: Boydell.

Williams, Gareth. 2011b. "Silver Economies, Monetisation and Society: an Overview." In James Graham-Campbell, Søren M. Sindbæk and Gareth Williams (eds.), *Silver*

*Economies, Monetisation and Society in Scandinavia, AD 800–1100*. Aarhus: Aarhus University Press.

Wilmart, Mickaël. 2016. "Travailler pour les autres dans un village de la région de Meaux à la fin du XVe siècle". Forthcoming.

Winroth, Anders. 2000. *The Making of Gratian's Decretum*. Cambridge: Cambridge University Press.

Woods, Andrew. 2013. "Economy and Authority: a Study of the Coinage of Hiberno-Scandinavian Dublin and Ireland." 2 vols. PhD. thesis, University of Cambridge.

Woods, Andrew. 2014. "Monetary Activity in Viking-Age Ireland: the Evidence of the Single-Finds." In Naismith, Allen and Screen 2014.

Wormald, Patrick. 1977. "*Lex scripta and verbum regis*: Legislation and Germanic Kingship, from Euric to Cnut." In Peter Hayes Sawyer and Ian N. Wood (eds.), *Early Medieval Kingship*. Leeds: University of Leeds.

Wright, F.A. 1930. *The Works of Liudprand of Cremona: Antapodosis, Liber de Rebus Gestis Ottonia and Relatio de Legatione Constantinopolitana*. London: George Routledge and Sons Ltd.

Zingerle, I.V. 1877. *Reiserechnungen Wolfger's von Ellenberchtskirchen Bischofs von Passau, Patriarchen von Aquileia*. Heilbronn: Henninger.

Zucchini, Stefania. 2008. *Università e dottori nell'economia del comune di Perugia. I registri dei Conservatori della Moneta (sec. XIV-XV)*. Perugia: Dep. Storia Patria Umbria.

# INDEX

*Italic* numbers are used for illustrations.

Abd al-Malik 112, *113*, 127
Abelard, Peter 131
accidental losses 81
accounting systems. *See* exchange rates
Acre, Israel 94, 113, *113*
Adalard of Corbie 53
Adalbert, Bishop of Prague 46, *47*
adaptations of coins 102–4, *102*, *104*, 166, 168–9, *170*
Æthelwulf, King of Wessex 44
afterlife, coins for 165, 167
Agathias 137
Alan of Lille, *De planctu naturae* 125
Albert the Bear, Margrave of Brandenburg 166
Alcuin 133
alienation of church goods 73–4
alms-giving 133, 134, 136, 168, *169*
Anastasius I, Byzantine Emperor 102
*Anglo-Saxon Chronicle* 167
Anglo-Saxon coinage 83, 84, 87, 88, 107, 118, 144, *144*
 *See also* penny (England)
Anselm of Canterbury 130, 132
Antioch, Turkey 91
apocalyptic signs 137
Aquinas, Thomas 130, 132
archaeology of early medieval money 41–3, 80

architects, payment of 53
*argenteus* (Spain) 44–5
aristocratic consumption 40, 41, 51
armbands 102–3, *102*
army, Byzantine 109
Arne, Bishop of Stavanger 130
art and representation 99–124
 authority of coins 107–14
 intended audience 101–7
 makers of coins 114–19
 unintended audience 119–23
art, concept of 99
Artuqid coinage 118, 121–3, *122*
Asia Minor 96
assaying process 30, 31, 32
audiences for coins 101–7, 119–23
Augustine of Hippo 62, 63
authority of money 107–14, 159–64

Balducci Pegolotti, Francesco 106–7
Baltic towns 96
barter 37, 38, 40, 48, 50
bent coins 169, *170*
Bergen, Norway 135–6
Bernard of Pavia, *Summa decretalium* 73–4
Bible and money 129
 *See also* parables of money
billon coins 8, 91
bills of exchange 4–5, 10, 159

bimetallic ratios 23, 158–9
Black Death 18, 137
Blackburn, Mark 82
blanks 33, 111, 116–17
Boccaccio, Giovanni 52
Body of Christ 58, 61, *61*, 64
Bohemia 86, 89, 94, 96
Boleslaw, King of Poland 46
Bolton, Jim 80
Bote, Hermen 32
bracteates 8, 94
bread, consecrated 58, 61, *61*
Britnell, Richard H. 80
bullion 24–7, 33
bullion economy 87, 156
bullionist policies 25–6
burials, coins found in 121, 165–6
Byzantine coinage 8–9, 83, 85, 89, 108–11, 120–1, *120*
Byzantine court, gifts of money 104–5

Calais, France 95
Canal, Martin da 48, 49
Canterbury, England 30
Carolingian Empire 115
Caronno, Italy 171
Cassian, John 129
cattle, value of 141, 152, 156–7
*cens* (land taxes) 45–6
*champart* (harvest share) 50–1
charity 46, 133
    See also alms-giving
Charlemagne, Holy Roman Emperor 6–7, 84–5, 105
Chartres, France 138
checks 10
China 128
Christ 58, 61–4, *61*, 106, *106*
Christian interpretation of money. *See* interpretation of money in the *societas Christiana*
Christianity and credit 68, 70–7
church goods 73–4
churches, coins found in 135–6, 169, 171
cider prices 19
circulation of wealth 41
Clement V, Pope 131
clipping of coins 87, 88, 93, 148, *148*
clothing 52, 53

Code of Justinian 65, 73
collateral for loans 52
Commercial Revolution 17, 19, 23, 68, 125
commercialization 80, 132
commodities
    food products 21, 40, 44, 50–1
    objects, monetary value of 37, 38, 52–3, 58–9
    sacred 66–7, 72, 75
    as units of value 5, 127–8, 141–2, 152, 153, 154, 156–7
Conrad II, Holy Roman Emperor 171
Constans II, Byzantine Emperor 111, *112*
Constantine III, Byzantine Emperor 109–10, 122, *122*
Constantine Heraclius 110–11
Constantinople, Turkey 137
construction sites 53–4
contracts 71, 74–5
cooperative mints 29
copper-alloy coinage
    Byzantine 8, 111, *112*
    post-Roman 5, 6, 154
    Sri Lankan 116, *117*
counterfeit currency 140–1
countryside, use of money in 45, 91, 98, 136, 154
Coupland, Simon 85
cow, foundation deposit of 171
cows, value of 141, 152, 156–7
Cragh, William 169
credit 4–5, 19, 68, 70–7, 159
crises, responses to 137
Crusader states 91, 94, 113–14, *113*
crusades, financing of 131
currency borders 26–7
Cusanus, Nicholas, *The Ball Game* 78
cutting of coins 87, 88, 93, 148, *148*
Cyprus 94, 96

Dante Alighieri, *La Divina commedia* 146, *147*
David II, King of Scotland 95
Davies, W. 44–5
debasement of coinage 8, 26, 27, 145, 146, 163–4
debt, notion of 57–8, 63
Della Valle, Pietro 134

denarii 48
*denarius* (Francia) 18–19, 46, 105
*denier* (France) 20, *20*, *85*, 88
*deniers de l'aumosnerie* (France) 136
Denmark 9, 91, 94, 96, 130, 146
denominations, expansion of 9, 19–24
Devroey, J.-P. 44
dies 34, 115
*dinar* (Abd al-Malik) 112, *113*
dinars 88
*dirham* (Acre) 113, *113*
*dirham*, adapted 168–9, *170*
Domesday Book 115
Dorestad, Netherlands 84
double-entry bookkeeping 10
Duby, Georges 41, 44
ducat (Venice) 163
ducats 23, 127

Eadgar, King of England 86
earthquakes 137
Ecchard, Count of Mâcon 41
ecclesiastical lifestyle 68, 69, 132
ecclesiastical mints 130
ecclesiastical wealth 64–6, 73–4
economic life 41
economic metaphors 61–2, 67, 68
economic revolution of the Middle Ages 17, 19, 23, 68, 125
economy, sacred 66–7, 68
*écu d'or* (Saint Louis) 23
Edict of Pîtres 115
Edward I, King of England 149
Edward III, King of England 114
Einaudi, Luigi 44
Einhard 44, 45
Eligius, Saint 105
elite audiences for coins 102, *102*
*emporia* 42, 43
England
   bullionist policies 25–6
   centralization of production 115
   coinage 88, 90, 92–3, 95
   denominations, expansion of 19
   halfpenny 88
   hoards *81*, 82
   Long Cross penny 148, *148*
   mints 30, 161, 162
   penny 7, 19, 83, 85–6, 107, 166

   recoinage 90, 92, 148–9
   ritual deposits 121, 165, 171
   royal place 80
   Short Cross penny 90, *90*
   trading centers 42–3
European coinage 79–98
   sixth to eleventh centuries 82–9
   twelfth to fourteenth centuries 89–96
exchange in the early Middle Ages 17, 37–8, 40–1
exchange rates 23, 26, 54, 159
Exeter, England 42
extrinsic value of money 128

faith and money 66–70
farming out of mints 29–30, 31
farthing (England) 19
feudal coinages 162
flans 33, 111, 116–17
Flixborough, England 43
Florence, Italy 23, 96, 151–2
*florin* (Florence) 23, 96
florins 23
food products 21, 40, 44, 50–1
   *See also* commodities
forms of money 153–9
   *See also* commodities; European coinage; hacksilver
foundation deposits 169, 171
fractions of metals 33
fragments of coins 87
France
   alms 136
   billon coins 8
   coinage 23, 86, 90, 92, 95
   cooperative mints 29
   debasement of coinage 145, 146, 163–4
   *denier* 20, *20*, *85*, 88
   *gros tournois* 20, *20*, 92, *92*, 127
   money-changing 138
Francia
   coinage 114
   *denarius* 18–19, 46, 105
   distribution of coinage 85
   fineness of coinage 83
   gold and silver coinage 6, 18
   gold coinage 160
   mints 42, 161

*obol* (halfpenny) 8, 85, 88
silver coinage 28, 157, 162
*tremissis* 5, 18, 28, 83
Francis of Assisi, Saint 131–2
Frederick I, Holy Roman Emperor 89
Frisian coinage 42, 107, 118
Frothaire, Bishop of Toul 45–6
Fulk, Abbot of Fontenelle 44

Ganz, David 135
Geminiano, Saint 166
Gerald of Wales, *Topography of Ireland* 134
Germany
   bracteates 8
   coinage 23, 29, 86, 88, 89, 96
   foundation deposits 169
   grain prices 21
   mints 130
*gewerken* (mining organizations) 25
ghost money 44–5, 54
gifts of money 45, 104–5, 166
Gildas 156
Girard, A. 27
Girolami, Remigio di 151–2
gold
   as metal of worldly payments 109
   sources of 25, 50, 92, 94
gold coinage
   post-Roman 5–6, 160
   tenth century 86
   *c.* 1200–1400 9–10, 127
   persistence of 154
   and silver currency 22–4
goods of equivalent value 3
grain, land exchanged for 44
graves, coins found in 121, 165–6
Great Jubilee (1300) 137–8
Greece 91, 96
Gregorian Reform 69
Gregory I, Pope 129
Grierson, Philip 81–2
Gritille, Turkey 91
groat
   English 19, 92, 95
   Scandinavian 94
   Scottish 95
*gros tournois* (France) 20, *20*, 92, *92*, 127
*grosso* (Venice) 9, 48, *49*, 93, 158
*gulden* (Lübeck) 23

hacksilver 4, *4*, 87, 155–6, *155–6*
halfpenny (England) 88
Halldórr Snorrason 142–3
Hamburg, Germany 21
hammered coinage 33–4
Harald Hardrade King of Norway 142–3, *142*, 145
Henry II, King of England 90
Henry of Segusio, *Summa aurea* 75–7
Heraclius, Byzantine Emperor 108–11, *108*, 122, *122*
Heraclius Constantine 109–10, 122, *122*
Heraclonas 110–11
*hexagram* (Byzantine) 108–9, *108*
Hildebert of Lavardin 129
Hincmar, Archbishop of Rheims 131
hoards 81–2, *81*, 83, 165, 166–8
Holy Roman Empire 27, 31
Honorius of Autun, *Gemma animae* 59, 61
horizontal exchange 41
host, Eucharistic 58, 61, *61*
House of the Vestal Virgins, Rome 166
hucksters 21–2, *22*
humans as coins 62, 129–30
Hungary 89, 94, 96, 139

Iceland 141
ideas of money 37–55, 126–8
   archaeological evidence 41–3
   currency and payment methods 43–6
   forms of payment 39–41
   goods, wages, and the poor 51–4
   monetization of the economy 46–50
   prices, taxes, and merchandise 50–1
imaginary currency 44–5, 54
imitation coins
   of Byzantine coins 120–1, *120*
   of English coins 163
   of florin 10, 23
   of Frankish coins 121, *121*
   of John III Vatatzes 106, *106*, 108
   of a late Roman *nummus* 117
   of nobles 27
   of pennies 93, 95
   in Scandinavia 87
   in Spain 88
immoral use of money 131
improvement of coinage 146, 148–9
inalientation of church goods 73–4

indebtedness, notion of 57–8, 63
India, Byzantine coins in 120–1, *120*
inflation 21, 50, 145
ingots 8, 46–8, 138
interest 71, 72, 75–7, 132, 133
  See also usury
interpretation of money in the *societas Christiana* 125–50
  church as force for monetization 149–50
  cultural context 129–39
  idea of money and coinage 126–8
  kings and secular transactions 139–49
investment of church goods 74
Ireland 88, 90, 93, 95, 134, 157
iron bars 48
Isidore of Seville, *Etymologiae* 152
Islamic coinage
  influence of 9, 88, 91, 127
  inscriptional model 112, *113*
  movement of 87
  rating of 4
  See also Artuqid coinage; Umayyad Caliphate
issues of the age 151–72
  authority of money 159–64
  forms of money 153–9
  using money 164–72
Italy
  banking systems 10
  coinage 6, 84, 85, 88–9, 93, 95–6, 158, 161
  ducat 163
  *florin* 23, 96
  *grosso* 9, 48, *49*, 93, 158
  *mancus* 45
  mints 29, 30, 91, 162
  monetary system 5
  See also Caronno; Florence; Perugia; Rome; Venice

jewelry 102–4, *102*, *104*, 166
Jewish Volga Bulgars 9
Jews, roles of 139, *139*, 148–9
John III Vatatzes, Emperor of Nicea 106, *106*
John XXII, Pope 11
Judaism, value of 63

Judas Iscariot 64
Justinian I, Eastern Roman Emperor 65, 73, 143

Kingdom of Jerusalem 91
Kiser, Edgar 30
Koenwald, Bishop of Worcester 168

labor service 37, 46, 48–9, 50
land taxes 45–6
language of economics and religion 58–9
lead-based coins 116, *117*
lead for church roofs 44
lending of money 132
  See also usury
León, Spain 44–5
Levant 91, 94
Liutprand of Cremona 104–5
livestock, value of 141, 152, 156–7
living conditions 51–2
loans, collateral for 52
London, England 42
Long Cross penny 148, *148*
Lopez, Robert S. 17, 18
lost coins 81
lost money, parable of 60
Louis I the Pious, King of the Franks 6–7
Louis IX Saint Louis, King of France 20, 92
love for money 129, 131
Low Countries 91, 93–4, 96
  See also Netherlands
Lübeck, Germany 23
Lupus Servatus, Abbot of Ferrières 44
luxury goods 40, 41, 51

makers of coins 27–31, 114–19
*mancus* (Italy) 45, 157
manumission of slaves 171–2
mark (Viking) 158
markets 17, 42
marriage belts 103, *104*
mathematical skills 33, *34*
Maximilian I, Holy Roman Emperor 15–16, *16*, 35
Mayhew, Nick 50
medieval, definition of 1–2
Meinwerk, Bishop of Paderborn 41
mendicant orders 131–2

Merovingian coinage 28, 83, 115, 118, 121, *121*
metal-detecting 41–2, 80
metallurgy 31–5, 116
metaphors for money 61–2, 67, 68
mines 25, 50
*ministeriales* and minting 28–9
mint masters 26, 29, 31, 115
mint-places, expansion of 158, 161, 162
minting on the move 117–18
minting, organization of 27–31, 115, 116–18, 130
Miskimin, Harry 18
monasteries, wealth of 64–5
monetary substitutes. *See* commodities
monetization of the economy 46–50, 80
money of account 127
money-changers 129–30, 138–9
money-offerings 131, 134–7, 166–8
money, varieties of 2–5, *4*
moneyer-based minting 28, 161
moneyers 114–15
multiple currencies 26–7, 163
Murray, Alexander 125
Muslim world coinage 8–9

Naismith, Rory 83, 126, 129
names of coins 157
necklaces 103, *104*
Netherlands 27, 35
Norman coinage 88, 89, 91
Norway 94, 130, 133, 135–6, 140–5, 146
*nummi* (copper-alloy coins) 82

objects, monetary value of. *See* commodities
*obol* (halfpenny) (Francia) 8, 85, 88
Offa, King of Mercia 84
offerings of money 131, 134–7, 166–8
Olaf II, King of Norway 143–4
ora (Viking) 158
Oresme, Nicholas, *De Moneta* 145, 163–4
Oswald, Archbishop of York 137

pagan offerings 167
Papal See, money received by 131, 138, 166
paper money 128
parables of money 59, *59*–60, 129, 136, 152–3

Paris, Matthew 148–9, *148*
Parva Mahumeria, Kingdom of Jerusalem 91
Passion of Christ 62, 63
Paul, Saint 137–8
pawning 52
payment forms in the early Middle Ages 39–41, 43–50, 80
payments in kind 39, 49, 51, 53
peasant economy 37, 40, 41, 51
pedlars 21–2, *22*
Pegolotti, Fransesco, *Pratica della Mercatura* 139
penance, paid for 133–4
penny 6–9, 87, 155, 157
penny (England) 7, 19, 83, 85–6, 90, *90*, 107, 148, *148*, 166
   *See also* sceattas
penny, multiple. *See* groat; *gros tournois* (France)
Pepin, King of the Franks 84
percentages of metals 33
Persia 134
Perugia, Italy 54
Peter, Saint 137–8
Peter Cantor 132
Petershausen, Germany 169
Petrarch, Francesco 52
*Pfennig* (Holy Roman Empire) 145
Philip II Augustus, King of France 90
Philip IV the Fair, King of France 20, 145, 146
Phocas, Byzantine Emperor 103
piedforts 115–16, *116*
pierced coins 120–1, *120*
pilgrimages 137–8, 171
Pirenne, Henri 6
plague 18, 137
plurality of money 152
Poland 89, 94
Polo, Marco 128
popes, minting by 130
portraits on coins 109–10
Portugal 94
post-Roman centuries (*c*. 500–750) 5–6, 153–4, 156, 157
   *See also* Anglo-Saxon coinage
poverty 68, 69, 132
*pragergroschen* (Bohemia) 96

prayers, payments for 44, 134
Price of Redemption 62, 63
Procopius of Caesarea 143, 160
production costs 19, 20–1
production standards for coins 118
productive sites 41–2, 43, 83–4
prototype coins 115–16, *116*
Prussia 21, 26, 30

quality control for coins 118
quarter-penny (England) 19
Quentovic, Francia 42

recoinage 90, 92, 148–9
relics, payment for 46
Rendlesham, England 80
representations on coins. *See* art and representation
reputation and coinage 145
*res valentes* (goods of equivalent value) 3
Rhinegulden 27
Ribe, Denmark 84
riots 146
ritual and religion 57–78
    credit and Christianity 70–7
    management of money and wealth 63–6
    money and faith 66–70
    money, debt and value 57–63
ritual uses of coins 165–72
Rome, Italy 137
rural use of coins 45, 91, 98, 136, 154

sacred economy 66–7, 68
sacred wealth 64
Sahagún, Spain 44
Saint Louis, France 23
salaries 38, 39, 48–9, 53
salvation of the soul 133–4
Sarris, Peter 102
Sasanian Empire 115
*sceattas* 42, 83, 107, 118, *119*
    *See also* penny
Scotland 88, 90, 93, 95
seignorage 21, 24, 30, 31
Serbia 94
shipyard of Venice 48–9
Short Cross penny 90, *90*
shortages of coinage 3, 45, 154

silver
    as metal of God 109
    sources of 25, 50, 92, 94–5
silver coinage 6, 20, 22–4
    *See also* penny
silver ingots 8, 46–8, 138
simony, sin of 67, 68, 69
slaves 157, 171–2
Slavic coinage 87
small change 4, 8, 21, 45, 136
Snorre Sturlasson, *Heimskringla* 142
social unrest 146
*solidus* 5, 82, 143, 153–4, 157
sources of metals 25, 50, 92, 94–5
Southern, Sir Richard 133
Spain
    coinage 6, 94, *119*, 161
    commodities 50, 156
    imaginary currency 44–5
    minting 162
    shortage of coins 3, 154
    taxes 48
speculative crazes 32
Spufford, Peter 23–4, 47, 86, 127, 145, 149
Sri Lanka 116, *117*
St John, monastery, Bergen, Norway 135–6
St Peter's, Rome 171
sumptuary laws 51–2
supply of coins 3, 21, 23, 158
Sutton Hoo ship burial, England 121, 165
Swabia 21
Sweden 94, 96, 136–7

talents, parable of 59
tax collecting 30, 48
tax systems 50–1
teachers 54
technologies 15–35
    bullion 24–7
    currencies and denominations 18–24
    metallurgy 31–5
    minting, organization of 27–31
testing of coins 31–2, *32*, 144–5, *144*
Teutonic Order, Prussia 26, 30
text tradition of coin design 112–14, *113*
Theodebert I, Merovingian King 114, 160, *160*

Theophanes 109
Thomas Aquinas (saint) 130, 132
Thomas de Cantilupe, Saint 169
time, price of 133
tombs, offerings at 166
touchneedles 31, *32*
touchstones 31
Toulouse, France 138
town mints 28–9
towns, growth of 18
towns, use of money in 97
trade
    balance of 25–6
    growth of 17–18, 21–2, 23–4, 42
    local 40
transubstantiation 58
*tremissis*
    Francia 5, 18, 28, 83
    Spain 118, *119*
    value of 153–4
trust (*fides*) 70–1
trust in money 139–49
    commodities, value of 141–2
    counterfeit currency 140–1
    debasement of coinage 145, 146
    improvement of coinage 146
    recoinage 148–9
    reputation of rulers 145
    testing of coins 144–5
    value of coinage 142–4
Turnemire, William 29–30
Tutbury hoard, England 82

Ukraine 9
Umayyad Caliphate 108, 112
uniform coinage 33
Uppsala, Sweden 137

uses of money 164–72
usury 49, 71–3, 75, 77, 132–3

Valencia, Spain 48
Value, divine 58, 64
value, of objects 52–3, 58–9, 64
Venice, Italy 9, 48–9, *49*, 93, 96, 158, 163
vertical exchange 40–1
Vestfold, Norway 87
Vikings
    bullion and hacksilver, use of 3–4, 156
    coin testing by 144–5
    coinage of 87, 88, 142, 158
    commodities, use of 157
    impact of 86–7
Visby, Sweden 136–7
Visigothic coinage 118, *119*
vocabulary of money 157
Volga Bulgars 9

wages 38, 39, 48–9, 53
war of the gold 'nobles' 27
water as a metaphor for money 67
Weber, Max 126
weight, units of 33
West Whelpington, England 82
wheat prices 21
Whithorn, Scotland 171
Wickham, Chris 1–2
widow's mite, parable of 129, 136, 152–3
Wipo of Burgundy, *Gesta Chuonradi imperatoris* 171
Wolfger, Bishop of Passau 138
wool trade in England 25, 95
Worcester, England 171
workshop mints 31
Wulfad, Archbishop of Bourges 134